Law of Partnership

Second Edition

BY

CHARLES D. DRAKE

M.A., LL.B. (CANTAB)

of the Middle Temple;
Barrister; Professor of English Law
and Dean of the Faculty
of Law, University of Leeds

LONDON
SWEET & MAXWELL
1977

First Edition   1972
Second Edition   1977

Published in 1977 by
Sweet and Maxwell Limited
of 11 New Fetter Lane, London,
and printed in Great Britain
by The Eastern Press Ltd. of
London and Reading.

ISBN 0 421 22130 5

AD S. S.

PREFACE

THE second edition of this book has given me the opportunity to try to increase its utility to law students, to professional students and to practitioners who seek a statement of the law of partnership within reasonable compass. For the reasons recited in the Preface to the first edition, it is no longer necessary to rebut the heresy of those who assert that the importance of a subject can be measured by the number of reported cases; it is clear that partnership continues to occupy an important place in the law of business associations. In the past few years the arguments in favour of size have come to wear a slightly jaded look and it is noticeable that regulation of the registered company, not excluding the private company, is likely to increase rather than diminish.

In this edition, I have attempted to realise certain objectives. First, the text has been substantially rewritten in order to accommodate changes in the law and to reflect certain developments which have relevance for partnership, such as accession to the European Communities, and the pressure to allow corporate association and limited liability to those professional persons denied the benefit of each, or both—matters which will fall for consideration by the recently established Royal Commission on Legal Services.

Secondly, whether one likes it or not, it has become difficult, if not impossible, to consider partnership in isolation from the law of taxation. Accordingly, the chapter on taxation has been expanded to include a comparison of the personal income tax régime as it bears upon partnership and the corporation tax régime as it bears upon the company, together with outlines of capital gains tax and capital transfer tax, all of this in addition to the more detailed discussion of the taxation of partnership profits which alone figured in the first edition.

Thirdly, I have substituted for the Appendix on Partnership Precedents, an Appendix which sets out the Partnership Act 1890, thereby, it is hoped, meeting the wishes of students who complained of the omission from the first edition.

Fourthly, because confession is supposedly good for the soul, I confess that I have changed my mind on one or two questions, particularly on the question of the criminal liability of partners, on which I now give brief treatment despite my conclusion that this is a topic outside the purview of the Partnership Act 1890.

In the preparation of this edition I have received help and advice on a scale so generous as to defy verbal recompense. Miss Ann Spowart, LL.B. (Leeds), LL.M. (Dal.), who had recently returned from her postgraduate studies in Dalhousie, Canada, occupied the summer of 1976 in reworking the greater part of the text, before taking up her appointment as Lecturer-in-Law in the University of Sheffield. Experts in textual analysis will be able to identify the replacement of some rhetorical passages by lucid and pungent exposition, or the curbing of male imagination by feminine pragmatism. It is a pleasure to record my debt to her. Another substantial debt is owed to my friend and former colleague, Mr. N. S. Todd, F.C.A., Principal Lecturer in Accountancy in the Polytechnic of Newcastle-upon-Tyne, who helped with the revision of the tax chapter and contributed the worked examples both on the taxation of partnership profits and on the tax comparisons between the partnership and the company. Without his invaluable assistance one of the distinctive features of this book, namely, the importance placed upon the tax element, would have emerged as something less distinctive and, possibly, less distinguished. With regard to tax I was doubly fortunate in that I was able to call on the advice and guidance of Mr. G. N. Glover, LL.B., Solicitor, who, as a colleague and tax expert with a considerable reputation as a teacher and writer in tax affairs, gave advice and suggestions in the ready manner which I have come to expect of him. My brief excursion into the criminal law was witnessed by another of my colleagues, Professor Brian Hogan, who steered me with a kindness and longanimity which the learned do not always bestow upon the ignorant. Mrs. D. Bray of the Companies' Registration Office kindly looked at the material on the registration of business names and for this I am most grateful. In acknowledging my debts to those named above, and others, unnamed, who helped me but who I know will not hold the omission against me, I am happy to issue the customary indemnity against errors for which I am insurer and, accordingly, responsible.

Last, but by no means least, I wish to pay my thanks to Mrs. Susan Batchelor, my secretary, who showed resilience and good humour in coping with the task of typing and arranging this book for publication.

Leeds
October 20, 1976

CHARLES D. DRAKE

CONTENTS

TABLE OF CASES

xi

TABLE OF STATUTES

CHAPTER ONE

INTRODUCTION

PARTNERSHIP AND OTHER FORMS OF BUSINESS ORGANISATION

IN English law, the basic, but by no means only, forms of business organisation, excluding the so-called " sole trader," are the partnership and the corporation. The single person conducting business on his own account must provide capital, labour and skill himself. In contrast, the partnership provides a ready means whereby two or more persons may join in business, each providing capital, labour and skill either together or separately. In modern society, these two elementary forms of business organisation, both embodying the conjunction of proprietorship and enterprise, have, to a large extent, been overtaken by corporate forms of business organisation, chiefly, the company registered under the companies' legislation and having a limited liability share capital. The advantages of incorporation have induced many sole traders and partnerships to undergo the legal metamorphosis into the registered company which, in its private form, requires only two members. The public company in search of the so-called economies of scale can, by means of a quotation for its shares and securities on the stock exchanges, obtain access to the capital market. The larger public companies have during this century witnessed the separation of ownership and control and this, in turn, has led to an examination of the structure of the modern company and the obligations and accountability of those who run it. Prominent amongst the questions now being discussed in this context is the question of " worker participation." In addition to the legal and economic aspects of incorporation, there is the increasingly obtrusive tax aspect, a topic dealt with in Chapter 8.

The genesis of the modern registered company is to be found in the unincorporated joint-stock company which was widely used until the Bubble Act of 1720 put a halt to their use and thereby to the consistent development of company law. Thereafter, the joint-stock company (in effect a large partnership with a common transferable stock) languished until revived in the "deed of settlement " company which made use of the trust concept. In such a company the joint stock might be vested in trustees and the management of the business

1

in directors (some, or all of whom, might also be trustees). Nevertheless, despite the ingenuity lavished on these companies, they remained unincorporated partnerships in the eye of the law. During the nineteenth century different committees turned their attention towards the possibility of achieving the twin objectives of transferability of stock and limited liability by adapting the partnership to meet these needs. Although there were those who favoured such an adaptation by combining some form of registration with limited liability for those providing capital only (borrowing from the commandite partnerships of continental law), there was resistance to limited partnerships and in the end the twin objectives were achieved by permitting the incorporation of companies with a limited liability share capital by the simple device of registration.

Statutory restrictions in 1844 and 1856 on the maximum number of persons who might form a company, association or partnership to carry on business for gain gave the *coup de grâce* to the partnership with a large and fluctuating membership. The dichotomy of partnership and company conceals the existence of a congeries of associations such as the building society, the friendly society, the unit trust, the industrial and provident society, the trustee savings bank and the cost-book company, each with its own peculiar legal status and attributes. Discussion of these associations lies beyond the provenance of this book.

As a sub-species, partnership shares with the unincorporated association the lack of any legal existence separate from its members. As Farwell L.J. put it: " In English law a firm as such has no existence; partners carry on business both as principals and as agents for each other within the scope of the partnership business; the firm name is a mere expression, not a legal entity." [1] This reluctance to ascribe separate existence to the firm is exemplified in *Commissioners of Customs and Excise* v. *Glassborow* where notwithstanding section 22 (1) of the Finance Act 1972 (which permits VAT registration in the name of the firm irrespective of " any change in the partnership ") the court considered that section to be " permissive and procedural only " so that the registration of the firm was in reality the registration of the names of the individuals trading under the firm name [2] (see p. 24).

Members of unincorporated bodies, such as members' clubs, are, as a general rule, only liable to the extent of their agreed contributions. " It is upon this fundamental condition " said Lord Lindley,

" not usually expressed but understood by everyone, that clubs are formed; and this distinguishing feature has often been judicially recognised." [3] The committee of a club does not have power to affix members with unlimited liability for its acts as a necessary implication of law, whereas the essence of partnership is the power of a partner to bind himself and his co-partners by acts in the ordinary course of the partnership business, notwithstanding any private limitation of authority which may have been agreed between them. The extent of the liability resulting from the exercise of that power is illustrated by the case of *Mercantile Credit Co. Ltd.* v. *Garrod* [4] where a partner was held liable for the acts of his co-partner " *of a like kind* to the business carried on by persons trading as a garage " (italics added: ss. 5–18 are discussed in detail in Chap. 3). To use the rather dated phrase in the Report of the Select Committee on Partnership (1851), each partner is liable to the extent of " his last shilling and his last acre " a consideration which indicates that, as in marriage, the first canon is to pick one's partner with care.

Section 1 (2) of the Partnership Act 1890 differentiates the partnership from certain types of companies or associations, in particular the registered company:

" But the relation between members of any company or association which is:

(*a*) Registered as a company under the Companies Act 1862, or any other Act of Parliament for the time being in force and relating to the registration of joint stock companies [5]; or

(*b*) Formed or incorporated by or in pursuance of any other Act of Parliament or letters patent, or Royal Charter [6]; or

(*c*) A company engaged in working mines within and subject to the jurisdiction of the Stannaries [7]:

is not a partnership within the meaning of this Act."

The registered company is the offspring of partnership, but now exhibits marked differences from its progenitor. Such a company is a discrete legal *persona* set apart from its members and able to own property, real or personal, to grant leases or charges, to enter contracts, to commit torts, crimes and breaches of trust, save when its artificial nature makes this impossible. It is free of the procedural embarrassments which beset the unincorporated association in litigation and because of its perpetual existence (*i.e.* until wound up) it is also free of those difficulties in the holding and transmitting of property which affect societies and trusts. In *Saloman* v. *Saloman and Co. Ltd.*,[8] the House of Lords set its seal on the reality of corporate existence when it gave to a debenture-holder, who was virtually the proprietor of the company capital, priority over unsecured creditors in a winding up, despite the latter's protests that Saloman and his company were in truth the same person.

Partnership property, on the other hand, is held jointly by the partners who cannot, in general, create a floating charge over the firm's assets comparable to the company floating debenture. The partners may, admittedly, grant a mortgage over partnership assets, but this will lack the ability of the floating debenture to float like a cloud over assets as they fluctuate from day to day until such time as an event occurs sufficient to cause the charge to crystallise, as well as lacking the transferability of the company debenture. A written mortgage over goods will normally be governed by the Bills of Sale Acts 1878 and 1882, and will need to be registered as a conditional bill of sale together with a schedule or inventory of the goods comprised therein—a requirement which precludes a statutory bill of sale over after-acquired property. In addition to the peculiar commercial opprobrium which seems to attach to the bill of sale in commercial circles, there is the risk that by virtue of the " reputed ownership clause " (Bankruptcy Act 1914, s. 38) the goods covered by a conditional bill of sale may be available to satisfy the borrower's creditors in the event of bankruptcy because the goods are held to be in the possession, order or disposition of the bankrupt in his trade or business by the consent and permission of the owner at the commencement of the bankruptcy. The Consumer Credit Act 1974, s. 192 (3) (*a*), Sched. 4, para. 6 added a new section 38A which, though it is not yet in force, provides that goods subject to certain credit agreements are not to be treated as the property of the bankrupt until the default notice has expired or been complied with. The Crowther Committee on Consumer Credit in its recommendation of a radical reform of credit law proposed that either a fixed charge over shifting assets or a floating charge should be made generally available. The extension of the floating charge to non-corporate borrowers would go far to eradicate some of the anomalies which exist in this area of the law of credit, but so far these proposals have not been implemented.

Perhaps the greatest attraction of the limited liability company is the limitation of the shareholder's liability to the amount, if any, unpaid in respect of the nominal value of his shares. Little use has been made of the limited partnership introduced in 1907 because of the ease with which a private company with limited liability could, by virtue of the Companies Act 1907, be registered from that year. The unlimited joint liability [9] of partners for partnership liabilities is one of the major hazards in ordinary partnership, liabilities swelled by the liability for negligent misstatements as the result of the *Hedley Byrne* decision,[10] although the degree of risk obviously depends on the type of business undertaken and may, in some cases be covered by insurance.

As we have seen, agency is the essence of partnership in that each partner is endowed with the power to bind the firm under section 5 of the Partnership Act 1890. The individual shareholder as such has no equivalent power to bind the company, the management of which is entrusted to directors who act as its agents. The separation of ownership and control in the larger company following upon the decline of proprietor-capitalism and the emergence of a new managerial class, as predicted by Max Weber, have left the shareholder, both individually and collectively, with little direct say in the running of the company. The partnership by contrast continues to afford scope to the proprietor-entrepreneur since section 24 (5) of the 1890 Act confers upon every partner a prima facie right to participate in the management of the firm's business.

As regards freedom to do business, it looked for a while as though the new registered companies would, like the old common law corporations, have the powers of a natural person, except where such powers were patently inappropriate, but this notion was decisively rejected in *Ashbury Railway Carriage Co. v. Riche*,[11] where the House of Lords held that such companies were only incorporated " with reference to a memorandum of association "; once they entered into contracts outside the powers conferred by the memorandum they became, so to speak, *non personae*. In practice the doctrine of *ultra vires* has not inhibited company freedom to do business. So far as persons dealing with the company are concerned, such restrictions as remain have been further reduced by section 9 (1) of the European Communities Act 1972, which, in certain circumstances, permits of the enforcement of *ultra vires* transactions *against* a company. So far as partnership is concerned, there is no impediment to a complete change in the nature of the partnership business, provided all the partners agree.

Accession to the European Communities has provided both for the company and the partnership a right of establishment and, in the case of professional partnerships, there has been pressure for the mutual recognition of qualifications and diplomas and perhaps ultimately for common qualifications. British partnerships which intend to open offices or branches in Europe are subject to exchange control by the Bank of England which includes provision for repatriation of a proportion of profits, dividends and fees (details of which are given in the Bank of England's booklet, *A Guide to United Kingdom Exchange Control*). A British firm proposing to conduct business in a Member State will need to take account of the law in that State (including the types of business entity prevailing there) and of any professional restrictions in that State. Valuable advice for British firms wishing to open a business abroad is available from the British Overseas Trade Board. Doubtless, considerations such as these have led some British firms to utilise the services of existing firms in the Member State, although it is noticeable that several firms now operate branches within the Community.

The proposal for a European Co-operation Grouping (O.J. No. C. 14/30 of February 15, 1974) is based on the need to allow persons, firms and companies to have at their disposal a trans-national legal vehicle freed from the " legal, fiscal and psychological difficulties " involved in the national laws of Member States. If promulgated as a Regulation the Grouping will provide a type of " European Partnership " as an alternative to the " European Company " which, despite a long gestation, is still being discussed.

Above all, the partnership, and the same applies to many private companies, is a personal relationship founded on mutual confidence and trust. Contrasting it with the depersonalised relationships which characterised the joint-stock company, James L.J. said that it was " essentially composed of the persons originally entering into the contract with one another." [12] In the absence of provision in the articles of partnership, the death or retirement of a partner works a dissolution of the firm. Whilst there is nothing to prevent a partner creating a sub-partnership with regard to his share in the partnership, he cannot foist a new partner on his co-partners without their concurrence. The small shareholder in a large public company, although technically co-proprietor, is, for all practical purposes, merely the owner of a contingent right to periodic dividends. Despite the greater degree of legal regulation affecting the registered company, it is undeniable that the advantages of incorporation—separate legal personality, limited liability (if so desired), transferability of shares in the case of a public company and possible tax advantages (see Chapter 8, below)—have induced partners and sole traders to convert their businesses into corporate form.

Nevertheless, partnership remains important. Mutual trust and confidence may be more highly esteemed than the benefits of incorporation. Subject to a few exceptions, partnership is the usual and, in many cases, the mandatory form of association for professional persons. Most of the professions prohibit association in the form of the limited liability company for fear that to allow this would erode the principle of individual professional accountability towards the client—a notion which lies at the heart of the professional ethos. It is true that some professions permit the unlimited liability company to be used, and it is also true that in recent years there has been pressure in certain professions to relax professional rules to allow use of the limited liability company with safeguards such as a minimum capital subscription from the professional members of the company, restriction on the capital participation of non-professional members and some requirement as to professional indemnity insurance. In the cases of solicitors, the prohibition on corporate association is statutory and is supported by criminal sanctions (Solicitors Act 1974, s. 24 (2); for the restrictions on dentists, see Dentists Act 1957, s. 38). No person other than a company or industrial and provident society may carry on business as the promoter of a trading stamp scheme, admittedly not a professional activity so-called (Trading Stamps Act 1964, s. 1 (1)). The individualistic professional ethos finds its apotheosis in the Bar and the Royal College of Physicians of London which deny even the partnership to their members. It is interesting to note that the possibility of partnerships for barristers, and incorporation with limited liability for solicitors, will be amongst the matters to be considered by the Royal Commission on Legal Services, recently appointed at the time of writing.

Professional partnerships denied the benefits of incorporation may be attracted to the device of the " service company," a company (usually unlimited) separate and distinct from the partnership, but consisting of shareholders and directors from the partnership, with or without members and directors who are non-partners. Such a company can take over from the partnership responsibility for premises, staff and equipment leaving the partnership free to concentrate

on professional or business work freed from problems of administration and discontinuity (where the partnership membership changes).
The service company is entitled to make a charge (the " service fee ")
for its services and a reasonable profit which the partnership can set
off against its profits for tax purposes. A service company which
charges a high service fee in the opening years of a partnership
(including the " new " partnership consequent upon a change of
partners) will reduce the partnership's profits in the early vital years
(see p. 197 below) although *Stephenson* v. *Payne, Stone, Fraser and
Co.* [13] shows that there is not complete freedom in this respect. In
that case, it was held that a service charge in excess of the actual cost
of the services including a nominal profit could not, so far as the
excess was concerned, be attributed to the partnership's profits so as
to reduce the partnership's assessments in the opening years. Against
the advantages of the service company needs to be set possible tax
disadvantages including the possibility that the service company will
be a " close company."

In recent years the lure of incorporation has grown less. The
Companies Act 1967 has provided for the increase in the maximum
number of persons who may be members of certain professional
partnerships and has plucked away the fig leaf with which the exempt
private company could keep its financial affairs secret. The result is
that in those cases where privacy is the paramount consideration,
the exempt private companies, now abolished, have either re-
registered as unlimited companies or become partnerships, either
ordinary or limited. One can discern in domestic legislation a trend
towards greater legal regulation of the company as opposed to the
partnership, as in the Industry Act 1975, and the signs are that
membership of the Communities will bring with it increasing
regulation of corporate forms of organisation, notably structural
changes in the company to accommodate hitherto continental ideas
of co-determination involving workers. Whether or not the partnership will escape these changes remains to be seen. The tax aspects of
company *versus* partnership are sufficiently important to merit
separate consideration in Chapter 8.

The House of Lords has now recognised for certain purposes the
existence of that hybrid creature, the " incorporated partnership,"
or, as it was formerly known, the " quasi-partnership." In *Ebrahimi*
v. *Westbourne Galleries Ltd.,*[14] a director who had been removed
from office in strict conformity with section 184 of the Companies

Act 1948 was nevertheless held to be entitled to an order for the winding up of the company on the " just and equitable " ground as though it were a partnership. The "just and equitable" ground allows the court to look behind the corporate façade to see if there are rights, expectations and obligations which are not wholly subsumed in the company structure. Lord Wilberforce in that case declined to give an exhaustive list of those indicia which point to an incorporated partnership and stressed that the fact that a company is small or private is not enough. However, his Lordship pointed to certain elements which permit equitable considerations to be superimposed on the company structure, *viz.* (i) an association formed or continued on the basis of personal relationship involving mutual confidence, as where a pre-existing partnership is converted into a limited company; (ii) an agreement or understanding that all, or some (for there may be sleeping partners) of the shareholders are entitled to participate in the conduct of the business; and (iii) restriction on the transfer of the members' interest in the company, so that if confidence is lost, or one member is removed from management, he cannot take out his stake and go elsewhere.[15] His Lordship accepted that " quasi-partnership " is a convenient description of such a company but considered that it might obscure or deny the fact that the company " however small, however domestic, is a company not a partnership or even a quasi-partnership and it is through the just and equitable clause that obligations, common to partnership relations, may come in." It will be seen therefore that the concept of the incorporated partnership is so far limited to the context of winding up on the " just and equitable " ground.

THE PARTNERSHIP ACT 1890

The aims of the Partnership Act, as originally intended, were to codify the law of partnership, to introduce something comparable to the *société en commandite* of Continental law, and to establish universal and compulsory registration of firms. Described by Harman L.J. as " that model piece of legislation " [16] the Act certainly achieved the aim of codification and has influenced the law in Commonwealth and American jurisdictions. The *commandite* partnership however had to wait until 1907 and registration (on a limited scale) only came in 1916. Drafted by Sir Frederick Pollock, the Act governs the law of partnership, so that where its provisions are unequivocal they must be applied. The Act is no more a complete code than companies' legislation is a complete code of the law regulating companies. Where a provision in the Act is unclear, resort may be had to pre-1890 cases to elucidate its meaning. Section 46 preserves the rules of equity and common law applicable to partnerships except so far as they are inconsistent with the express provisions of the Act. Much of the law relating to the nature of partnership, dealings with third persons, mutual rights and duties of the partners *inter se* and dissolution, is to be found in case law. The mutual rights and duties of the partners whether ascertained by agreement or defined by the Act may be consensually varied under section 19 of the Act, an important provision which accepts the rights of the partners to settle their own terms.

[1] *Sadler* v. *Whiteman* (1910) 79 L.J.K.B. 786 at p. 799. The firm-name is discussed below, p. 24.

[2] [1975] Q.B. 465.

[3] *Wise* v. *Perpetual Trustee Company Ltd.* [1903] A.C. 139 at p. 149.

[4] [1962] 3 All E.R. 1103.

[5] Now the Companies Acts 1948 and 1967.

[6] Generally, but not necessarily, incorporated. By the Chartered Companies Act 1837 the Crown may establish companies by letters patent without incorporation.

[7] Cost-book companies were unincorporated companies regulated by local custom and the Stannaries Acts.

[8] [1897] A.C. 22.

[9] Associations in which the members accept several liability to third persons are not partnerships. Examples are insurance syndicates and mutual insurance companies.

[10] *Hedley Byrne & Co.* v. *Heller & Partners* [1964] A.C. 465.

[11] (1875) L.R. 7 H.L. 653.

[12] In *Smith* v. *Anderson* (1880) 15 Ch.D. 247 at p. 273.

[13] [1968] 1 W.L.R. 858.

[14] [1973] A.C. 360.

[15] *Ibid.* at p. 379.

[16] In *Keith Spicer Ltd.* v. *Mansell* [1970] 1 W.L.R. 333 at p. 335.

CHAPTER TWO

NATURE AND DEFINITION OF PARTNERSHIP

Partnership is defined by section 2 as: " the relation which subsists between persons carrying on a business with a view of profit."

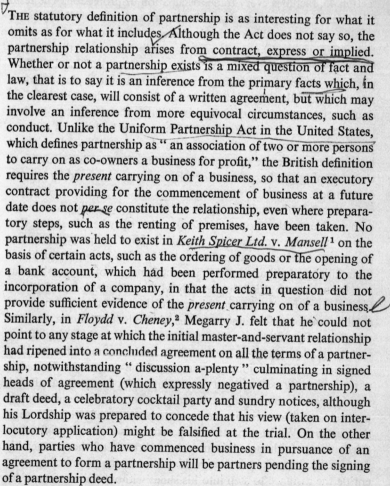

THE statutory definition of partnership is as interesting for what it omits as for what it includes. Although the Act does not say so, the partnership relationship arises from contract, express or implied. Whether or not a partnership exists is a mixed question of fact and law, that is to say it is an inference from the primary facts which, in the clearest case, will consist of a written agreement, but which may involve an inference from more equivocal circumstances, such as conduct. Unlike the Uniform Partnership Act in the United States, which defines partnership as " an association of two or more persons to carry on as co-owners a business for profit," the British definition requires the *present* carrying on of a business, so that an executory contract providing for the commencement of business at a future date does not *per se* constitute the relationship, even where preparatory steps, such as the renting of premises, have been taken. No partnership was held to exist in *Keith Spicer Ltd.* v. *Mansell*[1] on the basis of certain acts, such as the ordering of goods or the opening of a bank account, which had been performed preparatory to the incorporation of a company, in that the acts in question did not provide sufficient evidence of the *present* carrying on of a business. Similarly, in *Floydd* v. *Cheney*,[2] Megarry J. felt that he could not point to any stage at which the initial master-and-servant relationship had ripened into a concluded agreement on all the terms of a partnership, notwithstanding " discussion a-plenty " culminating in signed heads of agreement (which expressly negatived a partnership), a draft deed, a celebratory cocktail party and sundry notices, although his Lordship was prepared to concede that his view (taken on interlocutory application) might be falsified at the trial. On the other hand, parties who have commenced business in pursuance of an agreement to form a partnership will be partners pending the signing of a partnership deed.

In contrast to the more usual partnership between natural persons, where mutual trust and confidence play an important part, a

11

partnership may consist of, or include, incorporated companies subject to any restriction to be found in the " objects clause " of the company's memorandum of association (for the tax position of partnerships with incorporated partners, see below, p. 206).

Business

Partnership cannot exist without a business which, according to section 45, includes every trade, occupation or profession. The term " business " is of potentially wide import and in its ordinary sense signifies almost anything which is an occupation or duty as opposed to recreation or pleasure. It may formerly have been the case, as Shaw suggested, that the aristocratic classes worked hard at their pleasures but even a Kantian sense of duty towards pleasure does not transmute the latter into business; their attitude to business no doubt being accurately described by Wilde's dictum that " Work is the curse of the drinking classes." There may be business without profit and, conversely, there may be the hope of profit without business as where the owners in common of a race-horse agree to share winnings and expenses [3] or where a house is leased by tenants in common.

Section 2 (1) formally recognises that there is nothing in our law comparable to the Roman *societas unius rei* when it states that " joint tenancy, tenancy in common, joint property, common property, or part ownership does not of itself create a partnership as to anything so held or owned." The active nature of partnership was well brought out by Sir John Romilly M.R. in *Kay* v. *Johnston*,[4] when he explained that " a partnership means this: that the joint property shall be employed for some purposes which shall produce a return in the shape of profits, or so as to add to its value; but nothing of that sort took place here. It was in fact, nothing more than a joint occupation, under a joint ownership of the property." Indeed, a partnership may exist without the employment of property at all and, should property be employed, it need not necessarily be partnership property at all but remain the separate property of one or more of the partners. Whilst a partner may assign his share of profits to a third person (although this may be a breach of the partnership agreement), he cannot so assign his share in the partnership as to entitle the assignee to step into his shoes without the consent of his co-partners.

In the ordinary course of events the carrying on of business denotes a degree of continuity. This was the view taken in *Smith* v. *Anderson* in which an investment trust (the forerunner of the modern unit trust) was held not to offend against section 4 of the Companies Act 1862, Brett J. suggesting that the " expression ' carrying on any business ' . . . implies a repetition of acts, and excludes the case of an association formed for doing one particular act which is never to be repeated." [5] Ignoring the other grounds upon which that case was decided, it would not appear to represent the position in partnership law. In Scotland, a distinction is drawn between ordinary partnership and the " joint adventure," the latter being a limited partnership often without any firm-name and confined to a particular adventure, speculation, course of trade or voyage. Such a partnership is somewhat more circumscribed in the sense that the implied authority of each partner is not as extensive as in ordinary partnership, and also because it is dissolved on the completion of the adventure. The English cases do not single out the joint adventure for particular treatment and there is no reason in English law why a joint enterprise for some special and discontinuous object should not, in the absence of contrary indications, carry with it the attributes of an ordinary partnership.

The Act requires that the business must be carried on with a view to profit. The fundamental meaning of profit is the amount of gain made during the year or other accounting period and this can only be ascertained by comparing the value of the assets of the business at the two dates.[6] Strangely, although the Act requires the carrying on of business with a view to profit, it says nothing concerning the division of such profit. Tindal C.J. voiced the opinion in *Green* v. *Beesley* [7]: " I have always understood the definition of partnership to be a mutual participation in profit and loss "—an opinion echoed in several other cases decided before 1890. Lord Lindley, however, in a somewhat tentative discussion in his treatise on partnership considered the omission to indicate that participation in profits is not an essential element in partnership, a view from which Pollock (who drafted the original Partnership Bill) dissented. Lord Lindley's view seems difficult to support since the omission of any reference to the sharing of profits could well be rectified by the common law (see s. 46) and is hard to equate with the prima facie right to an equal share in profits as conferred by section 24 (1). Of course the partners may work to make a profit yet decide to allocate those profits to some third person or a charitable or philanthropic institution, but nevertheless the fact remains that they are disposing of a right to share in profits. Because they have decided to forgo a share of profits for themselves it does not follow that they have no right to profits.

Gross returns

Section 2 provides that:

> " The sharing of gross returns does not of itself create a partnership, whether the persons sharing such returns have or have not a joint or common right or interest in any property from which or from the use of which the returns are derived."

The distinction between profits and returns was pointed out by Kay L.J. in *Sutton and Co.* v. *Grey*,[8] where the court considered an agreement between a firm of stockbrokers and Grey under which Grey was to receive half commission on business introduced by him and bear half of any losses on such business. " The commission received in respect of any transaction might not be all clear profit; the expenses of the office establishment would have to be provided for. . . ." Returns therefore represent that which is obtained by the business; the excess of what is obtained over the cost of obtaining it being the profit. A person sharing gross returns necessarily shares profits, but not losses, unless there is agreement to this effect, as in the *Sutton* case. The rule concerning gross returns (which antedates the Act of 1890) provided a welcome escape from the rigour of the old rule that those who shared profits were liable as partners.[9] Now that the old rule has been modified, the rule concerning gross returns is to that extent unnecessary. In *Lyon* v. *Knowles*,[10] where the sharing of gross returns between the proprietor and manager of a theatre on the one hand, and the manager of a theatrical company on the other, was held not to constitute a partnership, Blackburn J. distinguished cases where a person has a specific interest in the profits themselves as opposed to a claim on the gross takings.

Sharing of profits

Under the old law a person lending capital to a business at a high rate of interest ran the risk of falling foul of the usury laws; if, moreover, he took a share in the profits, cases such as *Waugh* v. *Carver*[11] showed that he might find himself affixed with unlimited liability. During the nineteenth century various committees considered this dilemma, including the Mercantile Law Commission, which recommended the repeal of the usury laws and adverted " to the expediency . . . of enabling capitalists to lend money to traders at a rate of interest, and agents and servants to receive remuneration for their services by money payments, varying with the profits of the business, without being exposed to the hazard of being rendered liable as partners to the creditors of the concern." [12]

It was not until the leading case of *Cox* v. *Hickman* [13] that the test of participation in profits lost its position of primacy. In that case, the House of Lords held that an arrangement whereby a trader assigned his property to trustees representing creditors of his business, to enable the latter to superintend the conduct of the business so that the creditors might be paid off out of profits, did not raise a partnership between the debtor and his creditors. Lord Cranworth warned against the fallacy of assuming that participation in profits necessarily raises a partnership saying: " This, no doubt, is, in general, a sufficiently accurate test; for a right to participate in profits affords cogent, often conclusive evidence, that the trade in which the profits have been made, was carried on in part for or on behalf of the person setting up such a claim. But the real ground of liability is, that the trade has been carried on by persons acting on his behalf. It is not correct to say that his right to share in the profits makes him liable to the debts of the trade. The correct mode of stating the proposition is to say . . . that the trade has been carried on on his behalf, *i.e.* that he stood in relation of principal towards the persons acting ostensibly as the traders."

Although *Cox* v. *Hickman* was imperfectly understood for a while, it received statutory confirmation in section 2 (3) of the Act, as follows:

" The receipt by a person of a share of the profits of a business is prima facie evidence that he is a partner in the business, but the receipt of such a share or of a payment contingent on or varying with the profits of a business, does not of itself make him a partner in the business; and in particular:

(a) The receipt by a person of a debt or other liquidated amount by instalments or otherwise out of the accruing profits of a business does not of itself make him a partner in the business or liable as such:

(b) A contract for the remuneration of a servant or agent of a person engaged in a business by a share of the profits of the business does not of itself make the servant or agent a partner in the business or liable as such:

(c) A person being the widow or child of a deceased partner, and receiving by way of annuity a portion of profits made in the business in which the deceased person was a partner, is not by reason only of such receipt a partner in the business or liable as such:

(d) The advance of money by way of loan to a person engaged or about to engage in any business on a contract with that person that the lender shall receive a rate of interest varying with the profits, or shall receive a share of the profits arising from carrying on the business, does not of itself make the lender a partner with the person or persons carrying on the business or liable as such. Provided that the contract is in writing, and signed by or on behalf of all the parties thereto:

(e) A person receiving by way of annuity or otherwise a portion of the profits of a business in consideration of the sale by him of the goodwill of the business is not by reason only of such receipt a partner in the business or liable as such."

Sharing of profits is evidence, but not conclusive evidence, of partnership despite the subsection's preoccupation with profits. It is now clear that the court will ascertain the real intention and contract of the parties as shown by the whole facts of the case. Thus, in *Badeley* v. *Consolidated Bank*,[14] B advanced money to C to enable the latter to construct a railway, C assigning to B machinery, plant and securities, and agreeing to pay to B 10 per cent. on the money advanced plus 10 per cent. on the net profits of the venture, subject to an allowance of £1,000 per year which C might draw for his services in carrying out the construction contract. Looking at the agreement as a whole it was held that B had made a bona fide loan upon security and was not, despite his share of profits, a partner; it was true that B's capital was required to be *employed* in the venture but it was not *risked* in the construction contract in any sense since it could have been recovered from C if the venture had failed. Lindley L.J. warned against the fallacy of seizing upon a particular provision for the sharing of profits in order to raise a presumption in favour of partnership, which might then be rebutted by other provisions in the agreement, indicating that the proper course was to look at the whole of the evidence, including documents, in order to draw the proper inference, although the same judge accepted that it was probably true to say that where the only facts are that A carries on business and B shares the profits of that business, the presumption is that the two are partners.

A contrary inference was drawn from the facts of the earlier case of *Pooley* v. *Driver* [15] in which B and H had entered into partnership for 14 years and, in order to raise further capital, had transferred shares to a third person whose contributions were to be considered as loans. It was held that the " loans " were colourable inasmuch as the true relation between B, H and the " lenders " was that of active and dormant partners rather than that of borrowers and lenders. After a careful examination of the documents, the court was struck by the unusual rights given to the " lenders," such as their right to share in the capital (which was to be employed in the business during the subsistence of the partnership and to be repaid preferentially at its conclusion); their right to share in profits and surplus profits on a final settlement of accounts (with a corresponding duty to refund within limits any distribution of profits found to be excessive—" a wonderful provision if it is a bona fide loan," exclaimed Jessel M.R.); their right to insist that the partners conduct the business to the best of their ability (which they might enforce by means of a suit for damages); their right to interest varying not only with profits but also in proportion to the total capital employed, and the right to have differences arbitrated. If the " lenders " became bankrupt or compounded with their creditors, the two partners, B and H, might pay them off—" a very astonishing provision in an ordinary contract of loan. What has the bankruptcy of the creditor got to do with it? " was Jessel M.R.'s pertinent question, the same distinguished judge finding that the arrangement was merely " an ingenious contrivance, for giving these contributors the whole of the advantages of the partnership, without subjecting them, as they thought, to any of the liabilities." Jessel M.R. showed that the situations set forth in Bovill's Act (on which see below), are not litmus-paper tests of partnership. Once you have decided that the relationship is that of creditor and debtor " you do not want the Act at all, because the inference of partnership deriving from the mere taking a share of profits, not being irrebuttable, is rebutted by your having come to the conclusion that they are in the position of debtor and creditor." Although this was said in 1876 it is as true now as then.

Many of the most difficult problems in partnership have turned upon the question of categories, such as those of partner, creditor, servant, trustee, etc. Careful drafting of the agreement can do much to clear up ambiguity, but the courts have refused to be side-tracked by any verbal smokescreens. In the words of Lord Halsbury: " If a partnership in fact exists, a community of interest in the adventure being carried on in fact, no concealment of name, no verbal equivalent for the ordinary phrases of profit and loss, no indirect expedient for enforcing control over the adventure will prevent the substance and reality of the transaction being adjudged a partnership . . . and no ' phrasing of it ' by dextrous draftsmen . . . will avail the legal consequences of the contract." [16] In determining whether or not a partnership exists, it is important to remember that this question may conceal two quite different questions, *viz.* does a partnership exist so far as the outside world is concerned and—the separate question—so far as the parties *inter se* are concerned? *Stekel* v. *Ellice* [17] shows that a person who is termed loosely a " salaried partner," may be (1) a partner by " holding out," yet merely an employee within the partnership; (2) a partner in the true sense, both as regards third persons and his co-partners, and with all the rights of a true partner, *e.g.* to have the partnership wound up and its assets distributed; and (3) a " qualified partner " who is a partner in relation to the outside world and the other partners, save that he lacks a sufficient proprietary interest in the firm's assets entitling him to move for a winding-up under section 39 of the Act (the category into which the salaried partner was considered to fall in the *Stekel* case itself).

It may be noted here that the criticism of the old law had led to the passing of Bovill's Act in 1865 which was " An Act to amend the Law of Partnership." Confusion was made worse in that this Act was in turn criticised for failing to take account of the clarification of the law in *Cox* v. *Hickman*, and for giving rise to the false impression that new types of limited or *commandite* partnerships had been fathered. The Act was repealed and reproduced with some changes and additions, the most significant addition being the words preceding the five cases in section 2 (3).

Five cases

The five arrangements in section 2 (3) do not *of themselves* create a partnership, although, as we have seen, the court may conclude from all the circumstances that a partnership in fact exists. *Cox* v. *Hickman* itself is an example of paragraph (*a*), above. Another is to be found in *Kilshaw* v. *Jukes* [18] where A was held not to be liable as a partner with B and C by reason of advancing money and supplying goods to B and C for a building speculation on terms that he would be repaid out of the profits, the remainder of which, if any, were to go to B and C. Paragraph (*b*) allows servants and agents to participate in profit-sharing schemes with their employers without ranking as partners with the latter. [19] The problem of categories is illustrated by the case of *Walker* v. *Hirsch*, [20] in which the plaintiff, previously a clerk in the firm, agreed to advance £1,500 to the firm in return for a salary of £180 and one-eighth of net profits (or losses). It was held that he remained a servant, and, as such, could not move for a winding up of the firm, Lord Lindley saying of the document containing the arrangement that " it is not a mere contract of loan; it is not a mere contract of service; it is not a mere contract of partnership " but, rather, had some of the elements of all of those contracts. The third case (paragraph (*c*)) permits a widow or child annuitant of a deceased partner to receive an annuity out of profits without ranking as a partner purely by reason of the receipt of such annuity. [21]

The fourth and most important case (paragraph (*d*)) deals with the person advancing money by way of loan and receiving a share of profits [22] or interest at a rate which varies with the profits. If, unlike *Pooley* v. *Driver*, [23] an advance of money by way of loan *simpliciter* can be made out, then paragraph (*d*) comes into play. [24] Read literally, the proviso to paragraph (*d*) would appear to indicate that if the contract in question is not in writing, or not signed, then the lender is prima facie a partner with the borrower [25]; but the better view would appear to be that the absence of a duly signed memorandum is a formal deficiency which cannot be seized on to the exclusion of the true intention of the parties as it appears from the interpretation of the agreement as a whole. The last case, contained in paragraph (*e*), provides that the seller of goodwill who receives in return an annuity or portion of the profits, is not, by reason only of such receipt, a partner in the business. Where a medical practitioner assigned his medical practice by deed to a purchaser on the terms that he would continue to reside in the house for three months and introduce the patients to the purchaser, the earnings and expenses during the three months to be shared equally, it was held that the two medical practitioners were not partners and that the practice was the purchaser's from the date of the assignment. [26]

Postponement in insolvency

A person who is able to pray in aid section 2 (3) and show that despite participation in profits he is not a partner must take the benefit of section 2 (3) with the burden of section 3,[27] *viz.*:

" In the event of any person to whom money has been advanced by way of loan upon such a contract as is mentioned in the last foregoing section, or of any buyer of a goodwill in consideration of a share of the profits of the business, being adjudged a bankrupt, entering into an agreement to pay his creditors less than twenty shillings in the pound, or dying in insolvent circumstances, the lender of the loan shall not be entitled to recover anything in respect of his loan, and the seller of the goodwill shall not be entitled to recover anything in respect of the share of profits contracted for, until the claims of the other creditors or buyer for valuable consideration in money or money's worth have been satisfied."

The creditor who has advanced by way of loan or who has transferred goodwill within the terms of section 2 (3) cannot compete with other creditors, and it is immaterial that the latter were or were not creditors during the continuance of the loan or that they were not creditors of the business. The postponed creditor cannot prove his debt in the bankruptcy until all the other creditors have been paid.[28]

In *Re Fort* (which concerned the operation of section 3 in relation to the proviso to case (*d*) of section 2 (3)) S, under an agreement not in writing, had advanced £3,000 to F to enable the latter to set up business as a jeweller on the terms that he would receive 5 per cent. plus a half share of the profits of the business. A receiving order having been made against F, S tendered proof of the debt, but was held to be postponed on the ground that section 3 applied to contracts governed by section 2 (3) (*d*) ignoring the proviso. " I cannot well see why, if the contract is in writing, the lender is to be postponed, but is not to be postponed if the contract is by parol," said Smith L.J.[29]

It is possible that the creditor under section 2 (3) may have lent other sums at a fixed rate of interest, in which case he may recover those sums like any other creditor,[30] unlike a continuation of substantially the same advance with a variation of terms which will not necessarily fall outside the subsection, such as the continuance of a loan to one partner who has taken over the business after the dissolution of the firm and then become bankrupt.[31] It is also possible that the advance of a small sum in return for a large share of profits and of a large sum at a fixed rate of interest by the same person might be adjudged to be an evasion of the Act rendering the creditor a partner with the debtor, or, at the least, bringing him within section 3 as to both loans. Section 3 " does not apparently deprive the lender of his right to retain any security he may take for his money; nor of his right to foreclose such security." [32] Another provision which may be noted here is section 36 of the Bankruptcy Act 1914 under which a loan by one spouse to another for the purpose of a trade or business is postponed even where there is no arrangement for the sharing of profits. In *Re Meade*, Mrs. H lent money to her lover X for use in the latter's business, but was unable to prove with X's ordinary creditors on the ground that this was not a loan at all but " her contribution to the capital of a business enterprise in which she plainly had an interest herself."[33]

TYPES OF PARTNERS

General partners

Unlike the Limited Partnerships Act 1907, which distinguishes between " general " and " limited " partners, the 1890 Act does not differentiate between different kinds of partners, but assumes that the normal type of partner will be a " general " or " active " partner who has the right to take part in the management of the partnership business in the absence of any agreement, express or implied, to the contrary. It is not unusual to provide in the articles of partnership that there shall be some internal division of labour, or that certain partners, *e.g.* junior partners, shall have limited rights in certain matters, such as the signing of bills of exchange or the ordering of goods. We have seen from *Stekel* v. *Ellice* (p. 18, above) that a person may be termed a " partner " with different consequences in different contexts. In that case a salaried partner was held to be a partner both as regards the outside world and as regards the partner *inter se*, without, however, possessing all of the plenary powers conferred by the 1890 Act and, in particular, the right to have the partnership property applied under section 39 of the Act.

" Dormant " or " sleeping " partners

A distinction is commonly drawn between " active " partners and " dormant " partners; a distinction not without legal effect, although nowhere mentioned in the Act. A dormant partner takes no active part in the management of the business. We have already seen that the distinction between those who advance capital and on whose behalf the business is conducted, and those who rank as creditors *simpliciter*, is sometimes a fine one. As Jessel M.R. pointed out in *Pooley* v. *Driver*,[34] there may be a dormant partner " who puts nothing in—neither capital, nor skill nor anything else." If his name does not appear in the firm's business name, then the latter must be registered under the Registration of Business Names Act 1916.[35]

A dormant partner is commonly, but not necessarily, a concealed partner. His concealment however does not give him any special immunity from the liability of partners for acts performed by any partner within the scope of apparent authority. A concealed partner will be liable in the same way as an " ordinary " partner, subject to the proviso to section 5 of the Act which makes an exception in those situations in which the third person does not know or believe that the person with whom he is dealing is a partner. The difficulties raised by the wording of the proviso are discussed below at p. 35.

Partner by " holding out "

A partner by " holding out " is not a partner in the true sense but someone who is adjudged to be a partner for particular purposes by reason of the doctrine of estoppe'. Lord Esher M.R. explained it as follows: " If a man holds himself out as a partner in a firm and thereby induces another person to act upon that representation, he is estopped as regards that person from saying that he is not a partner. The representation may be made either by acts or by words; but the estoppel can be relied upon only by the person to whom the representation has been made in either way, and who has acted upon the faith of it." [36] Liability by reason of " holding out " is dealt with in section 14 (below), which deals with liability to those who give credit to the firm on the faith of the representation made to them. Whilst it is true that a partner by " holding out " is not necessarily a " true " partner within the firm, although the holding out may be evidence that this is the case, it is possible that a person may be held out as a partner *e.g.* a salaried partner and, at the same time, be a true partner so far as the firm itself is concerned; on the other hand, he may be a partner by holding out to those dealing with the firm within which he is merely an employee.

MAXIMUM NUMBER OF PARTNERS

Under the Companies Act 1948, s. 434, no company, association or partnership consisting of more than 20 persons may be formed for the purpose of carrying on any business having for its object the acquisition of gain, unless it is registered as a company under that Act, or formed under some other Act. In the case of a banking company, the maximum number is 10 (*ibid.* s. 429). These restrictions prevent the re-emergence of the old unincorporated companies with their attendant abuses, but have been lifted by the Companies Act 1967, and regulations made thereunder, in respect of certain professional partnerships which, presumably because they subscribe to a professional ethos which serves to protect the public, are not so likely to fall into evil ways. Subject to varying qualifications, partnerships consisting of (or in certain cases mainly consisting of) the following professional persons may exceed the limit of 20 persons, *viz.* solicitors, accountants (as defined), members of recognised stock exchanges, patent agents, surveyors, auctioneers, valuers, estate agents, land agents (including estate management), actuaries, consulting engineers and building designers. The limit of 10 persons applicable to banking companies was raised to 20, provided each member is for the time being authorised by the Board of Trade to be a member of a partnership so enlarged.

Sexual discrimination against a person in relation to a position as partner in the firm is unlawful if the firm consists of six or more partners (s. 11 of the Sex Discrimination Act 1975): otherwise partnerships are liable under the Act, *e.g.* for discrimination in employment.

The tendency towards larger business units is reflected in the emergence of large national and, sometimes, international firms, and the greater use of mergers. These have involved structural arrangements such as the main firm linked with a branch firm or the device of the group practice. In the former case, partners from the main firm appear as " representative " partners on the branch firm which commonly remits a fee to the main firm. Group arrangements arise where two or more separate firms form a separate firm to promote the collective interest, one or more of the partners from the constituent firms being members of the group firm. Another possibility is that firms may be able to collaborate without structural re-organisation as where they enter into agreements for mutual support or agency arrangements. Even though many professional firms are now emancipated from the restriction on numbers discussed above, the advantages of branch or group arrangements have caused them to make the necessary organisational changes. There has also been pressure, usually from outside the professions concerned, for " mixed partnerships " which can offer a spectrum of professional services. Thus, there is much to be said for an omnibus firm which can provide all the services concerned with house purchase, such as legal services, estate agency, valuing, insurance and mortgage broking. At the time of writing however mixed practices are unlikely in those areas in which professional rivalry runs high.

Mention has already been made of those associations which, though not partnerships, yet exist for the acquisition of gain by their members within the meaning of the Companies Act and which, like partnerships, are unlawful if not registered. On the other hand, societies formed for the purposes of investing money or buying property and re-selling it to members, which are neither partnerships nor formed for the acquisition of gain do not require registration, although some, such as Unit Trusts, are subject to control under the Prevention of Fraud (Investments) Act 1958. Certain professional firms, such as accountants, architects and stockbrokers/jobbers (who have been allowed to form unlimited companies known as stock exchange service companies) can now use the device of the unlimited company and we have seen that there is currently some pressure in other professions for corporate status.

MEANING OF FIRM

" 4 (1) Persons who have entered into partnership with one another are for the purposes of this Act called collectively a firm, and the name under which their business is carried on is called the firm-name.

(2) In Scotland a firm is a legal person distinct from the partners of whom it is composed, but an individual partner may be charged on a decree or diligence directed against the firm, and on payment of the debts is entitled to relief *pro rata* from the firm and its other members."

Unlike the law of Scotland, English law knows nothing of the firm as an artificial person distinct from the members composing it. It is incorrect to say that a firm carries on business; it is the members of the firm who carry on business in partnership under the name or style of the firm. Nevertheless, there is little doubt that the firm is " personified " in business and accountancy practice,[37] whilst in law the partnership, although lacking discrete legal personality, does exhibit certain elements of " quasi-corporateness " which mark it off from unincorporated associations generally. Thus, the firm-name may be used in legal instruments both by the partners themselves and by other persons as a collective description of the partners in the firm at the time to which the description refers. The Rules of the Supreme Court permit of actions by and against the firm " in the name of the firm " and of the enforcement of judgments or orders against " any property of the firm." [38] At common law it was impossible for an action to be brought between a partner and his firm, or between two firms having a common member, but doubts remaining on this score until 1891 have been expressly removed by the Rules of the Supreme Court. [39] For the rather special purpose of income tax, the firm may be treated as a separate entity. [40] The distinctions between partnership property and separate property, and between partnership debts and separate debts are further complications from which the registered company is largely free.

The attribution of legal personality to the firm in Scotland has not been entirely free of difficulty, raising, as it does, the contrast between dealings with the firm or " house " and dealings with the partners at a particular moment in time, a contrast which has in its turn raised problems as to the effect of the death of a partner under section 33 (below) and as to the authority of partners under section 38 (below).

CHOICE OF NAME

Generally speaking, every person is by the law of England free to call himself by what name he chooses, or by different names for different purposes, so long as he does not use this liberty as the means of fraud or of interfering with the substantive rights of others. This freedom extends to commercial transactions. However, like most rights, the right to use any name is not unrestricted.

1. Registration of Business Names Act 1916 [41]

If partners select or use a business name which does not consist of the true surnames of all partners who are individuals, and the corporate names of all partners who are corporations, without any addition other than the true Christian names of individual partners or initials of such Christian names, they must, *inter alia*, register their true names with the Registrar of Business Names. The sanctions for non-compliance are criminal and civil; criminal, in that a fine not exceeding £5 *per diem* may be imposed on summary conviction, and civil, in that the rights of a defaulter arising out of contract are, subject to relief by the court, unenforceable (see ss. 7 and 8 of the Act, discussed below in Chap. 10). Section 14 of the Act, as enlarged by the Companies Act 1947, s. 116, gives the Registrar discretion to refuse the registration of misleading or undesirable business names.

2. Passing-off

" It is the law of this land," said Romer J.,[42] " that no man is entitled to carry on his business in such a way as to represent that it is the business of another." In this respect the prohibition is similar to that concerning the passing-off of goods, except that unlike the latter, a person may carry on business in his own name provided he acts properly, even though there may be some degree of confusion with the business of another. However, the present restriction may prevent persons from using their own names where such use is likely to deceive the public by making them believe they are dealing with someone else.[43]

3. Corporate names

The use of the descriptions " Company " or " and Company," which by common usage are applied to incorporated and un-incorporated associations alike, is permitted, but it has been said that it is an offence against the Prerogative for private persons to " assume to act as a corporation." [44] The last word of the name of a company registered with liability limited by shares or guarantee must be " limited," except for certain companies which may be relieved of this obligation. Section 439 of the Companies Act 1948 makes it an offence for persons to use a trade name ending with the word " limited " for an unincorporated association and this includes partnerships, whether ordinary or limited. There is, in fact, no require-ment that a limited partnership must have a firm name indicating the limitation of liability on the part of certain partners.

4. Exclusive right to trade name analogous to property in trade marks

Although in this country we do not recognise the absolute right of a person to a particular name to the extent of entitling him to prevent the assumption of that name by a stranger, nevertheless the law recognises a legal right to the exclusive use of a name in connection with a trade or business. This right is analogous to, but not identical with, the right to a trade mark proper which, under the Trade Marks

Act 1938, s. 68, means a mark used or proposed to be used in relation
to goods in order to indicate a connection between the goods and
some person having the right either as proprietor or as registered
user to use the mark. But one trader will only be entitled to restrain
another from using his trade name if both are engaged in a common
field of commercial activity. In *McCulloch* v. *May* [45] a BBC enter-
tainer known as " Uncle Mac " was held disentitled to restrain the
use of this name by another in connection with a breakfast cereal.
However, it may be noted that a " trade mark " includes, *inter alia*,
" a name " and sections 3 and 9 of the Trade Marks Act 1938 provide
that a firm-name, including that of a partnership, may be registered
as a trade mark for particular classes of goods where it is represented
in a special or particular manner.

CAPACITY

Although it is the general rule that everyone *sui juris* is competent to
enter into the partnership relation, some brief treatment is needed
of those special cases in which a person either cannot become a
partner (as with the alien enemy), or may become a partner, but with
peculiar attributes.

Aliens

So far as the law of partnership is concerned, an alien is as fully
capax as a British subject to become a partner. Because it is against
public policy to allow an alien enemy to maintain business relations
supported by the law of this country, a partnership which includes
an alien enemy is terminated on the outbreak of war, although the
rights of the alien enemy are not for ever extinguished. The term alien
enemy includes not only the subjects of hostile states resident therein,
but also other persons, including British subjects, who are also
resident or trading therein, thus demonstrating that the status of the
enemy alien is derived not from nationality or chauvinism but from the
place of residence or business.

The distinction between British subject and alien has been rendered
less stark in recent years, notably by United Kingdom accession to
the European Communities. Nationals of Member States of the EEC
can invoke Article 7 of the Treaty which prohibits " any discrimination on grounds of nationality " and, more specifically, can invoke
the right of establishment which we now know to be directly applicable and enforceable by national courts under Article 52, which

confers freedom of establishment upon firms under the conditions laid down for nationals of the country in which establishment is sought. A rude shock was administered to many, including the Government of the United Kingdom, when the Court of Justice of the European Communities held that Article 52 was directly applicable in Member States notwithstanding a national law which purported to restrict the right to practise as an *avocat* to nationals of that State (Reyners [1974] E.C.R. 631). As a result of the Van Binsbergen case ([1974] E.C.R. 1299) we also know that Articles 59 and 60 (which relate to freedom to provide services) are directly applicable so as to prohibit restrictions on legal practice based upon nationality or residence, although the Court of Justice in that case considered that specific requirements as to professional qualifications which are justified by the general good would not be incompatible with the Treaty depending upon the particular nature of the services to be provided. Taken in conjunction with the trend towards harmonisation of laws, such as the qualifications of road haulage operators, it will be seen that partnerships can cross national frontiers, so far as the EEC countries are concerned, with considerably greater ease than in the past.

Minors

It is clear, as Bayley J. pointed out in *Goode* v. *Harrison*,[46] that a minor may be in partnership until such time as he takes steps to disaffirm the partnership. It is also clear that a minor who is a partner cannot incur contractual liability for partnership debts, so that a judgment against the " firm " in respect of such a debt cannot be enforced against the " firm " as a whole but only against partners other than the minor.[47] The contract of partnership constitutes one of the class of voidable contracts which minors may repudiate either during minority or within a reasonable time of attaining majority. But the minor who effectively repudiates liability cannot recover money paid in respect of the contract unless he can demonstrate a total failure of consideration. In *Goode* v. *Harrison* itself it was held that the defendant, who had been in partnership with I.S., was liable in respect of goods delivered to I.S. after the defendant had attained the age of 21 years. Despite the absence of proof that the defendant had done any act as partner after reaching his majority, he was nevertheless held liable because he had failed in his duty to disaffirm the partnership when he came of age. The age of majority has been

18 years since January 1, 1970, by virtue of section 1 of the Family Law Reform Act 1969, a change to be borne in mind when reading the old cases.

Whilst the minor may repudiate the partnership, the adult partner is entitled to insist that the partnership assets should be applied in payment of the liabilities of the firm, and that until this is done, no part of such assets should be recoverable by the minor; to this extent, therefore, third parties may recover their debts out of the minor's property.

Married women

By virtue of the Law Reform (Married Women and Tortfeasors) Act 1935, the separate treatment of married women as a class of persons *alieni juris* is no longer justified. The married woman is as fully capable as the *feme sole* and may own property, incur liability in tort and contract, be made bankrupt for debt and bring and defend actions. Clearly, husband and wife may enter into a valid partnership agreement, but in view of the reluctance of the courts to presume that spouses living together in amity intend their discussions concerning money matters to have legal effect, it is doubly important that their wishes should be unequivocally set forth in a partnership deed.

Mental patients

A mental patient may enter into a partnership agreement, but this proposition must be qualified by two main considerations. First, at common law, such an agreement is voidable at the option of the person of unsound mind if he can prove, (a) that he did not appreciate the implications of the agreement into which he had entered, and (b) that this was known to the other party. Secondly, a partner's mental disorder (and this applies to supervening mental disorder) is a ground for the dissolution of the partnership under section 103 (1) (*f*) of the Mental Health Act 1959, which empowers a judge (as defined in the Act) to make such orders or give such directions as he thinks fit for the dissolution of a partnership of which the patient is a member. The Court of Protection may authorise the receiver as next friend to start proceedings in the Chancery Division which is obviously better fitted to deal with questions of property and accounts.

[1] [1970] 1 W.L.R. 333.

[2] [1970] Ch. 602.

[3] *French* v. *Styring* (1857) 2 C.B.(N.S.) 357, in which it was held that there was no partnership as to the horse; but a partnership as to the winnings was not ruled out. Thus, breeding from a mare has been held to constitute a business.

[4] (1856) 21 Beav. 536.

[5] (1880) 15 Ch.D. 247 at pp. 277–278.

[6] Fletcher Moulton L.J. in *Re Spanish Prospecting Co. Ltd.* [1911] 1 Ch.D. 92 at p. 98.

[7] 2 Bing.N.C. 108, at p. 112.

[8] [1894] 1 Q.B. 285 at p. 291.

[9] See for example *Waugh* v. *Carver* (1793) 2 H.Bl. 235.

[10] (1863) 3 B. & S. 556.

[11] (1793) 2 H.Bl. 235.

[12] First Report of Mercantile Law Commission (1854).

[13] (1860) 8 H.L.Cas. 268.

[14] (1888) 38 Ch.D. 238.

[15] (1877) L.R. 4 P.C. 419. See *Ex p. Delhasse* (1877–78) 7 Ch.D. 511.

[16] *Adam* v. *Newbigging* (1888) 13 App.Cas. 308 at p. 315.

[17] [1973] 1 W.L.R. 191.

[18] (1863) 3 B. & Sm. 847.

[19] " Co-partnership schemes " are not partnerships. *Ross* v. *Parkyns* (1875) L.R. 20 Eq. 331.

[20] (1884) 27 Ch.D. 460.

[21] *Cf. Re Jones, exp. Harper* (1857) 1 De G. & J. 180; *I.R.C.* v. *Lebus's Trustees* [1946] 1 All E.R. 476: 27 T.C. 136 (C.A.).

[22] Payment of a fixed sum " out of the profits " is equivalent to a share of profits: *Re Young, ex p. Jones* [1896] 2 Q.B. 484. *Cf. Re Pinto Leite and Nephews* [1929] 1 Ch. 221.

[23] (1877) 5 Ch.D. 458: see also *Ex p. Delhasse* (1877–78) 7 Ch.D. 511: *Syers* v. *Syers* (1876) 1 App.Cas. 174.

[24] *Bullen* v. *Sharp* (1865) L.R. 1 C.P. 86; *Re Howard, ex p. Tennant* (1877) 6 Ch.D. 303.

[25] Smith L.J. took this view in an *obiter dictum* in *Re Fort, ex p. Schofield* [1897] 2 Q.B. 495 at p. 501.

[26] *Pratt* v. *Strick* (1932) 17 T.C. 459.

[27] See Bovill's Act, s. 5, on which the decisions remain applicable.

[28] *Re Grason, ex p. Taylor* (1879) 12 Ch.D. 366 at p. 379; followed in *Re Mason* [1899] 1 Q.B. 810.

[29] [1897] 2 Q.B. 495.

[30] *Ex p. Mills* (1873) L.R. 8 Ch. 594.

[31] *Re Mason, supra.*

[32] Lindley, p. 96: *Ex p. Sheil* (1877) 4 Ch.D. 789.

[33] [1951] 1 Ch. 774, *per* Romer J. at pp. 783–784, who also held that she was not a partner or sharer in profits (a conclusion criticised in Pollock, 15th ed., p. 23).

[34] (1877) 5 Ch.D. 458 at p. 473.

[35] Discussed below, p. 229.

[36] *Re Fraser, ex p. Central Bank of London* [1892] 2 Q.B. 633 at p. 637.

[37] Proprietor's capital, even for a sole trader, is a " debt " owed by the firm to the proprietor.

[38] R.S.C., Ord. 81, r. 1. Actions are discussed below, pp. 162 *et seq.*

[39] R.S.C., Ord. 81, r. 6.

[40] Partners are liable to tax which is computed and stated as a joint liability of the partners quite separate from any individual liability which they may have apart from the partnership. See below, pp. 195 *et seq.*

[41] Chap. 10, *post.*

[42] In *Joseph Rodgers and Sons Ltd.* v. *W. N. Rodger & Co.* (1924) 41 R.P.C. 277 at p. 291.

[43] *Holloway* v. *Holloway* (1800) 13 Beav. 209.

[44] Pollock, 15th ed., p. 26.

[45] [1947] 2 All E.R. 845.

[46] (1821) 5 B. & Ald. 147 at p. 157.

[47] *Lovell and Christmas* v. *Beauchamp* [1894] A.C. 607.

CHAPTER THREE

RELATIONS OF PARTNERS TO PERSONS DEALING
WITH THEM

ACTUAL AND APPARENT AUTHORITY

AGENCY constitutes the central feature of partnership. Even before
the Partnership Act 1890, the common law had endowed each
partner with general authority to bind the firm (that is, himself and
his co-partners) by acts in the usual course of the partnership
business. "The liability of one partner for the acts of his co-partners
is in truth the liability of a principal for the acts of his agent," said
Lord Cranworth in *Cox* v. *Hickman*.[1] Throughout this case Blackburn J. treated the contractual liability of partners as one of the
branches of agency. We have seen that the power and authority of
the partner derive from the fact that the partnership business is run
on the partners' behalf, a state of affairs which puts a partner's
property, whether joint or separate, at the mercy of the skill, knowledge and integrity of his co-partners.

It is customary in agency law to draw a distinction between the
actual authority of the agent, whether express or implied, and his
apparent or ostensible authority, the former arising from express
consensual agreement or the inferences to be drawn from the conduct
of the parties or the circumstances of the case, the latter being an
authority which the agent appears to others to hold. As Lord Denning
M.R. pointed out in *Hely-Hutchinson* v. *Brayhead Ltd.*,[2] apparent
authority will often coincide in practice with actual authority, but
not necessarily on all occasions, as where a managing director binds
his company to the purchase of goods to the value of £1,000 despite a
limit of £500 on such purchases imposed by his board of directors.
It is interesting to note that Diplock L.J. in an earlier case had
defined apparent authority as " a legal relationship between the
principal and the contractor created by a representation, made by
the principal to the contractor, intended to be and in fact acted on by
the contractor, that the agent has authority to enter on behalf of the
principal into a contract of a kind within the scope of the ' apparent '
authority, so as to render the principal liable to perform any obligations imposed upon him by such contract." [3] Now, whilst it will

32

doubtless make little difference in practice whether one rests apparent authority upon the objective appearance of authority presented to third parties, or upon the so-called " estoppel " theory, with its emphasis upon a " representation," it must be confessed that the latter explanation fails to provide a satisfactory rationale for that phenomenon of English law—the undisclosed principal.[4]

The extent of the apparent authority of partners is spelled out in section 5 of the 1890 Act.

" Every partner is an agent of the firm and his other partners for the purpose of the business of the partnership; and the acts of every partner who does any act for carrying on in the usual way business of the kind carried on by the firm of which he is a member bind the firm and his partners, unless the partner so acting has in fact no authority to act for the firm in the particular matter, and the person with whom he is dealing either knows that he has no authority, or does not know or believe him to be a partner."

Registration of names under the Registration of Business Names Act 1916 does not operate as constructive notice for the purposes of section 5. The extent of the partner's authority, and the corresponding liability of partners resulting from its exercise, are well described by Sir W. M. James L.J. in *Re Agriculturist Cattle Insurance Co.*; *Baird's Case*, when he distinguished partnerships from joint-stock companies. " Ordinary partnerships are essentially in kind, and not merely in the magnitude of the partnership or the number of the partners, different from joint-stock companies. . . . As between the partners and the outside world (whatever may be their private arrangements between themselves), each partner is the unlimited agent of every other in every matter connected with the partnership business, or which he represents as partnership business, and not being in its nature beyond the scope of the partnership. A partner who may not have a farthing of capital left may take moneys or assets of this partnership to the value of millions, may bind the partnership by contracts to any amount, may give the partnership acceptances for any amount and may even—as has been shown in the most painful instances in this Court—involve his innocent partners in un-limited amounts for frauds which he has craftily concealed from them." [5]

Leaving on one side for the moment the problems posed by the dormant partner, section 5 shows that a partner's apparent authority is confined to acts connected with the business of the kind carried on by the firm and performed in the usual way. To allow a partner to enter into a *negotiorum gestio* on behalf of the firm, but outside the scope of its business, however convenient or necessary this might be, would be undesirable. In such a case section 5 would not apply and, in the absence of special arrangements, the acts of one partner would not bind the firm.

Whether or not a particular act falls within the scope of the partnership business is essentially a question of fact. Referring to certain usages which have been constantly recognised by the courts in connection with certain frequent and important transactions, the fifteenth edition of Pollock went so far as to say that such judicially recognised usages were " in effect rules of law." [6] The translation of custom into law is a familiar phenomenon and doubtless customs not hitherto judicially recognised will in due course receive their judicial acknowledgment. At the same time, it is well to realise that individual firms sometimes conduct their business in their own ways, whilst customs themselves may fall into desuetude and serve only as out-dated reminders of an earlier age.

An example of the objective manner in which the courts approach their task of determining the scope of the partnership business is to be found in *Mercantile Credit Co. Ltd.* v. *Garrod*,[7] in which A and his sleeping partner B had entered into agreement for the letting of garages and the execution of motor repairs, but expressly excluding the buying and selling of cars. A, without B's knowledge, purported to sell a car to which he had no title to a hire-purchase company for the sum of £700, which was in fact paid into the partnership account. Mocatta J., in holding that B was accountable for the £700, dismissed the argument that the transaction was not binding because of the exclusion of buying and selling in the partnership deed, preferring instead to look at the matter from " what was apparent to the outside world in general." A " was doing an act of a like kind to the business carried on by persons trading as a garage." [8]

The act in question must not only fall within the scope of the business carried on by the firm but it must also be executed " in the usual way " of such business. It is evident, therefore, that there may be circumstances of time, place or manner in which the act in question, although connected with the firm's business, lies outside the partner's apparent authority. In *Higgins* v. *Beauchamp*,[9] acceptance of an inchoate bill of exchange lacking the drawer's name was sufficiently unusual to put such an acceptance beyond the usual way of carrying on business.

Before examining some of the refinements which the cases have engrafted on the general rule set forth in section 5, two matters may be disposed of.

First, an act outside the scope of the partnership business may be binding on the firm by virtue of the application of the ordinary principles of agency law. Thus, the firm will be liable where it has specially authorised a partner to act outside the ordinary scope of the firm's business. The effect would be to constitute the partner a special agent lacking the penumbra of apparent authority. The firm will also be liable where it has ratified the unauthorised act of a partner but the ratification is only valid where the agent professedly acted as such.[10]

Secondly, there is the problem of the dormant partner's liability for the acts of active partners. No difficulty arises when the latter act within the terms of their actual authority, in which event all the partners, including dormant partners, are liable. The position is rather more difficult when an active partner exceeds his actual authority but acts within the scope of the apparent authority conferred by section 5. If the third party knows or believes that the person so acting is a partner, and is unaware that he is exceeding his authority, the firm, including the dormant partner, is liable. Conversely, if the third party is unaware of the excess of authority and does not know or believe the person acting to be a partner, the firm, including the dormant partner, is not liable. This latter conclusion seems to be at variance with the doctrine propounded in *Watteau* v. *Fenwick*,[11] a case which turned upon the ordinary law of agency and which has excited both approval [12] and disapproval.[13] There, the owner of a public-house sold it to brewers who permitted the former owner to remain in possession as manager and licensee, subject to an express prohibition against the purchase of cigars on credit. The brewers were held liable for the cost of cigars bought on credit by the manager, although the suppliers of the cigars had in fact dealt with the manager as a principal. Wills J. suggested, *obiter*, that apropos the question of limitation of authority as between the partners, " The law of partnership is . . . nothing but a branch of the general law of principal and agent." [14] Whatever may be the position with regard to the undisclosed principal in ordinary law, it does seem as though the concluding words of section 5 put partnership into a separate category, inasmuch as a partner not known or believed to be such by the third party cannot, by acts outside his actual but within his apparent authority, affix his co-partners with liability.

According to the late Professor Montrose, anomalous results can be achieved in determining the liability of a dormant partner in firms comprising more than two partners.[15] For example, a dormant partner would be liable for a purchase of goods by co-partner A within the scope of apparent authority (but in breach of the terms of the agreed actual authority) from a supplier who knew that A was a partner of B, but who was unaware of the dormant partner's membership of the firm. On the other hand, the dormant partner would not be liable for such a purchase, either by his sole co-partner A, or by his co-partners A and B who purchase *jointly* from the supplier, who knows that A and B are partners, but does not know that the dormant partner is a partner; a result which in this latter case is achieved by including the plural in the singular so that the concluding words of section 5 should be read as ". . . or does not know or believe [them] to be partners."

Another, although obviously rarer, problem posed by the dormant partner concerns *his* ability to bind the firm. If such a partner is given actual authority, *cadit quaestio*; the firm, of which he is a member, is bound by acts within the scope of such actual authority, ignoring the point that the entrusting of an active role to a dormant partner is something in the nature of a contradiction. As in the situation previously discussed, a dormant partner acting outside the ambit of his actual authority cannot, *quoad* a third person who neither knows or believes him to be a partner, bind the firm.

Apparent authority of partners in certain transactions

It is customary to group the cases illustrating the extent of apparent authority into three main categories, *viz.*:

   (a) powers which are prima facie held by all partners;

   (b) powers which are prima facie held by partners in trading firms (carrying with it the corollary that partners in non-trading firms lack such powers); and

   (c) powers which prima facie belong to no partner.

However useful such groupings may be for the purposes of exposition, it is well to realise that they may prove to be fallacious guides in particular instances. As previously indicated, the eclectic inquiry into the scope of apparent authority within a particular firm is ultimately a question of fact. This admonition administered, examples are given of powers normally associated (or not associated) with the three categories.

(a) *Powers normally held by all partners*

Every partner is presumptively entitled to bind the firm by means of the following acts:

  (i) He may sell any goods or personal chattels of the firm.

  (ii) He may purchase on account of the firm goods of a kind necessary for or usually employed in its business. The firm is bound even though the goods are misapplied by the partner who purchases on account of the firm.[16] Thus, a non-trading firm may be bound by a purchase of goods on credit but not by a partner's borrowing on behalf of the firm. Megarry J. uttered a reminder against being bewitched by words in *Mann* v. *D'Arcy*,[17] a case in which D, partner in a firm of produce merchants, D and Co., purported to commit his firm to a joint venture with the plaintiff for the disposal of part of a cargo of potatoes. Pressed with the argument that a partner possesses no implied authority to make his co-partners partners in another business,[18] Megarry J. preferred to hold that the arrangement was merely one mode of buying and selling goods which the partner had authority to buy and sell. The joint venture was a partnership but it did not rank as another business. D was only mitigating the expense inherent in the venture at the cost of reducing the profit.

  (iii) He may receive payment of the debts due to the firm, and give receipts or releases therefor.[19]

  (iv) He may engage employees for the purpose of the partnership business. In *Beckham* v. *Drake* [20] it was held that the plaintiff could sue the three partners for breach of an agreement between himself and the two active partners providing that he was to continue as foreman for seven years. It is thought that one partner may dismiss employees but not against the wishes of the other partners.

  (v) He may employ a solicitor to defend actions brought against the firm. The solicitor may enter an appearance in the names of each of the other partners and is not obliged to inform them of the progress of the action.[21] It is not certain whether a single partner may employ a solicitor to bring an action on behalf of the firm.

(b) *Powers normally held by partners in trading firms*

Partners in trading firms are said to have wider powers than their counterparts in non-trading firms. Unfortunately, this rather dubious distinction would now appear to have been consecrated by the cases. Without purporting to give an exhaustive definition of what constitutes a trader, Ridley J. in *Wheatley* v. *Smithers* [22] said that " one important element in any definition of the term would be that trading implies a buying or selling." Proceeding on this basis, the court held that an auctioneer was not a trader; he does not buy and, although he sells, he sells not his own goods but only those of other persons. The Court of Appeal declined to express any opinion on the status of the auctioneer in this context, but the distinction set out in the *Wheatley* case was approved in *Higgins* v. *Beauchamp*, [23] in which it was held that a partner in a firm of cinematographic theatre proprietors had no power to borrow on the credit of the firm. The partnership deed expressly negatived any such power to borrow and the non-trading character of the firm negatived an implied power to borrow. " In my opinion," said Lush J., " it would be wrong to say that every business which involves spending money is a trading business. To my mind a trading business is one which carries on the buying and selling of goods." [24] This brings to mind the following question. Would cinema proprietors who sell ice-cream during the intervals in performances be trading partners *vis-à-vis* the vending of ice-cream, but not *vis-à-vis* the provision of the film? The most comprehensive statement of the partner's powers is to be found in *Bank of Australasia* v. *Breillat*, where it was said that " each partner is *praepositus negotiis societatis*; and may consequently bind all the other partners by his acts, in all matters which are within the scope and objects of the partnership. Hence, if the partnership be of a general commercial nature, he may pledge, or sell the partnership property; he may buy goods on account of the partnership; he may borrow money, contract debts, and pay debts on account of the partnership; he may draw, make, sign, endorse, accept, transfer, negotiate and procure to be discounted, promissory notes, bills of exchange, checks [*sic*] and other negotiable paper in the name and on account of the partnership." [25]

Although the term " partnership of a general commercial nature " is clearly wider than " trading partnership," the later cases have tended to aequiparate the two. Consequently, a partner in the latter type of firm has been held able to bind the firm in the following ways:

(i) He may draw, issue, accept, transfer and indorse bills of exchange and other negotiable instruments in the name of the firm.

Section 23 (2) of the Bills of Exchange Act 1882 provides that " The signature of the name of a firm is equivalent to the signature by the person so signing of the names of all persons liable as partners in that firm." However, a partner cannot bind the firm by using a name which departs substantially from the firm name. Furthermore, section 25 of the Bills of Exchange Act 1882 states that a procuration signature binds the principal only within the actual limits of the authority conferred. If the name of the firm is also the name of an individual partner in that firm, the latter's signature to a bill prima facie binds the firm unless it can be shown (and the burden of proof is on the co-partners) that the person so signing did so in his personal capacity.[26] In the case of a non-trading partnership, those who seek to hold the firm bound must prove that such a course of dealing is necessary or usual in the particular business. So, for example, a partner in a banking partnership may have a customary power to act in relation to bills of exchange, but such a power will usually be lacking in the case of solicitors,[27] auctioneers [28] and farmers.[29]

(ii) He may borrow money on the credit of the firm, irrespective of any private limitation of authority between the partners unless, of course, such limitation is known to the third party. *Ex abundanti cautela*, section 7 reminds us that this power (any more than the other powers) is not unlimited in extent:

" Where one partner pledges the credit of the firm for a purpose apparently not connected with the firm's ordinary course of business, the firm is not bound, unless he is in fact specially authorised by the other partners; but this section does not affect any personal liability incurred by an individual partner."

(iii) He may for the purposes of the foregoing pledge any goods or personal chattels belonging to the firm. Thus, in *Brown* v. *Kidger* [30] it was held that a managing partner in a common trading partnership could bind his firm by borrowing for partnership purposes. This would be so even though he might wrongfully apply the money so borrowed to other than partnership purposes. However, as in all cases of apparent authority, it is otherwise if the lender knows that the partner offering partnership property intends to apply the proceeds to his own use.[31] This power was not implied in the case of *Higgins* v. *Beauchamp*,[32] which involved a non-trading firm. This latter type of firm is only bound if the agent is given actual authority or, lacking such authority, his act has been ratified by his co-partners.

(iv) He may for the like purposes make an equitable mortgage by deposit of title deeds or otherwise of real estate or chattels real belonging to the firm.[33] However, a legal mortgage requiring a deed cannot be executed by one partner so as to bind his firm.

(c) *Powers not normally held by partners*

No partner, whether in a trading firm or not, has apparent authority in the following respects:

(i) He cannot bind his firm by deed in the absence of express authority under seal (for which purpose the fact that the partnership agreement is under seal does not suffice).[34]

(ii) He cannot bind the firm by giving a guarantee in the firm's name, even where this is reasonable and convenient in relation to the partnership business.[35]

(iii) He cannot accept shares in a company, even if fully paid up, in satisfaction of a debt due to the firm.[36]

(iv) He cannot bind the firm by a submission to arbitration.[37]

Finally, it may be noted that there is no converse rule that the firm is the agent of the individual partners. Payment to the firm is not discharge of a separate debt due to one partner in the absence of proof that the firm had authority to receive payment for him.[38]

LIABILITY OF THE FIRM AND OF THE PARTNERS

So far we have discussed the power and authority of the partner to bind his firm. Attention must now be turned to the nature, extent and duration of the liability attaching to the firm and its members as a result of the partner's acts.

Section 6 provides that:

" An act or instrument relating to the business of the firm and done or executed in the firm-name, or in any other manner showing an intention to bind the firm, by any person thereto authorised, whether a partner or not, is binding on the firm and all the partners.

Provided that this section shall not affect any general rule of law relating to the execution of deeds or negotiable instruments."

The negative effect of this section is that the act of any agent even although it is related to the business of the firm and done for its benefit, will not bind the firm if the agent acted as principal on his own account. As Gurney B. put it in *Beckham* v. *Drake*,[39] the point to be considered in each case is whether the party is acting for himself alone or on behalf of the firm. In that case A and B, the " ostensible " partners in a firm which included C, had entered into a written agreement to continue the employment of X as foreman. Although C was not a party to the memorandum, it was held that, notwithstanding the parol evidence rule in contract (which in any case was held to be inapplicable), he could be sued along with A and B for breach of the agreement. At the same time, the court accepted that an agent may contract as principal. In the words of Lord Abinger C.B., " An agent may say to the person with whom he is dealing ' I am the person responsible in this particular transaction or the other party may say ' I hold you responsible to me ', though I know your principal.' " [40]

Except where his acts are unauthorised but later ratified, the agent need not act professedly as such; if in fact he was acting for the firm and within his authority, the firm will be bound even though its existence has been concealed. [41]

The proviso to the section preserves the special rules applicable to deeds and negotiable instruments. *Re Briggs and Co.*, [42] affords a useful reminder that a deed signed by a partner within his authority on behalf of the firm is not necessarily devoid of legal effect. In that case, it was held that an assignment by deed of book debts belonging to a firm by a partner therein operated as a good equitable assignment under the main part of the section, whatever its effect as a deed might be.

Section 7 sets the *ne plus ultra* to the scope of section 5 by making it clear beyond peradventure that a firm is not bound where a partner pledges the firm's credit for purposes apparently not connected with its business:

> " Where one partner pledges the credit of the firm for a purpose apparently not connected with the firm's ordinary course of business, the firm is not bound, unless he is in fact specially authorised by the other partners; but this section does not affect any personal liability incurred by an individual partner."

Persons who " have notice or reason to believe that the thing done in the partnership name is done for the private purposes or on the separate account of the partner doing it," [43] cannot be heard to say that they were misled by the partner's apparent, general authority.

In *Bignold* v. *Waterhouse* [44] a special favour was granted to a consignor of goods by one partner in a firm of coach proprietors operating between London and Norwich. It was held that where a customer of a trading firm stipulates with one of the partners for a special advantage in the conduct of their business with him, for a consideration which is good as between himself and that partner, but of no value to the firm, the firm is not bound by this agreement, and incurs no obligation in respect of any business done in pursuance of it. In *Shirreff* v. *Wilks* [45] a special application of this principle was made where two out of three partners gave an acceptance in the name of the firm for a debt incurred before the third had entered the partnership; this was held not to bind the new partner, for it was, in effect, the same thing as an attempt by a single partner to pledge the joint fund for his individual debts. The commonest case in which the principle is applied arises where a partner gives a negotiable instrument or other security in the name of the firm to raise money for his private purposes or for the satisfaction of his private debt to the knowledge of the person providing the money. Where a partner authorised to indorse bills in the partnership name and for partnership purposes indorses a bill in the name of the firm for his own private purposes, a holder who takes the bill not knowing the indorsement to be for a purpose foreign to the partnership, can still recover against the other partners, notwithstanding the unauthorised character of the indorsement as between the partners. [46] However, if he knows that the indorsement is in fact not for a partnership purpose he cannot recover. [47] In *Kendal* v. *Wood*, [48] the defendants received £1,000 of partnership money from W (the plaintiff's partner) in settlement of W's debt to them. It was held, on the dissolution of the firm, that the £1,000 could not be retained as against the plaintiff who had neither authorised its appropriation to W's own debt nor led the defendants to suppose that W had the necessary authority to dispose of partnership property in this way. Although W had appropriated partnership funds to the liquidation of his own debts some four years previously, the court declined to infer that the authority then conferred had continued. Cockburn C.J. put the matter in its strictest form when he said, " I am strongly of opinion that if a creditor of one of two partners chooses to take from his debtor what he knows to be partnership securities or partnership funds without ascertaining whether the debtor has the authority of his partners as to this application of the partnership funds, he does so at his own peril, and it is not enough that he has even reasonable cause to believe in the existence of the authority." [49] Blackburn and Montagu Smith JJ. did not go as far as this, the former stating that third persons can hold the partners accountable if they can show either actual authority conferred on the partner who has acted, " or probably, if they can show that the other partner whom he seeks to bind has so conducted himself that they had reasonable ground to suppose there was authority." [50] Even so, reasonable belief is linked with the conduct of the person whom it is sought to make liable, upon which an estoppel is raised which precludes him from denying authority.

Section 8 clarifies the pre-existing law when it states that:

> " If it has been agreed between the partners that any restriction shall be placed on the power of any one or more of them to bind the firm, no act done in contravention of the agreement is binding on the firm with respect to persons having notice of the agreement."

Lord Cranworth remarked in *Cox* v. *Hickman*,[51] that " Partners may stipulate among themselves that some of them only shall enter into particular contracts, or that as to certain of the contracts none shall be liable except those by whom they are actually made; but with such private arrangements third persons dealing with the firm without notice have no concern."

This section clears up a conflict between dicta of Lord Ellenborough in *Gallway* v. *Matthew* [52] and *Alderson* v. *Pope* [53] and the opinion of Lord Lindley in his extra-judicial capacity as a textbook writer. The former were to the effect that notice of a restrictive agreement between the partners precluded the third party from suing in breach of the restriction. Lord Lindley had suggested that " notice of an agreement between the members of a firm that one of them shall not do certain things is by no means necessarily equivalent to notice that the firm will not be liable for them if he does." [54] This view was drawn from cases such as *Greenwood's* case [55] and *Brown* v. *Leonard*,[56] in which it was held that the conduct of a partner in telling a third person that he had ceased to be a partner but that his name would continue in the firm for a certain time was not tantamount to a disclaimer of responsibility but meant that he would be responsible for the debts of the firm contracted during the specified time. Now, whilst it is clear that an agreement between the partners purporting to negate the essence of partnership, such as for example the attaching of limited liability for debts to certain partners, is inoperative to limit the rights of third persons whether they have notice of the limitation or not, section 8 comes down against Lindley's view. It was suggested in *Pollock on Partnership* (15th ed.) that restrictions might be of two sorts, namely, those which purport to limit the power of a partner to bind the firm and those which accept the power but render its exercise a breach of faith, it being a question of construction in every case to decide into which category a restriction falls. It is difficult to dissent from the view there expressed that " it is hard to see what rational motive there should be for giving any partner wider powers, as between the firm and third persons, than his co-partners are really willing to trust him with as between themselves." [57]

Liability for debts and obligations

A partner who succeeds in affixing his firm with liability *ex contractu* in effect subjects the firm to a single, joint obligation which is incumbent upon all the partners, including himself. Whatever may have been thought to be the position previously in equity, *Kendall* v. *Hamilton* [58] has put it beyond doubt that partnership debts and obligations are joint in nature, except in the case of a partner dying, in which event his estate is also severally liable for the debts of the firm. A and B were sued in respect of a loan by the plaintiff to the firm, in which A and B were partners, and judgment was signed against them but remained unsatisfied. Discovering that C, a solvent person, had been a partner in the firm at the relevant time, the plaintiff brought a second action against C in respect of the same loan, but failed on the ground that judgment in the previous action, even though unsatisfied, extinguished the obligation. The obligation to pay had been merged in the previous judgment. Thus, a company's debt from a firm cannot, even under strong temptation on the peculiar facts, be set off against one partner's claim against the company in liquidation. Similarly, an executor cannot retain a legacy to one partner of a firm by virtue of a partnership debt to the estate. The rule in *Kendall* v. *Hamilton*, and indeed joint liability in general, has evoked little enthusiasm. As one distinguished commentator has put it: " What is needed is that joint liability as a legal conception should cease to exist, and that every obligation now read as joint should be read as joint and several." [59] Nevertheless, the rule has received statutory confirmation, as follows, in section 9 of the Act:

" Every partner in a firm is liable jointly with the other partners, and in Scotland severally also, for all debts and obligations of the firm incurred while he is a partner; and after his death his estate is also severally liable in a due course of administration for such debts and obligations, so far as they remain unsatisfied, but subject in England or Ireland to the prior payment of his separate debts."

The section deals not only with contractual obligations but also " debts," a term wide enough to include non-contractual debts such as a judgment debt or value added tax (see s. 22 (2) of the Finance Act 1972 which assumes that s. 9 covers tax liability: see s. 152 of the Income and Corporation Taxes Act 1970, and pp. 195–196, below, for joint liability to income tax). It will doubtless be observed that, in so far as it applies, joint liability only attaches with regard to debts and obligations of the firm incurred while the partner whom it is sought to make liable was a member of the firm. In *Bagel* v. *Miller*,[60] a deceased partner's estate was held to be free from liability in respect of goods ordered for the firm whilst he was a partner, but delivered after his demise; no debt accrued under the contract until such time as the goods were delivered. Section 20 of the Sale of Goods Act 1893 states that, unless otherwise agreed, delivery and payment are concurrent conditions. The decision would have been different if the contract had provided for prepayment of the price and the deceased had died after the date set for such prepayment.

Despite the fresh lease of life given to the rule by section 9, certain exceptions go some way towards ridding it of some of its noxious features.

(a) It will be noted that the rule does not apply in Scotland, where joint and several liability for partnership debts and obligations is preserved.

(b) The section also preserves the joint and several liability of the estate of the deceased partner for debts and obligations of the firm incurred whilst the deceased was a partner. Even before *Kendall* v. *Hamilton*, this exception had long prevailed in equity: *jus accrescendi inter mercatores locum non habet*. It matters not in what order the partnership creditor chooses to pursue his concurrent remedies, provided two conditions are substantially satisfied. First, he is not allowed to compete with the deceased's separate creditors, to whose claims he is postponed.[61] Secondly, the court will require the presence of the surviving partner or partners in some way so that the partnership accounts may be taken.[62]

(c) Although judgment against one or more of several obligees extinguishes further rights of action, it may be that two rights of action are not *in eadem causa*, as where one of joint guarantors is sued on a cheque given by him in discharge of the guarantee; if judgment on the dishonoured cheque is not satisfied, the guarantee may still be enforced against the guarantors.[63] As Grose J. put it in

Drake v. *Mitchell*,[64] " The note or bill, not having been accepted as satisfaction for the debt, could only operate as a collateral security; and though judgment has been recovered on the bill, yet not having produced satisfaction in fact, the plaintiff may still resort to his original remedy in the covenant."

(d) The harshness of the rule is alleviated by Order 81, rule 1, of the Rules of the Supreme Court, which permits an action to be brought against the partnership in the firm-name, provided it carries on business within the jurisdiction. The use of the firm-name is merely a convenient method of suing those persons who composed the firm at the date when the cause of action accrued; the effect is that the plaintiff sues the partners individually just as much as if he had set out all their names.[65]

Liability of the firm for wrongs

Discussion so far has turned on the liability of the firm for contracts entered into on its behalf by a partner. But the firm (and, again, this is merely a compendious way of referring to the partners) may be liable for wrongs done to a third person by a partner, either because the wrong has been authorised by the partners (as where they authorise one of their number to commit a trespass), or because the wrong has been committed in the course of the partnership business (as where one of the partners negligently injures a third person whilst about partnership business). Section 10 sets out the broad rule governing liability for wrongs:

" Where, by any wrongful act or omission of any partner acting in the ordinary course of the business of the firm, or with the authority of his co-partners, loss or injury is caused to any person not being a partner in the firm, or any penalty is incurred, the firm is liable therefor to the same extent as the partner so acting or omitting to act."

Hamlyn v. *Houston and Co.*[66] illustrates the operation of this section. H, the active partner in a firm consisting of himself and S, bribed a clerk in a rival firm to disclose confidential information concerning the contracts and tenders of his employers. Rejecting the argument that the end (obtaining information concerning competitors) and the means (inducing the clerk to break his contract) were both illegal, it was found that the obtaining of information lay within the firm's business and that the means employed were sufficiently related to that end to make the firm liable. The partner's act, therefore, may be wilful or negligent, tortious and even criminal. " It is too well established by the authorities to be now disputed," said Collins M.R., " that a principal may be liable for the fraud or other illegal act committed by his agent within the general scope of the authority given to him, and even the fact that the act of the agent is criminal does not necessarily take it out of the scope of his authority." [67] The false currency given to the notion that the agent's act must have been committed for the principal's benefit [68] was dispelled by the House of Lords in *Lloyd* v. *Grace, Smith and Co.*, in which it was held, in the words of Lord Macnaghten, that " a principal must be liable for the fraud of his agent committed in the course of his agent's employment and not beyond the scope of his agency, whether the breach be committed for the principal's benefit or not." [69]

In *Meekins* v. *Henson*, Winn J. suggested, *obiter*, that section 10 deals only with the secondary liability of the partners, that is to say the liability which attaches in respect of the act of another committed in the course of his employment or as agent, and pointed out a contrast between " liability falling directly upon a man who is a partner in a partnership firm, and a liability falling upon him because he is an employer or principal whose employee or workman or agent has done a tortious act." [70] In that case, a libellous letter signed by A had been sent on behalf of the firm (consisting of A, B and C) to a borough treasurer. Because liability was personal to the partners, C alone was held liable inasmuch as the occasion attracted qualified privilege and C alone had acted with malice.

It is generally assumed that section 10 deals solely with the question of the civil liability of the firm despite the reference in that section to " any wrongful acts " and to the liability of the firm for " any penalty incurred " by reason of such wrongful act or omission by a partner in the ordinary course of the business of the firm. The word " penalty " has an uncertain connotation since it covers both a criminal punishment, *e.g.* a fine, and liquidated damages containing a punitive element. In the context of a civil statute it is, perhaps, unlikely that the word " penalty " refers to criminal conduct, although presumably it would formerly have covered the " penal action," which, prior to its abolition by the Common Informers Act 1951, was in essence a civil action brought by a common informer to whom the penalty was payable. An example of such an action is to be found in section 9 of the Truck Act 1831 which allowed a member of the public to sue for and recover a penalty from any employer who entered into " trucking " contracts against the terms of that Act. However, section 13 of the same Act, which remains extant, precludes the conviction of a partner of an offence under the Act committed by a co-partner without the former partner's knowledge, privity or assent, subject to the rider that the partnership property may be made available to satisfy any fine or sum of money awarded.

If, as seems unlikely, the section refers to crime, it is clear that it does not *create* criminal liability.[71] It goes without saying that a partner may be liable for crime as a primary party or a secondary party in the same way as anyone else. In *Parsons* v. *Barnes*,[72] a partner in a building and roof-repairing business was held to have committed an offence under the Trade Descriptions Act 1968 because he was present when his co-partner made a false statement concerning a process to be applied to a customer's roof. Declining to commit itself to any large proposition that one partner was necessarily liable for the acts of a co-partner under the Act, the Divisional Court found that the defendant's presence at the initial inspection and discussions justified his conviction by the justices who had found that he and his co-partner had acted in concert throughout. Similarly, partners who break a duty imposed on them by law may incur criminal liability as, for example, breach of the general duties laid down in the Health and Safety at Work Act 1974. A partner prosecuted for breach of those duties could not escape liability by showing that the responsibility of complying with the requirements of that Act had been delegated to one or more of his co-partners since each partner is an " employer " for the purposes of that Act. If criminal liability attaches to partners it attaches to them personally and not, at least in England and Wales, to their firm, since this lacks legal personality. There is nothing comparable to the use of the firm-name as in civil actions, or the procedure to enforce criminal liability against corporations. If the use of a now-judicially condemned phrase may be allowed, the partners are not the *alter ego* of their firm.

Quite apart from the personal liability of partners for crime, a partner may be vicariously liable in crime, the familiar example being the vicarious liability of the partner for the crimes of his employees in the course of employment. The cases show, less familiarly perhaps, that one partner may be vicariously liable in crime for the acts or omissions of his co-partner, as in *Davies* v. *Harvey*,[73] in which a poor law guardian was held to have been properly convicted of supplying a bedstead for parish relief to his own profit despite the fact that the guardian knew nothing of the transaction which had been effected by his co-partner in business.

Such vicarious liability in crime as a partner may incur by reason of the acts or omissions of a co-partner in the course of business rests upon the relationship of principal and agent which exists between them. Whether or not a partner is vicariously liable for the acts of his co-partner will depend on the nature of the crime involved. Thus, where A and B were partners, it has been held that A could not be properly convicted of the offence of " using " a vehicle in contravention of section 64 (2) of the Road Traffic Act 1960 merely by reason of the fact that his co-partner, B, in A's absence, drove a tractor on partnership business (*Garrett* v. *Hooper* [74]). Similarly in *Crawford* v. *Haughton*,[75] it was held that the owner of a stock-car driven on the road by another person in contravention of the Road Traffic Act could not be convicted of " using " the stock-car although it is interesting to note that the Divisional Court considered that the driver's *employer* would have been liable if the use of the vehicle had taken place in the course of employment. It would appear that a partner who is liable for an employee who drives a vehicle will not, so far as this particular offence is concerned, be responsible for a co-partner who drives the vehicle on partnership business, although he might be responsible for " causing " or " permitting " the use of the vehicle if the necessary *mens rea* can be made out. Apart from cases involving resort to what has been termed " the dictionary of judicial semantics," it has been suggested that " by and large in cases where a man would normally be liable for the acts of his servant the presumption must be that a partner would be liable for the acts of his co-partner in the course of business." [76] However, as indicated above, the foregoing discussion of the criminal liability of partners probably goes beyond the scope of the 1890 Act; which is not to say that the topic itself is therefore without relevance to partnership.

The generality of section 10 contrasts with the particularity of the two situations described in section 11, both of which concern the misapplication of money or property received for or in the custody of the firm. Section 11 provides:

" In the following cases; namely:

    (*a*)   Where one partner acting within the scope of his apparent authority receives the money or property of a third person and misapplies it; and

(b) Where a firm in the course of its business receives money
or property of a third person, and the money or property
so received is misapplied by one or more of the partners
while it is in the custody of the firm;
the firm is liable to make good the loss."

In subsection (a), the same partner must be responsible for the
receipt and misapplication of the money or property; whereas,
in subsection (b), a misapplication by any of the partners will
suffice.

In practice, there will be little difference between the two cases in
that receipt by a partner within the scope of his apparent authority
will normally constitute a receipt by the firm in the course of its
business. It matters not whether the receipt of money or property in
either case was in the first instance perfectly proper, or was improperly
obtained, if in fact the receipt can be brought within the ordinary
scope of business. As one might expect, the decisions as to what
constitutes the ordinary course of business provide a veritable
embarras de richesse.

(a) *Acts within the ordinary course of business*
An act which is within the apparent authority of a partner is
therefore binding on the firm except as regards third persons having
knowledge that the person so acting lacked actual authority. Thus,
in *Rapp* v. *Latham*,[77] decided in 1819, the "innocent" partner was
held to be bound by representations made by his co-partner that
wine had been bought and sold on behalf of a third person who had
employed the partnership (engaged in the business of wine and
spirits merchants) to make purchases and sales of wines on commission. It was held that the third person could keep a sum of money
which he had received in respect of fictitious sales of wines and also
recover "advances" of money for the purchase of wine upon which
there had been no returns. An interesting feature of the decision in
this case was the fact that the plaintiff, who had advanced £126,000,
had received £130,000 in respect of fictitious sales, but was nevertheless held entitled to recover advances for other fictitious sales on the
basis that this was "the mode most favourable for the plaintiff."
The obligation of the "innocent" partner to "make good the loss"
within section 11 would in these circumstances extend to a notional
"loss" on the supposed sales, ignoring the fact that the plaintiff in
the instant case had received more than he had advanced. It is

arguable that the case would now be decided under section 10 which is free of any requirement as to a receipt of money or property by a partner although that section requires some " loss or injury " to the third person.

In *Blain* v. *Bromley* [78] money was paid into the joint account of a firm of solicitors for investment. One partner represented it to have been invested accordingly, but he had in fact appropriated the money for his own use. It was stated that it was within the ordinary course of business for a solicitor to receive money for investment in a specific security, and the court held the " innocent " partner liable for the misapplication of money by his co-partner and for the latter's representation that the money had been invested. On the other hand, the receipt of money for the purpose of general investment is not normally an incident of the ordinary business of solicitors. [79] As was said in *Harman* v. *Johnson*, " I think that an attorney, *qua* attorney, is not a scrivener; that his business is to act in a Court of Law, to prepare conveyances, to execute titles, and so on; but not to act as a scrivener." [80] At this point it might be observed that it is most unwise to seize upon dicta of this nature in order to erect them into immutable, *ex cathedra* pronouncements as to what constitutes, or does not constitute, the ordinary course of business in particular trades or professions. It is worthy of note that cognisance was taken in the *Harman* case of the practices of certain attorneys who did act as scriveners, but it was found that there was no evidence of such practices in that case. Much will depend upon the nature of the retainer and the expertise of the firm. Thus, in *Earl of Dundonald* v. *Masterman*, [81] a firm of solicitors was retained to manage and settle the affairs of a client who was being pressed by his creditors, and, as is usual, one of the partners in the firm became responsible for looking after the client's affairs, which necessitated the assignment of property upon trust for creditors and the receipt of money. The solicitor acting in these respects having absconded with moneys received, it was held that the innocent partners were liable. Sir W. M. James V.-C., in rhetorical style, said " It is surely within the ordinary everyday practice of a firm of solicitors or attorneys to receive moneys from a client for the satisfying the demands of the creditors whom they are employed to arrange with. It is surely within the ordinary everyday practice of a firm of solicitors and attorneys to receive from a client, an executor, moneys—sometimes to pay the demands of government, sometimes to pay legatees, and sometimes to pay into Court—in short, to receive money for any specific purpose connected with the professional business which they have in hand." [82]

Rhodes v. *Moules*,[83] demonstrates that in determining what constitutes the ordinary course of business in a particular case, account may be taken of ancillary services performed in relation to transactions themselves unmistakably within the scope of the business. In that case, a solicitor was held accountable for the misapplication of share warrants which had been handed over to a co-partner on the faith of the latter's false representation that the mortgagee (to whom the client hoped to mortgage his freehold land) needed additional collateral security. Lindley L.J. had no doubt that the receipt of the bearer share warrants fell under both sub-sections (*a*) and (*b*) of section 11, saying, " So far [*i.e.* prior to the misapplication of the share warrants] the transaction was an ordinary business transaction, and such as solicitors are in the daily habit of conducting. It is everyday practice for a solicitor to act for both borrower and lender in a mortgage transaction, and to receive from the lender the money to be lent to the borrower in order to hand it to him, and to receive from the borrower the deeds and other securities on which the money is raised, and to keep those deeds and securities for the lender until he wants them, or until the loan is paid off." [84] There was also evidence that share warrants had been deposited by the same client on two previous occasions in connection with similar transactions. This case may be compared with that of *Sims* v. *Brutton* [85] where the receipt of principal money by a solicitor without the authority of the mortgagee-client was held to lie outside the ordinary course of business. Lindley experiences some difficulty with this latter case, inasmuch as the receipt of the principal money was shown in the firm's books, as was payment of interest, although it appeared that the co-partner was unaware of these entries.[86] In the *Earl of Dundonald* case [87] it was recognised that it had become common for attorneys to receive money on the completion of mortgage and purchase transactions, and further, that whilst an attorney might not possess apparent authority in relation to his client to receive money, it is otherwise where express authority to do so is given.

Care must be taken not to perpetrate the *non sequitur* that because an act is not part of the *normal* business of a firm, the firm is therefore free from liability. In the Australian case of *Polkinghorne* v. *Holland*,[88] a firm of solicitors was held liable for the loss of two sums of money by a client who had invested in the shares of two companies on the advice of one of the partners. In a useful passage the court said, " Solicitors possess, in virtue of their profession, no special skill in the valuation of real property, or shares, or of marketable securities. It is not in the course of their professional duties to advise on such matters. . . . But it is one thing to say that a valuation or expression of his own judgment upon a commercial or financial question is not within the scope of a solicitor's duties, and another to say that when he is consulted on the wisdom of investing in the shares of a company of which his client knows nothing, it is outside his province to inquire into the matter and to furnish his client with the information and assistance which the facts upon the register will give, to point out what inquiries may be made, and, if required, to undertake them or invoke the aid of those who will." [89] This approach is in line with that taken in the English case of *Blythe* v. *Fladgate*,[90] in which a firm of solicitors was held liable for loss caused by the inadequacy of a security upon which a client's trust money had been advanced, the omissions of the solicitor acting in this respect being imputed to the co-partners. Stirling J. commented that " It is, therefore, the duty of a solicitor not so much himself to form, or express an opinion on the value of the property offered to a trustee as security for an advance (although the law does not prohibit him from so doing, if he thinks fit), as to see that the trustee has before him the proper materials for forming a judgment of his own." [91]

(b) *Acts outside the ordinary course of business*

The partnership is not liable for acts outside the apparent authority of a partner or unconnected with its ordinary business in the sense described above. The following cases illustrate acts *dehors* the partnership business—the removal of securities other than those authorised from a box deposited with a banking firm for safe custody by a partner who subsequently misappropriated such securities (*Ex p. Eyre*) [92]; the receipt of principal moneys from a mortgagor without the consent of the client-mortgagee (*Sims* v. *Brutton*) [93]; the receipt of money for general investment by a partner in a bank (*Bishop* v. *Countess of Jersey*) [94]; and the receipt (concealed from co-partners) of bearer bonds by a solicitor for safe custody (*Cleather* v. *Twisden* [95]—*aliter* if co-partners had known that the bonds were in the safe custody of the firm). In *St. Aubyn* v. *Smart*,[96] a co-partner was held liable for the act of his partner who had received money by means of a power of attorney, executed in favour of the solicitors jointly and severally, which money he had misappropriated. " It is immaterial in such a case," said Sir W. Page Wood L.J. " whether the receipt of the money was or was not in the ordinary course of their business as solicitors. The money was received by Buller [the absconding solicitor] with the knowledge of his co-partners. The two partners had agreed to do a particular thing." In the Australian case of *Polkinghorne* v. *Holland*, to which reference has already been made, the firm was held to be free of liability with respect to a guarantee which the client had given in relation to a company's overdraft acting on the advice of a partner (himself a director in the company). To make his co-partners answerable, said the court, " it is not enough that a partner utilises information obtained in the course of his duties, or relies upon the personal confidence won or influence obtained in doing the firm's business. . . . Harold Holland [the partner dealing with the plaintiff] used the influence which, as a member of the firm, he had gained over the appellant, and abused the confidence which she reposed in him in that capacity, in order to obtain her suretyship. But he did nothing which was part of his business to do." [97]

The firm will not be liable if the partner's act was not performed *qua* partner. In *Tendring Hundred Waterworks Co.* v. *Jones*, a solicitor-partner, who was secretary to a company (the secretaryship being part of the business of the partnership) received a title-deed in respect of land conveyed to himself for the company's convenience, which deed he later used to secure a debt of his own. The co-partner was adjudged free of liability despite the employment of his firm in connection with the conveyance: he had been unaware of the partner's fraud and the latter's act in receiving the deed was referable to his trusteeship and not to his duties as secretary.[98]

A particular transaction may lie within the ordinary course of business of a firm but the firm will not be liable if the third person has elected to deal with a partner as principal. A leading example to support this proposition is *British Homes Assurance Corporation Ltd.* v. *Paterson*, in which it was held that a third party, who had elected to continue his dealings with a solicitor, could not sue a person whom the solicitor had taken into partnership. The third party had received notice of the admission of the new partner, but had nonetheless taken no notice of it and continued to deal with the solicitor. As Farwell J. explained it, the partners are liable " because the individual partner has acted as agent for them as either disclosed or undisclosed principals;

if disclosed, because the act or contract is avowedly with them or on their behalf; if undisclosed, because the law gives the other contracting party the option of proceeding against the undisclosed principal when discovered. But where A, knowing B and C to be partners, refuses to contract with them jointly and insists on contracting with B alone he cannot afterwards treat C as liable." [99]

The *British Homes* case was distinguished in the Scottish case of *Kirkintilloch Equitable Co-operative Society Ltd.* v. *Livingstone* [1] which shows that a partnership can incur liability for the act of a partner who alone was competent to perform a particular type of business. In that case, an accountancy partnership was held liable for the negligence of a partner who had been appointed official auditor to an industrial and provident society which had paid the audit fee to the partnership. Although the law regulating industrial and provident societies only permitted the appointment of an individual, and not a firm, as official auditor, it was held that the partner's negligence fell within the ordinary business of the partnership and within the authority conferred by his co-partners. Referring to the relevant legislation, Lord Cameron could see nothing " which implies that co-partners cannot give authority to one of their number to perform, as a partner, acts which they themselves may not be legally qualified to perform," the word " authority " denoting factual or objective control, direction or knowing approval on the part of the co-partners. It is likely that an English court, confronted with the same facts, would follow this persuasive authority.

A solicitor who acts as agent for trustees does not thereby become a constructive trustee by reason of incautious acts of which a court of equity would disapprove; to incur liability as constructive trustee it must be shown that the solicitor has received and become chargeable with some part of the trust property or that he assisted with knowledge in a dishonest and fraudulent design on the part of the trustee.[2] Nor does it follow that because a partner has incurred liability as a constructive trustee by reason of some act of intermeddling in the trust property his partners are therefore liable; the latter will not be liable if they are ignorant of the intermeddling and have not become chargeable with the trust property.[3]

Liability for wrongs joint and several

" 12. Every partner is liable jointly with his co-partners and also severally [4] for everything for which the firm while he is a partner therein becomes liable under either of the two last preceding sections."

The joint and several liability of the partners in tort is in contradistinction to their joint liability in contract. In the case of " pure tort," the distinction, however anomalous, gives rise to little difficulty; but the same cannot be said of liability arising out of contract, such as negligence by a professional adviser, or negligence by an employer in relation to the physical safety of his employees.[5] Leaving on one side the effect of contracts such as that in the *British Homes* case,[6] which differentiates the individual tortious liability of a partner and thereby excludes other partners, it would appear that in those cases where the tort of one partner may be laid at the door of all, such tort, even though it arises *ex contractu*, gives rise, at the option of the victim, to joint and several liability until the right of action has been cumulatively satisfied.

In *Blyth* v. *Fladgate* [7] the partners were held to be jointly and severally responsible for breach of trust by one of their number who had advanced trust money upon inadequate security. The latter had acted within the scope of his authority and his knowledge of the inadequacy of the security was imputed to the firm. As a result, judgment against the solicitor who had acted did not discharge the other partners. This case may be compared with that of *Re Biddulph, ex p. Burton* [8] in which a trustee had paid trust moneys to a firm of bankers who had knowledge of the trusts. One partner invested part of this fund without the consent of the trustee. The court held that, on the bankruptcy of the partners, the trustee could only prove against their joint estate; they had incurred a liability as between banker and customer and were not liable as trustees.

Improper employment of trust property for partnership purposes

Strictly speaking, section 13 deals with a question which does not appertain to the law of partnership as such. Nevertheless, it is not uncommon for a partner, particularly a solicitor, to be appointed a trustee, thus raising the question of the liability of his co-partners should he commit a breach of trust by employing the trust property in the partnership business. Section 13 helps to clarify the position:

" If a partner, being a trustee, improperly employs trust-property in the business or on the account of the partnership, no other partner is liable for the trust-property to the persons beneficially interested therein:

Provided as follows:

(1) This section shall not affect any liability incurred by reason of his having notice of a breach of trust; and

(2) Nothing in this section shall prevent trust money from being followed and recovered from the firm if still in its possession or under its control."

Therefore, the partnership is not liable to a *cestui que trust* merely because a partner-trustee has committed a breach of trust, even when this takes the form of employing the trust property in the partnership business.[9] For example, in *Ex p. Heaton*[10] father and sons were partners. The sons, who were trustees of a will, applied trust money to partnership purposes and on bankruptcy it was held that the amount so appropriated could not be proved against the joint estate. If it is wished to make the co-partners liable it is necessary to prove that they are implicated in the breach of trust either because they had knowledge of it or were culpably ignorant of it. In *Blyth* v. *Fladgate*[11] the knowledge of a solicitor who had acted *on behalf* of trustees was imputed to the other partners. Whether knowledge would be similarly imputed to co-partners of the trustee-partner would seem to depend upon whether he was a trustee in his personal capacity or in his professional capacity as a member of the partnership. In *Jacobs* v. *Morris*[12] Vaughan Williams L.J. felt that *Marsh* v. *Keating*[13] had decided that ignorance could not be relied upon where there was means of knowledge. In that case Park J. had equated actual knowledge with the means of knowledge, saying that there was no principle of law which protected those who by failing to use ordinary diligence as required in their calling did not obtain actual knowledge. Finally, it goes without saying that a co-partner who has knowingly assisted an express trustee in a fraudulent design upon the trust property is himself liable as a trustee *de son tort*.

The second proviso was intended to preserve the beneficial owner's right to recover trust property which had passed into the partnership fund. At the date of the Act, the right to trace trust property which had passed from the hands of the trustee was less developed than it is today and the proviso was therefore probably considered necessary to qualify the general freedom from liability conferred by section 13 on the non-trustee partners. Even today, the right to trace does not apply against a bona fide purchaser of the trust property without notice, but there is a right " *in rem* " which enables beneficiaries to recover " identifiable " trust property held by a volunteer and to have a charge over any property produced by a mixing of the trust property with the property of the volunteer. " Identifiable " trust property may be defined as property in its original form or, although in some other form into which it has been converted, still recognisable as the proceeds of the trust property. The advantage of the claim *in rem* is that, in the event of the bankruptcy of the partnership, the trust property is " separated " from the other assets and is not available to other competing creditors. In addition, there is a right " *in personam* " against a volunteer who has received and subsequently parted with the trust property, provided that the temporary possession and use of the property conferred some continuing benefit upon the volunteer so that a claim against him after he has parted with the trust property would not be inequitable.[14] The right to trace is only available when all personal remedies against the defaulting trustee have been exhausted and some claim by the beneficiaries remains unpaid.

One further aspect of the improper application of trust funds requires consideration. If a trustee pays money belonging to more than one beneficiary into an unbroken bank account where it is mixed with his own money, a problem arises if the account is subsequently reduced so that it cannot satisfy all of the claims upon it. As between the trustee and the beneficiaries there is a presumption against a breach of trust, so that if anything remains in the account it is presumed that the trustee used his own money first.[15] Similarly, if some of the fund has been invested and the rest dissipated, the presumption operates so that the trustee is deemed to have invested the trust property and dissipated his own property.[16] As between the beneficiaries it is presumed, in the event of the remaining funds proving to be inadequate, that money has been withdrawn in the order in which it was paid in.[17] It is less clear how these presumptions would apply when a trustee pays trust money into a partnership account where it is mixed not with his own money but with the partnership fund. It seems that the presumptions would apply as if the partnership account were the unbroken account of a trustee when the partnership account is used as the trust account or the trust property has been received as part of the business of the partnership. However, the position is not certain where the trust money is paid by the trustee partner as though it were his own beneficial property when presumably the presumptions would be inappropriate and the beneficiaries would have to rely on rights of tracing.

Persons liable by " holding out " SEE PAGE 22

A person who is not a partner may nevertheless be liable to third persons as though he were a partner by virtue of section 14, which provides:

" (1) Every one who by words spoken or written or by conduct represents himself, or who knowingly suffers himself to be represented, as a partner in a particular firm, is liable as a partner to any one who has on the faith of any such representation given credit to the firm, whether the representation has or has not been made or communicated to the person so giving credit by or with the knowledge of the apparent partner making the representation or suffering it to be made.

(2) Provided that where after a partner's death the partnership business is continued in the old firm-name, the continued use of that name or of the deceased partner's name as part thereof shall not of itself make his executors or administrators estate or effects liable for any partnership debts contracted after his death."

The liability created by this section rests upon estoppel. " Where a man holds himself out as a partner or allows others to do it, he is then properly estopped from denying the character he has assumed, and upon the faith of which creditors may be presumed to have acted. A man so acting may be rightly held liable as a partner by estoppel." [18] There is no harm in using the phrase " partner by estoppel " if it is apprehended that the section expresses a relationship between the person holding himself out and those who give credit on the faith of that representation; the section does not create a partnership relationship between the representor and others alleged to be co-partners with him. The term " apparent partner," which is used in the section, has been preferred as a better description, but this in its turn may cause confusion inasmuch as it is sometimes used to point the contrast with concealed or dormant partners. A person may fall into the category of concealed or dormant partner yet be an "apparent " partner to a particular individual to whom he has been held out as a partner. In *Martyn* v. *Gray* the defendant permitted the captain of a mine in Cornwall to represent him as a capitalist from London and was held liable to a merchant who gave credit on the faith of that representation which had been transmitted to the merchant by the captain of the mine without the defendant's consent, the evidence warranting the inference that the defendant was a partner and this notwithstanding that the merchant did not know the name of the defendant. " It was not necessary," said Erle C.J., " that this person should be identified by his Christian name and surname: it was enough that he should be so pointed at as to be distinctly identified." [19] Both section 14 and section 36 (below, p. 127) are indifferent to broad categories such as " notorious partners " or " profoundly secret partners " the test in either case being whether or not the person in question has been held out as a partner to the person relying on such holding-out.

If the third person giving credit is aware that the representor is not participating in the profits and losses of the firm it has been suggested that liability may still exist on the ground that " the lending of his name does justify the belief that he is willing to be responsible to those who may be induced to trust him for payment," [20] *Alderson* v. *Pope* [21] being distinguishable by reason of the fact that the third person in that case had notice of the stipulation between the three apparent partners that C should not participate in profit or loss " *and should not be liable as a partner* " (italics added and see s. 8 above, p. 43).

What amounts to " holding out "

" The holding one's self out to the world as a partner, as contradistinguished from the actual relationship of partnership, imports at least the voluntary act of the party so holding himself out. It implies the lending of his name to the partnership; and is altogether incompatible with the want of authority that his name has been so used. Thus, in the ordinary instances of its occurrence, where a person allows his name to remain in a firm, either exposed to the public over a shop-door, or to be used in printed invoices or bills of parcels, or to be published in advertisements, the knowledge of the party that his name is used and his assent thereto, is the very ground upon which he is estopped from disputing his liability as a partner." This passage from the judgment of Tindal C.J. in *Fox* v. *Clifton*,[22] shows that a person cannot be subjected to liability under this section unless there has been some voluntary act or assent on his part. The use of a person's name without his knowledge cannot suffice, as in the *Fox* case itself, where an applicant for shares in a company who had paid the first deposit thereon but was otherwise not interested in the concern was held not to be a partner merely because the secretary of the company had inserted his name in a book containing a list of subscribers. Not surprisingly, the defendants in *Collingwood* v. *Berkeley* [23] (who had received shares and an indemnity) were estopped from denying knowledge of the contents of a prospectus relating to a projected company formed to convey emigrants to the promised land of British Columbia in the light of their assent to the prospectus shown to them and subsequently published in *The Times* newspaper. The failure of the retiring partner in *Tower Cabinet Co.* v. *Ingram* (discussed in detail below at p. 128) to destroy the old note-paper of the firm was held not to amount to knowingly suffering himself to be held out as a partner when the old notepaper was inadvertently used after his retirement, thereby indicating that negligence or carelessness will not of itself raise liability. The words " knowingly suffers himself to be represented as a partner " do not mean that a person must take active steps to prevent another from lying or to contradict his assertions if the latter are made entirely without authority. Registration under the Registration of Business Names Act 1916 (see particularly ss. 6 and 18 of that Act at, respectively, pp. 232 and 240, below) does not constitute actual notice. Hence, the fact that a person is shown as a partner on the register will be irrelevant, unless it can be shown that the person seeking to establish liability against him actually searched the register or relied on the registration certificate (see s. 11 of the 1916 Act, below, p. 236), as occurred in *Bishop* v. *Tudor Estates*.[24] What amounts to a holding-out is a question of fact to be determined on the facts of the particular case, Lindley giving two cases in which on facts practically identical, different findings were returned by the jury in each case, findings which the court declined to alter.[25] The virtual disappearance of jury trial in civil cases and the increasing tendency of the courts to treat questions of fact as mixed questions of fact and law may in time occasion re-consideration of the old cases.

The second important requirement is that the use of the " representor's " name must have been made known to the person who seeks to make him liable. But there may be a " holding-out " without any direct communication by words or conduct between the parties. In the words of Williams J.: " If the defendant informs A B that he is a partner in a commercial establishment and A B informs the plaintiff, and the plaintiff, believing the defendant to be a member in the firm, supplies goods to them the defendant is liable for the price." [25] The defendant in such a case is liable if he makes the statement intending it to be repeated or acted upon or even under circumstances that it is likely that the statement will be repeated and acted upon by third persons who hear it.

The rule as to "holding-out" extends to administration in bankruptcy. If two persons trade as partners, and buy goods on their credit as partners, and afterwards both become bankrupt, then, whatever the nature of the real agreement between themselves, the assets of the business must be administered as joint estate for the benefit of the creditors of the supposed firm.[27]

Application on change in constitution of firm

The "holding-out" principle has its most frequent application on a change in the constitution of a firm (in which connection s. 36 should be read in conjunction with the present section). A partner who has retired from the firm may be liable on the principle of "holding-out" for debts subsequently contracted by the firm if he has omitted to give due notice of the retirement to those dealing with the firm. The leading case of *Scarf* v. *Jardine* [28] dealt with a situation in which A retired from a firm consisting of himself and B (the firm-name used names which were not those of A and B), his place being taken by a new partner, C. A customer of the firm dealt with the firm after the change but without notice of it and was held entitled to elect between suing A and B or B and C, but was held disentitled to sue, A, B and C, or to sue A after suing B and C. Lord Selborne L.C. explained that the choice lay between suing "those who were liable by estoppel, or . . . those who were liable upon the facts. Put it as I can," continued his Lordship, "I am unable to understand how there could have been a joint liability of the three. The two principles are not capable of being brought into play together: you cannot at once rely upon the estoppel and set up the facts; and if the estoppel makes A and B liable, and the facts make B and C liable, neither the estoppel nor the facts, nor any combination of the two can possibly make A, B and C all liable jointly." [29] It would be otherwise if A and B carried on business in their own names and A retired, without giving notice, and allowed C to come in, it being agreed that the name "A, B and C" might be used. A would be liable to someone dealing with the new firm on the strength of his membership thereof.[30] But, even so, liability cannot attach to a retired partner at the suit of a creditor of the firm who did not know him to be a member of the firm while he was such in fact, either by reason of dealings with the firm or because of knowledge of its composition. In *Court* v. *Berlin* [31] it was held that the retainer of a solicitor to prosecute an action continued after the retirement of a partner so that the latter was liable (in the absence of notice to the solicitor) for costs incurred in the action after retirement. However, in *Carter* v. *Whalley*,[32] it was held that a creditor of a firm named the " Plas Madoc Colliery Co.," whose dealing with that firm had arisen after the retirement of one of the partners (of which no notice, either to the creditor or to the public at large had been given), could not hold the retiring partner liable. Littledale J. explained that " where all the names in a firm appear, it may be presumed that everyone knows who the partners are; but where it is only a nominal firm, as in the present case, the fact of such knowledge must be ascertained by express proof." [33] It is upon this basis that it has been said that " a dormant partner may retire from a firm without giving notice to the world," [34] a statement which is at once true and too narrow inasmuch as the cases show that even an active partner who retires will escape liability for post-retirement debts to those creditors who were unaware of his membership of the firm. It is expressly provided by subsection (2) of the present section, as amplified by section 36(3),[35] that the doctrine of holding-out does not extend to bind the estate of a deceased partner or of a bankrupt partner, where, after his death or bankruptcy, the business of the firm is continued in the old name; and whether or not creditors of the firm know of the death or bankruptcy is immaterial.

The giving of credit to the firm

The giving of credit envisaged by the present section would appear to include not only the giving of credit in its narrow, business sense (as where a loan is made or goods are delivered against future payment), but the giving of credit in a wide sense so as to include the reception of property by the firm or the incurring of an obligation with the firm in circumstances in which its membership is relevant. One thing is now clear, and that is that the section does not encompass tort liability where the firm's composition is immaterial. In an early case,[36] a retired partner was held liable for damage done by a cart belonging to the firm and upon which his name still remained. It is now clear that to make a person liable in tort because he is an apparent partner involves a confusion of principles; liability by " holding-out " denotes that credit has been given to the firm on the strength of the apparent partner's name and this is clearly inconsistent with a cause of action independent of contract or trust. The earlier view has been overruled by *Smith* v. *Bailey*.[37]

Admissions and representations of partners

In consonance with the agency powers conferred upon partners by the Act, section 15 enacts that:

" An admission or representation made by any partner concerning the partnership affairs, and in the ordinary course of its business, is evidence against the firm."

An admission by a partner is not conclusive evidence against the firm. In *Hollis* v. *Burton* [38] an admission was made by the partner of a sole trustee that trust money had been received into the firm's banking account. This was followed by an application for leave to amend the defence. Leave was granted because the admission was shown to have been made by mistake. In *Stead* v. *Salt* [39] Best C.J. held that one partner cannot bind his co-partners by a submission to arbitration, even of matters directly germane to the business of the firm. He agreed that the admission of one partner is evidence against all the partners but went on to say that even in a general partnership one of the partners cannot bind the others without an authority, express or implied, the latter type of authority only being implied for what is necessary to enable the trade in which the partners are concerned to be carried on. Both an admission and a representation by a partner may amount to an estoppel against the firm. It is settled, however, that a partner cannot bind the firm either by a representation as to the extent of his own authority, or by a representation as to the nature of the partnership business; to allow of such representations would enable a partner to bind his firm merely by reason of his own *ipse dixit*. [40]

Notice to acting partner to be notice to firm

Under section 16, a notice given to an acting partner is tantamount to a notice given to the firm:

" Notice to any partner who habitually acts in the partnership business of any matter relating to partnership affairs operates as notice to the firm, except in the case of a fraud on the firm committed by or with the consent of that partner."

Before the Act, there seems to have been no clear authority for confining the rule to acting partners; but it would be neither just nor convenient to hold that a notice to a dormant partner operates, without more, as notice to the firm. Jessel M.R. treated the question of notice to a partner as an aspect of the law of agency in the case of

Williamson v. *Barbour*.[41] The same judge referred to the problem which arises when notice is given to a person who afterwards becomes a partner, saying, " It has not, so far as I know, been held that notice to a man who afterwards becomes a partner is notice to the firm. It might be so held." [42] Our suspense on this score (untouched by the Act) still remains. If notice is given to a servant of the firm who later becomes a partner therein, there is, perhaps, no need to invoke section 16 at all; the firm will be bound if the servant was an agent to receive the notice affecting his employer's business. As regards other classes of persons, such as those who have dealt with the firm or employees of such persons, it seems difficult to justify a rule by which notice to these classes of persons constitutes notice to the firm as and when they become partners. In *Goldfarb* v. *Bartlett* [43] notice of dishonour of a bill drawn by partners given to the continuing partner after the dissolution of the firm was held to constitute sufficient notice to the retiring partner under the Bills of Exchange Act 1882, s. 49 (11), which requires notice to be given to each of two or more drawers who are not partners, unless one has authority to receive notice for the others.

If a partner commits a fraud either upon the firm or upon one of the firm's clients, knowledge of his misconduct is not imputed to his co-partners. In the *Williamson* case (noted above), Jessel M.R. gave the example of a clerk who passes short-weight deliveries in return for presents from the vendor of the goods, saying that if the clerk is later taken into the firm his knowledge of the fraud is not deemed to be notice to the firm.

Liabilities of incoming and outgoing partners

The broad rule is that a partner is only liable in respect of partnership liabilities incurred whilst he is a member of the firm, a rule which carries with it the corollary that he is not prima facie liable for things done before he entered the firm or for things done after he has retired therefrom. Section 17 enumerates three rules, the first applying to new partners, the second and third to retiring partners:

" (1) A person who is admitted as a partner into an existing firm does not thereby become liable to the creditors of the firm for anything done before he became a partner.

(2) A partner who retires from a firm does not thereby cease to be liable for partnership debts or obligations incurred before his retirement.

(3) A retiring partner may be discharged from any existing liabilities by an agreement to that effect between himself and the members of the firm as newly constituted and the creditors, and this agreement may be either express or inferred as a fact from the course of dealing between the creditors and the firm as newly constituted."

It is possible, and indeed, not uncommon, for the three situations described in the section to occur together, as where one partner retires, to be succeeded by a new partner, the creditors agreeing to look henceforth to the firm as reconstituted.

Novation

In order to determine whether the liability of the new firm has been substituted for the liability of the old, two questions need to be considered:

(a) Has the new firm assumed liability?

(b) Has the creditor agreed to accept the new firm as his debtor and to discharge the old firm from its liability? [44]

An agreement between the old and new partners that the latter will assume liability for existing debts does not of itself confer any rights upon the creditors of the firm to proceed against the new partners. The rule of English law that not even an express intention by the parties to a contract to benefit a third person suffices to confer an actionable right upon the latter has, after a period of some doubt, received confirmation by the House of Lords in *Beswick* v. *Beswick*.[45] But, an incoming partner is liable for new debts arising out of a continuing contract made by the firm before he joined it, as in the case of *Dyke* v. *Brewer*,[46] where deliveries of bricks after the admission of a partner constituted performance of divisible contracts for which the new partner was held liable, each order for bricks being, in effect, a new contract. Nor is there anything in law to prevent a firm from stipulating with any creditor from the beginning that he shall look only to the members of the firm for the time being (in Scots law the contract " with the house " as opposed to the partners at the time of the contract) although such an arrangement will be *res inter alios acta* so far as new partners are concerned [47]; the term " novation " is not, however, properly applicable to such a case or to the type of case of which *Dyke* v. *Brewer* is an example.

The incoming partner will only be liable for existing debts where a novation has occurred, that is to say where the creditor has agreed with all concerned to accept the substitution of the new partner as his debtor in place of the old. The novation may be expressly agreed or, as section 17 (3) shows, be inferred as a fact from the course of dealing between the creditors and the firm as newly constituted. In determining what manner of dealing by the creditor amounts to an implied novation, Lord Eldon's dictum in *Ex p. Williams* [48] that " A very little will do to make out an assent by the creditors to the agreement " is sometimes cited. An examination of the cases, however, reveals that this dictum needs to be taken with great care. Implied novation is admittedly a question of fact, but something more than a mere scintilla of evidence is needed.

In one case, depositors with a banking firm, consisting of A and B, were unable to prove in A's estate when the bank got into difficulties. The depositors had been advised by means of a circular that X and Y were joining the firm; they knew that A had died but had continued to receive interest on their deposits from the new partners, in whose bankruptcy they had proved, all of which amounted to a " complete novation " absolving A's estate from liability.[49] Again, in *Rolfe* v. *Flower, Salting and Co.*,[50] the court found that something more than " slight circumstances " [51] was present so as to indicate a novation. There, partners took two of their clerks into partnership, but continued trading under the same name. The assets and liabilities of the firm were transferred to the new firm using the old books of account and the creditor was paid part of his debt from the assets so transferred. These circumstances, together with other acts and admissions and the creditor's continued dealing with the new firm (in itself probably not a conclusive factor, unless for a considerable period), were held to afford cogent evidence that a novation was intended. A customer of a banking firm who, knowing that one of the partners in the firm had died, drew out part of a sum left by him on deposit, taking a fresh receipt for the residue in the ordinary way, was held not to have relinquished his claim upon the deceased partner's estate.[52] *Per contra*, another customer of the same firm who wished to draw out the balance of his current account and was persuaded by the surviving partner to transfer the money to a deposit account was held to have accepted the surviving partner's sole liability and to have discharged A's estate from liability.[53] *Rouse* v. *Bradford Banking Co.*[54] serves to warn that evidence of a novation must be reasonably clear. In that case, dealing with the new firm and treating its members as debtors (including proving in their estates) were held on the facts to be consistent with not releasing the plaintiff. It was also held that the bank in that case had done nothing to release the plaintiff as surety. It should not be forgotten in talking of novation (*i.e.* substituting the liability of A for that of B) that the creditor might accept A's liability *in addition* to that of B, the latter remaining liable, provided, of course, that consideration can be shown.

The novation may affect not only a changed or enlarged firm, as in the *Rolfe* case (above), but also a firm reduced in numbers. In *Thompson* v. *Percival*,[55] A and B dissolved their partnership, having agreed that B should carry on the business alone and receive and pay all debts. C, a creditor of the firm, applied to A for payment, and was informed that he must look to B alone. C drew a bill on B which was dishonoured. In a subsequent action by C against A, it was held to be a question of fact for the jury whether C had agreed to accept B as his sole debtor and the latter's acceptance of the bill of exchange as satisfaction of the debt due from both. The fact that B had agreed to pay all partnership debts was evidence of an authority from A for B to make such an agreement. Although it seems that the decision remains law, it leaves some doubts. It is clearly true (as was said in the case) that a negotiable security from one of several partners might constitute good satisfaction [56] because of its negotiability and easy proof of dishonour, but it is not altogether easy to follow Lord Chelmsford's statement that the sole liability of one of two debtors might be more beneficial than the joint liability of the two because of factors such as convenience, the position in bankruptcy, survivorship and so forth, nor is it easily appreciated why the court should be precluded from inquiring whether the sole liability is in reality more beneficial than the joint liability. Notwithstanding the acceptance of *Thompson* v. *Percival* (which overruled two earlier cases),[57] it may be that its rationale is better put on the ground of equitable estoppel, than on a strained notion of substituted consideration.

The partner who retires

If a partner retires, leaving the existing partners to carry on the business and to be responsible for the liabilities of the old firm, a creditor of the old firm is not affected by the agreement between the partners and may look to the original partners, including the retiring partner. So also where partners instruct a solicitor to bring an action in the firm-name and then dissolve the partnership without revoking the solicitor's authority or informing him of the dissolution, they remain liable for costs incurred in the action after as well as before the dissolution, the retainer being an entire contract which continues until withdrawn or performed.[58] In *Welsh* v. *Knarston*,[59] a Scottish case, a firm of solicitors instructed to prosecute a claim for injuries sustained in a road accident allowed the claim to become time-barred. Two of the partners in the firm claimed that they were not liable in negligence since they had retired from the firm before the claim became time-barred, but were nevertheless held liable, a decision rested not on section 17 of the Act but upon section 38 (see below, p. 131) despite the facultative wording of the latter section, which was held to impose a duty as well as conferring a right. Another example of liability attaching to a partner notwithstanding his withdrawal from the firm is given in *Oakford* v. *European and American Steam Shipping Company*,[60] in which a firm, consisting of A, B and C, entered into a three-year contract with D. After one year. A retired from the firm, taking a covenant from B and C to indemnify him from all liabilities under the contract. D knew of A's retirement. It was held that A remained liable to D even after his retirement for acts properly done under the contract by B and C. Nevertheless, in such a situation A is in the position of a surety so that he is discharged if D varies the contract with B and C, *e.g.* by giving time to B and C. Lord Lyndhurst explained that such a variation places the " surety" "in a new situation and exposes him to risk and contingencies which he would not otherwise be liable to." [61]

Of the cases concerning a running or current account between a partnership and those dealing with it, one, *Clayton's Case* [62] has established a rule which transcends the law of partnership and provides a rule of general application in commercial law. According to that rule, payments into an unbroken current account are deemed to discharge the earliest items in that account standing to the debit of the payer; conversely, withdrawals from that account are offset against deposits in order of date. " First in, first out " expresses therefore an artificial method of offsetting credit and debit items in a current account, although it should be noted that the appropriation of payments produced by the rule in *Clayton's Case* may only take effect subject to the prior right of first, the debtor and secondly, the creditor, to make an express appropriation of a payment or payments. In *Clayton's Case* itself, A, who was a partner in a banking firm along with B and C, died, B and C continuing the business. Customers continued to deal with the bank knowing of A's death. The firm became insolvent. It was held that A's estate was liable for balances owing to customers at the date of his death, less sums subsequently paid out by the bank. The firm's indebtedness to a customer, *i.e.* the amount standing to the latter's credit, will therefore be reduced or even extinguished by drawings subsequent to the death of the partner (itself causing a dissolution of the firm). The rule was applied in *Deely* v. *Lloyds Bank Ltd.*[63] where a bank, holding a mortgage as security for an overdraft, omitted to close the account upon receiving notice of a second mortgage of the same security. It was held that subsequent payments in must be appropriated to earlier drawings, thus extinguishing the secured debt so that the bank was unsecured in relation to subsequent advances.

Revocation of continuing guarantee by change in firm

Section 18 is a substantial re-enactment of provisions of the Mercantile Law Amendment Act of 1856 for England and Scotland respectively:

> " A continuing guaranty or cautionary obligation given either to a firm or to a third person in respect of the transactions of a firm is, in the absence of agreement to the contrary, revoked as to future transactions by any change in the constitution of the firm to which, or of the firm in respect of the transactions of which, the guaranty or obligation was given."

This section shows that it cannot be inferred from the mere fact of primary liability being an indefinitely continuing one, such as a guarantee given for sums to become due on a current account, that the promise is to continue in force notwithstanding a change in the membership of the firm. Rejecting such an inference in *Backhouse* v. *Hall*,[64] Blackburn J. required an express stipulation or some necessary implication from the nature of the firm or otherwise to support such an inference. In *Metcalf* v. *Bruin*,[65] the nature of the firm indicated that the guarantee was to continue *non obstante* a change in the composition of the firm requiring the guarantee. There, a person became surety by bond for another's faithful services to the Globe Insurance Company and all members thereof. The Court of King's Bench held that it appeared sufficiently that the obligor was to be answerable for the good conduct of the person employed to the individuals who constituted the company (itself not a body corporate) for the time being. On the facts of this particular case, the same result would have ensued had the debt, default or miscarriage of the Globe Insurance Co. been guaranteed by the guarantor.

[1] (1860) 8 H.L.Cas. 268 at p. 304.

[2] [1968] 1 Q.B. 549 at p. 583.

[3] *Freeman & Lockyer (A Firm)* v. *Buckhurst Park Properties (Mangal) Ltd.* [1964] 2 Q.B. 480 at p. 503.

[4] *Watteau* v. *Fenwick* [1893] 1 Q.B. 346. See also *Mercantile Credit Co. Ltd.* v. *Garrod, infra*, p. 34.

[5] (1870) L.R. 5 Ch.App. 725 at p. 733.

[6] Pollock (15th ed.), p. 31.

[7] [1962] 3 All E.R. 1103.

[8] *Ibid.* at pp. 1106 and 1107, respectively.

[9] [1914] 3 K.B. 1192, discussed *infra*, p. 38.

[10] *Keighley Maxsted & Co.* v. *Durant* [1901] A.C. 240.

[11] [1893] 1 Q.B. 346: see also *Edmunds* v. *Bushell* (1865) L.R. 1 Q.B. 97; *Daun* v. *Simmins* (1879) 41 L.T. 783, showing the more restricted apparent or usual authority of a non-licensed manager: *Kinahan and Co. Ltd.* v. *Parry* [1910] 2 K.B. 389, reversed on fact.

[12] Stoljar, *Law of Agency*, pp. 55–59; the author, however, accepts that s. 5 is at variance with the decision. Powell, *op. cit.*, p. 78, suggests that the main ground for criticising *Watteau* v. *Fenwick* is removed if the decision is based on usual authority and " not upon a liability arising from a distorted application of estoppel or of apparent authority."

[13] Underhill, *Principles of the Law of Partnership* (10th ed.), pp. 48–49, doubting the decision because it does not accord with the estoppel basis of apparent authority (*cf.* Powell's view, in preceding footnote; also *Bowstead on Agency* (14th ed.), art. 82, pp. 257–258, noting that the *Watteau* case cannot be explained as apparent authority based on a holding out by the firm, and finding the Powell notion of usual authority useful in this context).

[14] [1893] 1 Q.B. 346 at p. 349.

[15] (1939) 17 Can. Bar Rev. 693.

[16] *Bond* v. *Gibson* (1808) 1 Camp. 185.

[17] [1968] 1 W.L.R. 893.

[18] Lindley (12th ed.), p. 180.

[19] Best C.J. in *Stead* v. *Salt* (1825) 3 Bing. 101 at p. 103.

[20] (1841) 9 M. & W. 79.

[21] *Tomlinson* v. *Broadsmith* [1896] 1 Q.B. 386 (C.A.).

[22] [1906] 2 K.B. 321 at p. 322.

[23] [1914] 3 K.B. 1192.

[24] *Ibid.* at p. 1195.

[25] (1847) 6 Moo.P.C.C. 152.

[26] *Yorkshire Banking Co.* v. *Beatson* (1880) 5 C.P.D. 109 at p. 123.

[27] *Hedley* v. *Bainbridge* (1842) 3 Q.B. 316.

[28] *Wheatley* v. *Smithers* [1906] 2 K.B. 321.

[29] *Greenslade* v. *Dower* (1828) 7 B. & C. 635.

[30] (1858) 28 L.J. Ex. 66.

[31] *Ex p. Bonbonus* (1803) 8 Ves. 540.

[32] [1914] 3 K.B. 1192.

[33] *Re Bourne* [1906] 2 Ch. 427 at p. 430, *per* Vaughan Williams L.J.

[34] *Steiglitz* v. *Egginton* (1815) Holt N.P. 141.

[35] See also s. 18.

[36] *Niemann* v. *Niemann* (1890) 43 Ch.D. 198.

[37] *Stead* v. *Salt* (1825) 3 Bing. 101; *Adams* v. *Bankhart* (1835) 1 C.M. & R. 681.

[38] *Powell* v. *Brodhurst* [1901] 2 Ch. 160.

[39] (1841) 9 M. & W. 79 at p. 99.

[40] *Ibid.* at p. 92.

[41] *Ibid.* at p. 92, *per* Lord Abinger C.B., recognising " the principle, that the parties really contracting are the parties to sue in a court of justice, although the contract be in the name of another."

[42] [1906] 2 K.B. 209.

[43] *Re Riches, ex p. Darlington etc.* (1864) 4 De G.J. & S. 581 at p. 585.

[44] (1813) 1 M. & S. 255.

[45] (1800) 1 East 48.

[46] *Lewis* v. *Reilly* (1841) 1 Q.B. 349.

[47] *Garland* v. *Jacomb* (1873) L.R. 8 Ex. 216.

[48] (1871) L.R. 6 Ex. 243.

[49] *Ibid.* at p. 248.

[50] *Ibid.* at p. 251.

[51] (1860) 8 H.L.Cas. 268 at p. 304.

[52] (1808) 10 East 264.

[53] (1808) 1 Camp. 404.

[54] Referred to in Lindley (13th ed.), p. 213.

[55] (1854) 3 De G.M. & G. 459.

[56] (1816) 2 Chitty 120.

[57] Pollock (15th ed.), p. 41.

[58] (1879) 4 App.Cas. 504.

[59] Glanville L. Williams, *Joint Obligations* (1949), p. 3: the nature and consequences of the distinction between joint and joint and several obligations are authoritatively discussed in this work.

[60] [1903] 2 K.B. 212.

[61] *Re McRae* (1883) 25 Ch.D. 16 (C.A.).

[62] *Re Hodgson, Beckett* v. *Ramsdale* (1886) 31 Ch.D. 177 (C.A.).

[63] *Wegg Prosser* v. *Evans* [1895] 1 Q.B. 108.

[64] (1803) 3 East 252 at p. 259.

[65] *Per* Lindley L.J. in *Western National Bank* v. *Perez and Co.* [1891] 1 Q.B. 304 at p. 314.

[66] [1903] 1 K.B. 81.

[67] *Ibid.* at p. 85.

[68] Arising from the remarks of Willes J. in *Barwick* v. *English Joint Stock Bank* (1867) L.R. 2 Ex. 259 at p. 265.

[69] [1912] A.C. 716 at p. 731.

[70] [1964] 1 Q.B. 472.

[71] See Prof. J. A. Andrews, " The Criminal Liability of Partners " (1974) *Justice of the Peace*, pp. 176–179. Lindley refers to some old cases concerning breaches of revenue law ((13th ed.), p. 188).

[72] [1973] Crim.L.R. 537.

[73] (1874) L.R. 9 Q.B. 433.

[74] [1973] Crim.L.R. 61.

[75] [1972] Crim.L.R. 788.

[76] See n. 71 at pp. 178–179.

[77] (1819) 2 B. & A. 795.

78 (1847) 2 Ph.354.
79 *Plumer* v. *Gregory* (1874) L.R. 18 Eq. 621.
80 (1853) 2 E. & B. 61 at p. 66.
81 (1869) L.R. 7 Eq. 504.
82 *Ibid.* at p. 516.
83 [1895] 1 Ch. 236.
84 *Ibid.* at p. 249.
85 (1850) 5 Ex. 802.
86 *Op. cit.* pp. 199, 200.
87 (1869) L.R. 7 Eq. 504.
88 (1934) 51 C.L.R. 143.
89 *Ibid.* at p. 158.
90 [1891] 1 Ch. 337.
91 *Ibid.* at p. 360.
92 (1842) 1 Ph. 227.
93 (1850) 5 Ex. 802.
94 (1954) 2 Drew 143.
95 (1883) 28 Ch.D. 340.
96 (1868) L.R. 3 Ch.App. 616 at p. 649.
97 (1934) 51 C.L.R. 143 at p. 157.
98 [1903] 2 Ch. 615 at p. 621.
99 [1902] 2 Ch.D. 404 at p. 408.
1 1972 S.L.T. 154.
2 *Barnes* v. *Addy* (1874) L.R. 9 Ch.App. 244 at p. 251, *per* Lord Selborne L.C.
3 *Mara* v. *Browne* (1896) 1 Ch. 199 (C.A.); explained in *Williams-Ashman* v. *Price and Williams* [1942] Ch. 219.
4 *Plumer* v. *Gregory* (1874) L.R. 18 Eq. 621; *Atkinson* v. *Mackreth* (1866) L.R. 2 Eq. 570.
5 *Matthews* v. *Kuwait Bechtel Corporation* [1959] 2 Q.B. 57. *Lister* v. *Romford Ice and Cold Storage Co. Ltd.* [1957] A.C. 555.
6 *Supra,* n. 99.
7 (1891) 1 ch. 337.
8 (1843) 3 Mont. D. & De G. 364.
9 *Ex p. Apsey* (1791) 3 Bro.C.D. 265; *Ex p. White* (1871) L.R. 6 Ch. 397.
10 (1819) Buck 386.
11 [1891] 1 Ch. 337.
12 [1902] 1 Ch. 816.
13 (1834) 1 Bing.N.C. 198.
14 For the limits of the equitable right see *Re Diplock* [1948] Ch. 465 (C.A.) and *Ministry of Health* v. *Simpson* [1951] A.C. 251 (H.L.), which deals with the claim *in personam.*
15 *Re Hallett and Co.* [1894] 2 Q.B. 237.
16 *Re Oatway* [1903] 2 Ch. 356; also *Re Tilley's Will Trust* [1967] Ch. 1179.
17 *Clayton's Case,* discussed below, p. 69.
18 *Per curiam* in *Mollwo, March and Co.* v. *Court of Wards* (1872) L.R. 4 P.C. 419 at p. 435.
19 (1863) 14 C.B.(N.S.) 824, at p. 839.
20 Lindley (13th ed.), p. 101.
21 (1808) 1 Camp. 404n.
22 (1830) 6 Bing. 776 at p. 794.
23 (1863) 15 C.B.(N.S.) 145.
24 [1952] C.P.L. 807.
25 (13th ed.), p. 102.

[26] *Martyn* v. *Gray* (1863) 14 C.B.(N.S.) 824 at p. 841.

[27] *Ibid.* at p. 841, *per* Williams J.

[28] (1882) 7 App.Cas. 345.

[29] *Ibid.* at p. 350.

[30] See Lindley, p. 107.

[31] [1897] 2 Q.B. 396.

[32] (1830) 1 B. & Ad. 11.

[33] (1830) 1 B. & Ad. 11 at p. 13.

[34] *Heath* v. *Sansom* (1832) 4 B. & Ad. 172 at p. 177, *per* Patterson J.

[35] See below, p. 128.

[36] *Stables* v. *Eley* (1825) 1 C. & P. 614.

[37] [1891] 2 Q.B. 403 (C.A.).

[38] [1892] 3 Ch. 226.

[39] (1825) 3 Bing. 101 at p. 103.

[40] *Ex p. Agace* (1792) 2 Cox 312.

[41] (1877) 9 Ch.D. 529: *cf. Lacy* v. *Hill* (1876) 4 Ch.D. 537 at p. 549.

[42] (1877) 9 Ch.D. 529 at p. 535.

[43] [1920] K.B. 639.

[44] *Rolfe* v. *Flower, Salting and Co.* (1865) L.R. 1 P.C. 27 at p. 38.

[45] [1968] A.C. 58.

[46] (1849) 2 Car. & Kir. 828.

[47] *Re European Assurance Society* (*Hort's Case* and *Grain's Case*) (1875) 1 Ch.D. 307.

[48] (1817) Buck 13.

[49] *Bilborough* v. *Holmes* (1876) 5 Ch.D. 255; *Evans* v. *Drummond* (1801) 4 Esp. 89; *Hart* v. *Alexander* (1837) 7 C. & P. 746.

[50] (1865) L.R. 1 P.C. 27.

[51] Lord Eldon's phrase in *Ex p. Peele* (1802) 6 Ves. 602 at p. 604, and indicating that little evidence was needed to show acceptance of the novation by the incoming partner.

[52] *Head* v. *Head* [1893] 3 Ch. 426.

[53] *Head* v. *Head* (*No.* 2) [1894] 2 Ch. 236.

[54] [1894] 2 Ch. 32.

[55] (1834) 5 B. & Ad. 925.

[56] The explanation of the decision given by Pollock (15th ed.), p. 60.

[57] *Lodge* v. *Dicas* (1820) 3 B. & Ald. 611.

[58] *Court* v. *Berlin* [1897] 2 Q.B. 396 (C.A.).

[59] 1972 S.L.T. 96.

[60] (1863) 1 H. & M. 182.

[61] In *Oakley* v. *Pasheller* (1836) 10 Bli.(N.S.) 548. See also s. 38 for the continuing authority of partners for purposes of winding up.

[62] *Devaynes* v. *Noble, Clayton's Case* (1816) 1 Mer. 529.

[63] [1912] A.C. 756.

[64] (1865) 6 B. & S. 507, 520.

[65] (1810) 12 East 400.

CHAPTER FOUR

RELATIONS OF PARTNERS INTER SE

IN this chapter, the internal relationships between the partners are examined to the extent that these are regulated by sections 19–31, inclusive, of the Act. Two pervasive principles need to be recognised at the outset in connection with the internal partnership relationships. The first is that the partners are free to make their own rules, so far as is consistent with the nature of partnership, within the considerable area which the law leaves to the partners themselves. Indeed, partners would be well advised to set out their real intentions in the form of a comprehensive agreement and this for a number of reasons. It is quite possible that the statutory rules, particularly the rule relating to profit-sharing, do not reflect accurately the true wishes of the partners who are more likely than not to be laymen. The statutory rules pass over certain important matters, such as the scope of the partnership business and the expulsion of a partner, so that partners who desire to make provision on these matters must do so in their agreement. It is not unknown for minor matters, such as holidays, to cause irritation when there is no clear agreement between the partners and the statutory rules do not provide an answer. If disputes occur, the paradox is that agreement is least obtainable when most desired.

The second principle is that of *uberrima fides*, which requires the utmost good faith between partners and which, although tacitly recognised in sections 28–30, inclusive, is nowhere explicitly stated in the Act.

The first principle, however, that of freedom of contract, is set forth in section 19:

> " The mutual rights and duties of partners, whether ascertained by agreement or defined by this Act may be varied by the consent of all the partners, and such consent may be either express or inferred from a course of dealing."

It is seen, therefore, that questions concerning relations between the partners are resolved by recourse to the agreement, failing which reference to the Act becomes necessary. The contract of partnership is a simple contract and, as such, may be concluded orally, in writing, or even as an inference from conduct. If it is intended to effect a conveyance of an interest in land or to dispose of an equitable interest, informality must bow to the requirements of section 53 of the Law of Property Act 1925, which requires such dispositions to be in writing and signed. Whether or not interests covered by section 53 are involved, it is common practice to use a deed for the purposes of the partnership agreement. However formed, the agreement may be varied or rescinded (with or without a new agreement) with the consent of all partners, either expressly, or as an inference from the course of dealing.

The flexibility of partnership as a legal vehicle was well established in the nineteenth century, as can be seen from the statement of Lord Langdale M.R. in *England* v. *Curling*: " for with respect to a partnership agreement, it is to be observed that all parties being competent to act as they please, they may put an end to or vary it any moment; a partnership agreement is therefore open to variation from day to day, and the terms of such variation may not only be evidenced by writing, but also by the conduct of the parties in relation to the agreement and to their mode of conducting their business." [1] In that case specific performance was decreed of a partnership deed as varied. Lord Eldon had earlier recognised the flexibility of partnership in *Const* v. *Harris*, stressing, however, that where a material, binding change is to be made all the partners must be consulted, even in those cases in which the consent of all is not required, but accepting that the partners might change the terms of their agreement by " a long course of dealing, or a course of dealing not long, but still so long as to demonstrate that they all agreed to change the terms of the original written agreement." [2] Lord Eldon gives the example of partners who agree that no single partner may draw or accept bills of exchange but who " slide into " the practice, which the courts will condone, of allowing this to be done as of course. The Scottish case of *Geddes* v. *Wallace* [3] concerned a partnership agreement which purported to render all the partners, including the manager, " subject to profit and loss," but which was held to have been transmogrified by a long course of dealing which showed that the manager, if a partner, was no longer bound to contribute to losses. As with other terms of the partnership agreement, terms dealing with the treatment of partnership accounts may be supplemented or modified by a course of dealing, particularly a long course of dealing, so that, for example, a practice whereby losses on capital assets were treated as attributable to the year in which they were discovered precluded surviving partners from re-opening the accounts to show that after the death of their co-partner and the making up of the accounts certain supposed assets were discovered to be bad.[4] Conduct may, however, prove to be an equivocal guide as in *Cruikshank* v. *Sutherland* where, dealing with the practice of including certain assets in the accounts at book values, Lord Wrenbury asked, " How could there be a practice and usage uniform and without variation to pay a deceased partner's share on the footing of book values and not of fair values, where no partner had died before and no partner had retired before?"[5]

PARTNERSHIP PROPERTY

Because each of the partners is personally liable for the debts and liabilities of the firm it does not follow that it is therefore a matter for indifference whether or not particular property is partnership property. In the first place, partnership property must be dealt with exclusively for partnership purposes and in accordance with the partnership agreement.

Secondly, on a dissolution of the firm, every partner, by virtue of section 39 of the Act, is entitled as against the other partners to have the property of the partnership applied in payment of the debts and liabilities of the firm and to have the surplus assets applied in payment of what may be due to the partners. *Robinson* v. *Ashton*[6] illustrates the proposition that a partner's capital contribution may enrich his co-partners on a dissolution of the firm. There, A, the owner of a cotton mill, joined in partnership with B and C for the purpose of cotton-spinning under the terms of an agreement which provided that the business should be carried on at the mill. The mill, fixed plant and machinery were valued and entered in the partnership books as A's capital contribution. The partners enlarged and improved the mill. Land and buildings were later acquired at the firm's expense. The mill, plant and machinery (together with land and buildings acquired later) were held to constitute partnership property, so that on a sale of such property any rise (or fall) in value would rank as a profit (or loss) to be shared by the partners (after providing for debts and liabilities). In *Noble* v. *Noble*[7] it was held that a partner was entitled to have the firm's capital assets, which had been continued in the balance sheets at their original value for some years, entered in the balance sheet at their real value. It may be noted here that the Companies Act 1967, s. 16 (1) (*a*) provides that the directors' report must give any substantial differences between the market value of those assets which are interests in land and the value at which they are included in the balance sheet.

Thirdly, partnership property and separate property are exigible for the satisfaction of the claims of partnership creditors and separate creditors according to certain priorities (see below, p. 170). Finally, by virtue of section 22 of the Act, partnership land is in the absence of a contrary intention subject to the doctrine of conversion. It is not, however, subject to the right of survivorship—the *ius accrescendi*.[8]

What is partnership property?

Sections 20 and 21 afford some (but by no means complete) guidance:

" 20.—(1) All property and rights and interests in property originally brought into the partnership stock or acquired, whether by purchase or otherwise, on account of the firm, or for the purposes and in the course of the partnership business, are called in this Act partnership property, and must be held and applied by the partners exclusively for the purposes of the partnership and in accordance with the partnership agreement.

(2) Provided that the legal estate or interest in any land, or in Scotland the title to and interest in any heritable estate, which belongs to the partnership shall devolve according to the nature and tenure thereof, and the general rules of law thereto applicable, but in trust, so far as necessary, for the persons beneficially interested in the land under this section.

(3) Where co-owners of an estate or interest in any land, or in Scotland of any heritable estate, not being itself partnership property, are partners as to profits made by the use of that land or estate, and purchase other land or estate out of the profits to be used in like manner, the land or estate so purchased belongs to them, in the absence of an agreement to the contrary, not as partners, but as co-owners for the same respective estates and interests as are held by them in the land or estate first mentioned at the date of the purchase.

21. Unless the contrary intention appears, property bought with money belonging to the firm is deemed to have been bought on account of the firm."

The phrase " all property and rights and interests in property," according as it does with property as the subject of rights and as the rights themselves, indicates that there is no limitation on what is capable of being " partnership property." Land (see s. 22 below), personalty, leaseholds, goodwill, profits of offices held by a partner, property acquired by a partner in breach of his duty of good faith, the benefit of contracts acquired after notice of dissolution but before dissolution and the goodwill of a " solus site " (see *R. W. Pathirana* v. *A. Pathirana* [9]) are examples of property which have been held to have been impressed with the label " partnership property."

Before dealing with the definition of partnership property, one preliminary heresy needs to be cleared out of the way, *viz.* that *because* property is *used* by the partnership it is *therefore* partnership property. The correct rule is that expressed by North J. in *Davis* v. *Davis* [10]: " It is not the law that partners in business, who are the owners of the property by means of which the business is carried on, are necessarily partners as regards that property. That conclusion is expressly negatived by subsection 1 of the Act of 1890." The cases of *Fromont* v. *Coupland* [11] and *Steward* v. *Blakeway* [12] were cited in support of this statement; the former holding that partners in a coaching business were not partners as regards the horses used to do the work, the latter holding that land belonging to co-owners as tenants in common and used for the purpose of quarrying was not partnership property in the absence of some further evidence to displace the effect of section 2 (1) of the Act and to indicate at what precise stage in time the tenants in common (owners of undivided moieties) became owners *qua* partners.

If it established *in limine* that persons are partners as to the profits made by the use of land without being partners as to the land itself, subsection (3) of section 20 shows that other land purchased out of such profits belongs to those persons as co-owners for the same respective estates and interests as they held in the land first mentioned and not as partners. In the *Davis* case, a testator left his residuary estate, comprising, *inter alia*, freehold premises and a business concerned with the manufacture of patent fans, to his two sons in equal shares as tenants in common. The sons entered into no partnership agreement, but it was held, nonetheless, that they were partners in the business which had been left to them and which they had carried on. The sons borrowed money on the security of premises adjoining those in which the business was carried on, using the proceeds to add part of those premises to the business premises. It was held that the facts did not show a partnership in the land and that adapting the land in the way in which it had been done, although not the same as buying additional land, was sufficiently similar.

According to the Act, partnership property consists of:

(a) All property and rights and interests in property " originally brought into the partnership stock." Whether or not property has thus been brought into the common stock may be the subject of express agreement in the partnership agreement. That property has not been expressly brought into the partnership as partnership property does not mean that the partnership has no interest in it, as is shown in *Pocock* v. *Carter*,[13] in which A, B and C were partners in a tailoring and outfitting business carried on in Salisbury under the terms of an indenture which expressly provided that the lease of the premises to be used for the business was to remain the property of A, for whose life the partnership was to last, the same indenture also providing that rents, rates and taxes were to be paid out of yearly profits (as was, in fact, done). It was held, notwithstanding A's continued ownership of the lease, that the partnership had, so long as it lasted, a tenancy in the premises, but not a mere tenancy at will or a tenancy from year to year which, it was said, would have permitted A to turn the other partners out of the premises before the partnership had ended. The decision itself has been doubted, particularly in the light of the 1925 property legislation and the greater emphasis upon certainty of duration in relation to leases, and would appear to create more problems than it solves. In the United States, where the treatment of partners as joint tenants has produced some confusion and uncertainty, it has been established that a new kind of estate, termed " a tenancy in partnership " has been created by the Uniform Partnership Act. The obscurity surrounding the partnership interest can be avoided by use of the device of the contractual licence for valuable consideration during the continuance of the partnership. It may be noted here that by virtue of section 41A of the Landlord and Tenant Act 1954 the retirement of one of the partners no longer precludes the renewal of a lease of business premises by the remaining joint lessees.

In an ideal world, the answer to the question of what is or is not partnership property would be provided by the partnership or other agreement, or by irrefragable evidence pointing one way or the other. For example, in *Pawsey* v. *Armstrong*,[14] where a partnership was held to exist between a master and his former clerk, Kay J. was spared the problem of ascertaining any partnership interest in a mill in the light of an express stipulation that the mill and premises were to remain the exclusive property of the master notwithstanding the partnership. In *Robinson* v. *Ashton* (above), another case in which the partnership agreement had not been reduced to writing, there was no express stipulation concerning ownership of the mill and machinery which, however, had been entered in the partnership books as the owner's capital contribution, a fact which, as we have seen, impressed them with the character of partnership assets. On other occasions in an imperfect world, such as ours, the courts have been invited to make bricks without straw. *Miles* v. *Clark*,[15] in which the partners had " just drifted on " without any clear agreement, is not untypical. There, partner A, who had started up in business as a photographer with premises and equipment but without much success, took in B, a successful freelance photographer possessing a substantial connection, as a partner. The business flourished, but personal difficulties (the Achilles heel of small businesses) supervened and necessitated the winding-up of the firm. Harman J. held that the assets (excluding the stocks of film used in the business), such as the lease of the premises, the equipment and goodwill, remained the property of the partner bringing them in (a conclusion which prevented either from charging depreciation against the firm's assets). The judgment is interesting for two reasons. First his Lordship was not prepared to imply any more agreement than was requisite to give business efficacy to the association between the two partners. On this footing, the use of the premises and cameras was consistent with the granting of a licence or a bailment to the firm. Secondly, little credence was placed in the partnership accounts which showed the lease and stock-in-trade as business assets. Harman J.'s faith in the accounts had been undermined by the " monstrous unreality " of an opening entry which had shown A's private overdraft as a liability of the firm.

A similar reluctance to ascribe a proprietary interest in favour of the firm was evinced in *Singh* v. *Nahar*,[16] a case which shows that the firm's interest in property may be protected by contractual provision in the partnership deed or in some other way. In that case, D.N. took two partners into his business, which was carried on at premises of which G. S. were chief tenants. G. S. claimed possession of the premises for breach of covenant by D.N., alleging that D. N. had assigned the tenancy to the firm without written consent. The partnership deed made no specific reference to the tenancy, but did provide that the partners were to be entitled to the capital consisting of the net value of stock-in-trade, book debts and " other assets of the business," in equal shares. Lord Pearce, delivering the advice of the Judicial Committee of the Privy Council, did not doubt that the premises were an asset of the business, but added that this did not bear on the question of whether the tenancy was an asset of the business which had been transferred to the partnership. His Lordship considered that if the tenancy had been assigned under the deed he would have expected to find clearer provision with regard to it. " The tenancy might have been dealt with by the tenant giving to his partners a licence to trade with him there or by his constituting himself a trustee for the partnership, or merely by giving the partners no express rights at all." [17] The finding that there had been no assignment did not mean that the partnership could be turned out of the premises at will, inasmuch as the partnership deed expressly made provision for the business to be carried on at the premises in question or some other place to be agreed by the partners.

The Court of Appeal in *Harrison-Broadley* v. *Smith* [18] declined to recognise the validity of a licence given by A in favour of A and B for the purpose of the Agricultural Holdings Act 1948. After the death of her husband, A had entered into a partnership agreement drawn up by accountants with B, a neighbouring farmer, and this agreement provided for the farming of some 170 acres on certain terms which, however, made no reference to the nature of the partnership interest in the land (or in a house, part of which B had been allowed to occupy). The court declined to find a licence for the purposes of the 1948 Act, although accepting that B himself had a licence to occupy the house and work the land. Lord Pearson noted that A might give a licence to B or to B and C as partners, but not to A and B. [19]

(b) Property acquired by purchase or otherwise (i) on account of the firm, or (ii) for the purposes and in the course of the partnership business. As regards the first of these, section 21 expressly provides that:

> " Unless the contrary intention appears, property bought with money belonging to the firm is deemed to have been bought on account of the firm."

In the *Bank of England* case, it was laid down that there is no inflexible rule to the effect that property bought by partners out of partnership assets necessarily becomes invested with the character of partnership property, although if bought for partnership purposes,

" it is," in Turner L.J.'s words in that case, " scarcely possible to
conceive a case in which there could be evidence to rebut the trust ";
the same judge added that, " accordingly in those cases we find the
decisions almost entirely uniform, that the purchased land forms
part of the joint-estate of the partnership." [20] The property may,
however, have been bought as a mere speculation on account of the
partnership and yet be partnership property. For example, in *Ex p.
Hinds* [21] the partners traded as merchants in Liverpool and Barbados.
The Liverpool partner, without the knowledge or authority of the
other, acquired railway shares using partnership money and intending
to acquire them on behalf of the firm. They were held to be partnership property. The case shows that a purchase on account of the
firm under section 20 (1) may relate to a purpose completely foreign
to the firm's business. In the *Bank of England* case itself, one of two
partners had bought land and offered a share therein to his co-
partner. The latter accepted the offer and the purchase money was
provided from partnership assets. The land on which the partners
had built houses at their own expense was held to be partnership
property. Yet another possibility is that property may be bought for
one partner out of partnership funds, either as an outright transfer
of partnership capital, or in order to make the partner a debtor for
the amount so advanced.

The form of the conveyance is not conclusive; property acquired
by one partner may be held in trust for the firm, a result which may
also ensue in those cases in which one partner brings in property at
the inception of the partnership. In *Re Rayleigh Weir Stadium* [22] M,
the tenant in fee simple of a greyhound racing stadium, entered into a
partnership with R, and was held to hold the legal estate in the
stadium in trust for himself and R in equal shares, a solution which
escapes the difficulties inherent in the *Pocock* v. *Carter* solution
(above.)

The cases in which land has been acquired by will or on intestacy
by two or more persons and then utilised in a joint business are not
easy to reconcile. *Waterer* v. *Waterer* [23] indicates that the degree to
which the land is involved in the business is a relevant factor. There,
W, a nurseryman, devised land on which his business had been
carried on, and bequeathed the goodwill of his business to his three
sons as tenants in common in equal shares. The sons carried on the
business in partnership after their father's death, two of them buying
the share of the third in the land and business. Holding that the land

so devised had become partnership property, Sir W. M. James L.J. made the factual observation that in nursery gardening it is practically impossible to separate the use of the soil for the trees and shrubs, from the trees and shrubs themselves, which are part of the freehold and, at the same time, stock-in-trade. It is therefore clear that when the same judge said [24] that he was of opinion that the case was governed by "that class of cases in which Lord Eldon said that where property became involved in partnership dealings it must be regarded as partnership property," he had in mind the employment of the land in the business in a substantial and integral way. In *Davies* v. *Games* [25] two brothers and their nephew carried on a farming business; they were tenants in common of the land employed. The nephew sold his one-third share to the brothers as joint tenants. On the death of one brother it was held that this one-third share had become involved in partnership dealings and must be regarded as partnership property. This case may be contrasted with that of *Morris* v. *Barrett* [26] in which land was devised to two sons as joint tenants and farmed by them on a common stock but without any agreement. The land was held not to be partnership land.

It would appear that property which is purchased for the purposes of a business is more likely to be adjudged partnership property than property of which persons are already co-owners and which they decide to put to business use [27]: the latter, said Lord Eldon L.C. is "a very difficult question." [28] *A fortiori*, it is even more difficult to prove that property is partnership property where one of the partners had a sole interest in it before the commencement of the partnership.[DD]

Nature of partnership property

We have seen that partnership property may consist of real or personal property and that such property may be owned by the partners as such, or owned by one, or more, or all of them but subject to a trust, lease, licence or bailment in favour of the firm. It would now appear, notwithstanding powerful arguments to the contrary,[30] that partnership land is deemed to be held in undivided shares and therefore on trust for sale under section 34 (and Sched. 1, Pt. IV) of the Law of Property Act 1925. In *Re Fuller's Contract*,[31] land was conveyed in 1892 to six persons collectively described as "the purchasers" (in fact the partners) with the following habendum: "to the use of the purchasers their heirs and assigns as joint tenants in trust for them the purchasers their executors administrators and assigns as part of their co-partnership estate." It was held that the survivors could make a good title as trustees for sale under the statutory trusts of the Law of Property Act 1925, Sched. 1, Pt. IV. If land is expressed to be conveyed to more than four persons in undivided shares, the conveyance operates as if the land had been conveyed to the four first named in the conveyance (Law of Property Act 1925, s. 34 (2)). Formerly, partners acquiring property were presumed to hold it as beneficial tenants in common, thereby displacing the *ius accrescendi*.[32] Whilst the partnership property may have to be dealt with in a particular way as regards the partners *inter se*, *quoad* the world at large the partners have the beneficial interest in the partnership assets which are held together as an undivided whole and in which they have undivided interests.[33]

The House of Lords decision in *Rye* v. *Rye* poses a difficulty in those cases in which co-owners wish to transfer an interest in the property co-owned to themselves as partners. Two brothers, who were in partnership as solicitors, purported to effect an oral letting of freehold premises of which they were tenants in common in equal shares to themselves as partners, but it was held that they had failed to create a tenancy in favour of the partnership. Two *rationes* can be extracted from the decision, the first resting on the abortive nature of the oral letting as a conveyance under section 72 of the Law of Property Act 1925, the second resting on the doctrine, referred to by Lord Denning, that *nemo potest esse tenens et dominus*, which the provisions of sections 72 (4) and 82 (1) of the 1925 Act did nothing to overturn, at least in those situations in which the persons " are the same on both sides." [34] If in this context the law of property seems to set its face against legal schizophrenia, the same cannot be said of the criminal law or the law of tort; a partner may commit the crime of theft and the tort of conversion against the partnership property.

In *R.* v. *Bonner*,[35] B and W were in partnership as demolition contractors. B, unknown to W, broke the lock of W's garage and stole partnership property, namely scrap metal, from inside. The Court of Appeal stated that if B took the metal with the intention of permanently depriving W of his share he was guilty of theft. In *Baker* v. *Barclays Bank Ltd.*,[36] a partner who had delivered partnership cheques to be paid into an account other than the partnership account was guilty of conversion. A partner who takes possession of partnership chattels does not commit conversion, inasmuch as he is entitled to take possession, but it is otherwise if he commits some act which can only be justified by the right to exclusive possession.

Although the requirements of the Statute of Frauds (now replaced by section 40 of the Law of Property Act 1925) as to writing and signature in connection with contracts for the sale or other disposition of land or any interest in land formerly occasioned some doubt, it now appears to be settled that once a partnership is proved to exist (and for this writing is not requisite) parol evidence may be adduced to show that it holds an interest in land.[37] For example, in the Scottish case of *Munro* v. *Stein* [38] a dance hall was held to have become partnership property without a probative deed of conveyance.

The partners may, by agreement, convert partnership property into the several property of any one or more of the partners, just as, conversely, a partner may, at any time, agree to bring his separate property into the partnership fund; such conversions, if made in good faith, are effectual, not only as between the partners, but also as against the creditors of the firm.[39] If the firm, or the partner whose separate estate is involved, becomes bankrupt or insolvent following upon any such agreement, and something remains to be done to make it operative, the property is not converted.[40]

Whatever the interest of partners in the partnership property, it is, at least, clear that a partner cannot, either during or after the dissolution of the partnership, point to specific property and say to his co-partners that it is his alone.[41] A partner has a " share " in the partnership property, defined by Lindley, as " his proportion of the partnership assets after they have been all realised and converted into money, and all the partnership debts have been paid and discharged." [42] If, as we have seen, the partnership land is held by the partners as joint tenants upon the statutory trusts for themselves as tenants in common, the legal estate thereto will devolve according to law on surviving partners as trustees, express or statutory, on trust for sale for the partners, including the personal representatives of any deceased partner, in their respective proportions. Formerly partnership property had been subject in equity to the doctrine of conversion and, in the absence of a contrary intention, had accordingly been treated as personal property. The equitable doctrine, which looked on that as done which ought to be done, received statutory recognition in relation to partnership property in section 22 of the Act:

> " Where land or any heritable interest therein has become partnership property, it shall, unless the contrary intention

appears, be treated as between the partners (including the
representatives of a deceased partner), and also as between the
heirs of a deceased partner and his executors or administrators,
as personal or moveable and not real or heritable estate."

This section has lost much of its importance for two main reasons.
First, the rules concerning succession on death to real and personal
property have been largely assimilated by the property legislation of
1925. Secondly, because partnership land is in all probability subject
to the statutory trusts set forth in section 34, and Schedule I, Part IV,
of the Law of Property Act 1925, it follows that after 1925 the words
" unless the contrary intention appears " in section 22 cannot operate
to prevent a conversion.[43] However, conversion will still be important
if there is a devise of " all my realty " to A and " all my personalty "
to B.

*Procedure against partnership property for a partner's separate
judgment debt*

" Section 23 is absolutely new," said Lindley L.J. in *Brown,
Janson and Co.* v. *Hutchinson,* without referring to the open secret
that the amendment introduced by that section was largely due to
his counsel. " It replaced a very cumbrous method of proceeding
when a creditor obtained a judgment against one partner and he
wanted to obtain the benefit of that judgment against the share of
that partner in the firm; the first thing was to issue a *fi. fa.,* and the
sheriff went down to the partnership place of business, seized
everything, stopped the business, drove the solvent partners wild, and
caused the execution creditor to bring an action in Chancery in order
to get an injunction to take an account and pay over that which was
due by the execution debtor. A more clumsy method of proceeding
could hardly have grown up." [44] No longer are the partners driven
wild; partnership property cannot be seized except on a judgment
against the firm. A charging order on a partner's interest in the firm
has no immediate effect on the co-partners, who are not subject to
harassment as they were formerly, although once a receiver has to
their knowledge been appointed they must take care not to pay over
to the partner whose share is charged his share of profits. Section 23
is as follows:

" (1) After the commencement of this Act a writ of execution
shall not issue against any partnership property except on a
judgment against the firm.

(2) The High Court, or a judge thereof . . . or a county court, may, on the application by summons of any judgment creditor of a partner, make an order charging that partner's interest in the partnership property and profits with payment of the amount of the judgment debt and interest thereon, and may by the same or a subsequent order appoint a receiver of that partner's share of profits (whether already declared or accruing), and of any other money which may be coming to him in respect of the partnership, and direct all accounts and inquiries, and give all other orders and directions which might have been directed or given if the charge had been made in favour of the judgment creditor by the partner, or which the circumstances of the case may require.

(3) The other partners shall be at liberty at any time to redeem the interest charged, or in the case of a sale being directed, to purchase the same.

(4) This section shall apply in the case of a cost-book company as if the company were a partnership within the meaning of this Act.

(5) This section shall not apply to Scotland."

Subsection 2 applies with respect to a foreign firm having a branch in England.[45] It does not, as a rule, entitle the judgment creditor to have accounts rendered to him by the other partners, because an express assignment would not (by s. 31) give him that right.[46] A charging order is not a completed execution against the goods of a debtor within the meaning of section 40 of the Bankruptcy Act 1914, although if given before the commencement of the bankruptcy it secures the rights of the judgment creditor.[47]

The contention of counsel in *Helmore* v. *Smith*[48] that the taking in execution of a partner's interest *ipso facto* determines the partnership was forcefully rejected by Bacon V.-C., and is now dealt with by section 33 of the Act. The same case decided that the purchase of the judgment debtor's chattel interest in the goodwill and effects of the partnership business by his co-partner at a sale by auction of that interest must be set aside on the ground that the co-partner had used partnership money. The latter could not say that partnership money belonged to him, nor could he say that half of such money was his because there had, as yet, been no division.

Kewney v. *Attrill*,[49] the reporting of which formerly caused some doubt, is now seen to have decided that if judgment has been given in an action in the Chancery Division for the dissolution of partnership, and a receiver has been appointed, a creditor who later recovers judgment against the firm in the Queen's Bench Division, can obtain, on application in the Chancery action, a charge for the debt and costs on the partnership money in the hands of or coming to the receiver, with the consequence that if there is a bankruptcy such creditor obtains priority over the general body of the partnership's creditors. But a charging order confers upon the judgment creditor no greater rights than were held by the judgment debtor, so that if the partner whose interest in the partnership is being charged assigns his interest after the judgment but before the charging order is made, the assignee need not concede priority to the judgment creditor.[50]

Under the procedure laid down by the Rules of the Supreme Court, Ord. 81, r. 10, every application to the court by a judgment creditor of a partner for an order under section 23 of the Partnership Act and every application to the court by a partner of the judgment debtor made in consequence of the first-mentioned application must be made by summons. Every summons issued by a judgment creditor under this rule and every order made on such a summons must be served on the judgment debtor and on such of his partners as are within the jurisdiction (or, if the partnership is a cost-book company, on the judgment debtor and purser of the company). A summons or order served in accordance with this rule on some only of the partners is deemed to have been served on all the partners in the partnership. (For procedure in the county court, see the County Court Rules 1936, Ord. 25; r. 4 deals with an application by a separate judgment creditor and r. 5 deals with an application by the partner of a judgment debtor.)

Rules as to interests and duties of partners subject to special agreement
Section 24 is a miniature code of rules which governs the internal partnership relationships to the extent that the parties have not excluded or varied such rules.

" The interests of partners in the partnership property and their rights and duties in relation to the partnership shall be determined, subject to any agreement express or implied between the partners, by the following rules ":
The first of the nine rules (each of which will receive separate treatment) is a statutory affirmation of the rule that " equality is equity," and can be justified in the present context not so much on the ground

of absolute justice as upon the empirical consideration that any fairer standard of commutative justice would be difficult to ascertain and apply.

" (1) All the partners are entitled to share equally in the capital and profits of the business, and must contribute equally towards the losses whether of capital or otherwise sustained by the firm."

Read literally, this subsection would appear to indicate that partners share equally in capital even though they have contributed capital unequally. But if partner A has contributed £100 capital, and co-partner B has contributed £200 capital, the fact that B has contributed twice as much as A is evidence of an implied agreement that each is to take out the same proportion of the available capital when the business is liquidated.

Inequality of capital contribution does not, however, raise the implication that profits or losses are to be shared in the same proportion. Since the early nineteenth century it has been clearly recognised that, in the absence of agreement or evidence to the contrary, partners, whatever their capital contribution, are entitled to share equally in profits. The presumption of equality was held to have been rebutted in *Stewart* v. *Forbes* [51] where an examination of the books and dealings showed an unequal division of profits, notwithstanding that some equal sharing had been conceded on occasions as an act of bounty. If, however, there is no agreement or course of dealing which can establish unequal shares, the rule as to equality, applies, as in *Warner* v. *Smith* [52] where, in an adventure for the supply of arms to a foreign government between A (who signed separately) and B and C in their firm's name, it was held that in the absence of evidence to the contrary, the profits must be shared equally between the firm (treated for this purpose as an entity) and A.

Nor does it make any difference if there is unequal contribution of labour and skill. A partner who performs more work in the partnership business than his co-partner is not, in the absence of evidence to the contrary, entitled to a share of profits reflecting his greater contribution and, as subsection (4) below shows, is not entitled to remuneration, other than his equal share of profits, for his greater burden. The solicitor who was jointly retained in the case of *Robinson* v. *Anderson* [53] was held to be entitled to only half of the net profits of the retainer in the absence of evidence to the contrary, notwithstanding that he performed more work than his jointly-retained colleague, a finding which contrasts with that in *Webster* v. *Bray* [54] in which, on a joint retainer, " inequality of labour was contemplated from the beginning" with corresponding recompense to the defendant, the court directing an inquiry into the latter, on which there was, admittedly, some vagueness.

So far as losses, including losses of capital, are concerned, Sir W. M. James expressed some rhetorical doubts in *Nowell* v. *Nowell* [55] whether a " capitalist partner " would consent to join in " the game of partnership " on the terms that he might share in profits but must shoulder all the loss—the principle of " heads, I win; tails, you lose." In more forthright fashion, Jessel M.R. gave his assent in *Re Albion Life Assurance Society* [56] to " the general proposition of law, that in ordinary mercantile partnerships where there is a community of profits in a definite proportion, the fair inference is that the losses are to be shared in the same proportion." From the example given above, this would mean that any profit will be shared equally in the absence of contrary indications and, likewise, if it is found that after all the debts have been paid only £200 remains the £100 loss of capital will be borne by A and B in equal shares on the dissolution of the firm (s. 44 (*a*)). Hence A will be entitled to £50 and B to £150 in respect of the capital sums which each had originally brought in to the partnership.

Lindley defines profits as " the excess of what is obtained over the cost of obtaining it " [57] or, in other words, the amount of gain made by the business during the year or other accounting period. Unless otherwise agreed, the increase in the value of the total assets over the accounting period, allowing for capital introduced or withdrawn, represents in strictness the profits of the business. In practice the revenue profits of the business over an accounting period are ascertained from a comparison of ordinary receipts with ordinary expenses over that period. Even so, it is as true of partnerships as it is of registered companies that " the method by which the profits of a company are to be ascertained depends on circumstances which may vary widely as between one company and another." [58] In *Cooke* v. *Benbow*,[59] a father in business had admitted his sons into partnership with him, and had also provided the capital, which included certain book debts. The debts were undervalued at the commencement of the partnership, but in the event realised nearly their full value. It was held that the difference between the realised and estimated values of the book debts did not constitute profits but had remained part of the father's capital. Partners may treat profits left in the business as capital if they so wish, otherwise such profits will not be treated as capital, nor will they attract any interest which might otherwise be payable on capital.[60] That undrawn profits have previously been used to purchase or improve capital assets of the firm does not of itself mean that undrawn profits standing to the credit of a partner are capitalised, as is shown in the recent case of *Smith* v. *Gale*,[61] where an agreement to dissolve the partnership provided for the ascertainment of the " undrawn profits " due to each partner. The plaintiff claimed as undrawn profits his balance of £2,237 on current account, a claim to which the other partners objected, arguing that undrawn profits had previously been left in the business to purchase capital assets. Goulding J. held that, on the facts of the case, there was no agreement to modify the ordinary construction of " undrawn profits " and that, accordingly, the plaintiff was entitled to the £2,237.

" (2) The firm must indemnify every partner in respect of payments made and personal liabilities incurred by him—

(*a*) In the ordinary and proper conduct of the business of the firm; or

(*b*) In or about anything necessarily done for the preservation of the business or property of the firm."

It has already been seen that the partner is a Janus-like creature, one of his faces being that of agent empowered to act on behalf of the firm, the other that of principal liable, with the other partners, for the liabilities of the firm. As agent, the partner is entitled to the limited right of indemnity vouchsafed by ordinary agency law. The present subsection goes further by allowing indemnity not only for liabilities arising from acts connected with the ordinary and proper conduct of the business, but also for transactions in the nature of a *negotiorum gestio* provided, however, that such transactions are necessary and not " voluntary " in relation to the preservation of the firm's business or property. The cases have established a somewhat delphic distinction between the incurring of a necessary debt or liability, and borrowing for a necessary purpose, the former, unlike the latter, attracting a right of indemnity. Thus, the directors of a deed of settlement company who had incurred liabilities in respect of miners' wages in order to prevent the seizure of the mine under German law, were enabled to throw the loss upon the members according to the latter's interests. As it was said in that case, " To

hold the shareholders liable for money borrowed by the manager
without their authority would be unjust, for then they would be
liable whether the moneys borrowed were expended upon the mine or
not: but there is not the same injustice in holding them liable for
wages incurred, and debts contracted for the purposes of the mine,
for then they have the benefit of the expenditure." [62]

The principle of indemnity does not apply if the partnership itself
is illegal, or if the partner claiming indemnity bases his claim upon
his own wrong, a term which includes misconduct or culpable
negligence. So, in a case in which the managing partner of a mine
incurred liability for trespass when he had recklessly extended the
mine-workings beyond their proper boundary, his co-partner was
held free of any obligation to indemnify the managing partner for the
damages which had been assessed by arbitration at £6,000.[63] On the
other hand, a partner who bears a loss arising out of the illegal act of
his co-partner for which the firm is liable is not precluded from
claiming contribution from the other partners in the firm.

Although indemnity and contribution are sometimes lumped
together in the present context, the two are quite different. Contribution arises when one of two or more persons liable (whether jointly,
or jointly and severally) in respect of the same liability has been, or is
being, called upon to bear more than his aliquot share of the liability.
Contribution (which is not dealt with *nominatim* in the Act) may be
claimed by a partner who is guilty of nothing more than masterly
inactivity but who has been called upon to meet a partnership liability
created by the act of a co-partner. A person who pays the rent in
respect of premises jointly hired,[64] or a shareholder in a joint-stock
mining company who pays more than his share of the joint liability
on a promissory note,[65] has been held able to claim contribution from
those who have derived benefit from the respective payments, showing that the notion of unjust enrichment lies at the root of the doctrine
of contribution. Now that equitable rules prevail if in conflict or
variance with common law rules, it is clear that the equitable right
to claim contribution arises before a loss has been sustained, and it is
also clear that if one of the joint obligees is unable to contribute, as
for example where he is insolvent, the total liability is shared between
those able to pay,[66] unless there is agreement to the contrary.

The amount recoverable by way of contribution is not necessarily
limited by the nominal capital of the partnership inasmuch as the
latter cannot, as a matter of law, provide an upper limit to the

partnership's liability to the outside world. In *Royal Bank of Australia, Robinson's Executor's* case, the Lord Chancellor said that, " by the general rules of law every partner is liable to the whole of the demands of the partnership. To put an extreme case, if there had been but one solvent shareholder there is no doubt a call might have been made on him for an amount equal to the debts of the partnership," adding that " the shareholder who has paid a sum exceeding his rateable proportion, calculated on the number of his shares, will have a right of contribution against the other shareholders." [67] On the other hand, the limit of contribution may be fixed beforehand by express agreement between the members of the firm, in which case no partner may call upon a co-partner to pay more than his agreed contribution, however great may have been the amount of his own outlay on behalf of the firm or however great the magnitude of the liability incurred.[68]

" (3) A partner making, for the purpose of the partnership, any actual payment or advance beyond the amount of capital which he has agreed to subscribe, is entitled to interest at the rate of five per cent. per annum from the date of the payment or advance."

This subsection provides for interest at 5 per cent. per annum on advances beyond the amount of agreed capital and on actual payments such as those which confer a right of indemnity under the foregoing subsection.[69] As Lindley points out: " An advance by a partner to a firm is not treated as an increase of his capital, but rather as a loan on which interest ought to be paid." [70] Apart from attracting simple interest at 5 per cent. per annum, an advance has the further contrast with capital in that it normally takes effect as a loan and is not intended to be risked in the business.

" (4) A partner is not entitled, before the ascertainment of profits, to interest on the capital subscribed by him.

It is, of course, open to the partners to agree that interest is to be payable on capital brought into the business. If they so agree, such interest is only payable whilst the partnership is extant, so that no interest is payable if the business is carried on after dissolution with a view to sale.[71] The partners are, however, at liberty to agree on interest after dissolution, as was found in *Barfield* v. *Loughborough*,[72] where simple interest after dissolution was allowed in contrast to the calculation of interest with yearly rests during the continuance of the partnership.

" (5) Every partner may take part in the management of the partnership business."

The rule that " one partner cannot exclude another from an equal management of the concern " [73] does not apply if there is agreement between the partners to exclude one or more of their number from active management (as in the case of dormant partners), or to restrict the area of a partner's authority (as may be the case with junior partners). If a partner who is entitled to participate in the management of the business, is obstructed in the exercise of that right by his co-partners, the court may, where such obstruction is persisted in, decree a dissolution under section 35. In the case of a registered company, a director is entitled to attend meetings of the board of directors and to exercise his right to participate in the management of the company. Unlike partnership, however, a director may be removed from office before expiration of his term of office by means of an ordinary resolution of the company under section 184 of the Companies Act 1948, notwithstanding any provision to the contrary in the articles of association. In the case of the small private company, devices such as weighted voting arrangements (as in *Bushell* v. *Faith* [74]), or voting agreements, may afford the director protection from removal. A director with a service contract, although still removable under section 184, is protected to the extent that his removal may prove to be expensive for the company. All said, however, the director remains more vulnerable to a " squeeze " than the partner. If company law affords little consolation to the director who is squeezed out of office in accordance with section 184 and the articles, the concept of the " quasi-partnership " or, to use the now-preferred term, the " incorporated partnership," may allow him to invoke the greater security of the partner. This was the situation in *Ebrahimi* v. *Westbourne Galleries Ltd.*,[75] where the notion of the incorporated partnership was successfully invoked to give a remedy to the director of a private company who had been removed from office under section 184 and the articles of the company. Lifting the veil of incorporation, the House of Lords perceived an incorporated partnership in which the mutual relationships of confidence and trust were paramount and found that notwithstanding the director's " lawful " removal from office, the removal was inequitable since it violated an underlying expectation that, so long as the business continued, the director, like a partner, would be entitled to participate in the management of the business. Accordingly, by analogy with partnership, he was held entitled to an order for the winding up of the company under section 222 (f) of the Companies Act 1948 (the " just and equitable ground ").[76]

It is, perhaps, desirable that the power of management conferred by the facultative wording of the subsection should be reinforced, where necessary, by the imposition of an express, positive duty to attend to the firm's business.

" (6) No partner shall be entitled to remuneration for acting in the partnership business."

However assiduous a partner may be in his devotion to the partnership business, he is not on that account entitled to remuneration over and above his entitlement to a share of profits. Conversely, the partner who fails to discharge his fair share of the firm's business is nevertheless entitled to his share of profits. The result may be that an active partner, who is quite prepared to " carry " a " capitalistic partner " or a dormant partner, may find that he has also to carry a " passenger " without recompense for his additional trouble—a phenomenon not confined to partnerships. Understandably, he will be reluctant to emulate the heroic example of Samson who brought down the temple, although as a last resort he may find that he has no other course than to apply for a dissolution. The moral is clear. The partnership agreement should spell out the positive duties of the partners and, where necessary, should provide a procedure to vary profit shares according to the shares of work and responsibility of the partners with the ultimate sanction of expulsion to coerce the partner who cannot or will not make his contribution to the business of the firm. Nowadays, it is common to find clauses of this nature in the partnership agreement, together with provision for the payment of salaries to active partners to be paid from the profits, the balance of which is shared by all the partners including the active partners. Occasionally, a partner is remunerated entirely by salary whilst remaining a " true " partner, subject to the possibility, adverted to in *Stekel* v. *Ellice* (above, p. 18), that the term " salaried partner," like the designation " associate director," may conceal someone who is merely an employee. The *Stekel* case shows that the exact status of someone who is undoubtedly a partner may still be a matter of difficulty. In *Marsh* v. *Stacey*,[77] a provision that the salary of a junior partner (also entitled to a share of profits) was to be a first charge on profits was read to mean that the salary was to be payable out of, but not irrespective of, profits. Where the salary is to be paid

out of profits without being a " first charge " on profits the facts
may justify the inference that the firm is bound to indemnify the
salaried partner to the extent that the profits are insufficient to meet
the salary, with the further inference that the salaried partner is
under no obligation to contribute to losses.

The position is rather more flexible on a dissolution, when the
court may show a greater readiness to entertain a claim for remuneration from a partner who has carried on the business after his co-
partner's departure [78] or after the death of a co-partner.

" (7) No person may be introduced as a partner without the
consent of all existing partners."

Because partnership is founded on the rock of mutual confidence,
a partner cannot assign his share in the partnership so as to enable
the assignee of such share to step into his shoes and become a
partner against the wishes of the other partners. We shall see that it
does not follow from this that a partner cannot assign his interest in
the profits of the firm.[79] The assignment of a partner's share does
not *ipso facto* work a dissolution of the firm, or (unlike the situation
covered by section 33 (2)) [80] confer upon the other partners any
absolute right to have the partnership dissolved, although the fact
that a partner has alienated his substantial interest in the firm would
be a relevant circumstance to be taken into account by the court
when deciding whether it is just and equitable to order a dissolution
under section 35. A partner is at liberty to create a sub-partnership
between himself and a stranger to the partnership, an arrangement
which establishes no privity of contract between the stranger and the
partner's co-partners.[81]

Shares transferable by agreement

The rigidity of the rule embodied in the subsection can be avoided
by express agreement to permit the interest of any or more of the
partners to be assignable. Indeed, the transferability of shares was
one of the main features of the old unincorporated trading companies
and one which the Bubble Act of 1720 suppressed only temporarily.
The law will enforce an agreement for the introduction of new
partners. Lord Chancellor Brougham's statement in *Lovegrove* v.
Nelson [82] still represents the law: " To make a person a partner with
two others, their consent must clearly be had, but there is no particular mode or time required of giving that consent; and if three enter
into a partnership by a contract which provides that, on retiring, one

of the remaining two, or even a fourth person who is no partner at all, shall name the successor to take the share of the one retiring, it is clear this would be a valid contract which the court must perform, and that the new partner would come in entirely by the consent of the other two, as if they had adopted him by name." By allowing sons or kinsmen, whether identified by description or *nominatim*, to come into the firm, scope is given to nepotism (using that term in a non-perjorative sense).

" (8) Any differences arising as to ordinary matters connected with the partnership business may be decided by a majority of the partners, but no change may be made in the nature of the partnership business without the consent of all existing partners."

The partners may come to an agreement to regulate the manner in which differences between them are to be resolved. For example, in *Clements* v. *Norris* [83] the articles of partnership had stipulated that the business was to be carried on at a specified place, or " such other place or places as the partners may agree upon " and this, it was held, entitled one partner to restrain another from carrying on the business in premises, the lease of which he (without his co-partner's permission) had managed to renew. Lindley treats this case as an illustration of the procedural rule *in re communi potior est conditio prohibentis* [84] but it may equally illustrate the power of the partners to elevate any issue to the status of one requiring unanimity. In the absence of such agreements the minority must bow to the *volonté générale* in matters falling short of a change in the firm's business. Examples of such matters are the manner of treating profits, capital and interest, the admission of one of the partner's sons into the business in order to be trained,[85] the purchase and sale of goods and the engagement of employees.

Where it applies, the principle of majority rule is subject to two important limitations. First, the majority must consult with the minority in order that any decision which might emerge is a joint, although not necessarily unanimous, decision. In *Const* v. *Harris* [86] Lord Eldon stressed that Const " had a right to be consulted; his opinion might be overruled, and honestly overruled, but he ought to have had the question put to him and discussed." Secondly, the majority must, as fiduciaries, exercise their power for the benefit of the whole firm, and not solely in order to advance their own exclusive interests.[87]

Unless there is agreement to the contrary, one partner may, like a

Roman tribune, interpose his veto if there is a proposal to change the nature of the partnership business. The assumption is that a person who has invested capital, skill or labour, is not to be committed against his will to some new venture in which his capital may be faced with new, although possibly profitable, risks and in which his skill or labour may well prove to be sterile. The *status quo ante* also prevails if there is an equality of votes on a proposal not involving a change in the nature of the partnership business. For example, in *Donaldson* v. *Williams* [88] the dismissal of a servant by one partner was invalid where the other partner wished to retain him.

" (9) The partnership books are to be kept at the place of business of the partnership (or the principal place, if there is more than one), and every partner may, when he thinks fit, have access to and inspect and copy any of them."

Unlike shareholders (who, unless the articles of association permit it, have no right to inspect the company accounts), the partners (including dormant partners) have a right to inspect the books and accounts and, if necessary, to take copies, provided the right is not exercised for a purpose which is hostile or injurious to the firm, *e.g.* copying lists of customers whom it is intended to solicit after leaving the firm.[89] A partner commits a plain breach of his duty of good faith if he removes partnership books and documents. Partners who are bent on breaking this rule ought to show greater discretion than the defendant in *Greatrex* v. *Greatrex* [90] who was seen in the company of a porter wheeling a wheelbarrow containing a box of partnership books from the place of business in Walsall down the road to Birmingham. It is also a breach of the duty of good faith for a partner to utilise confidential information pertaining to the partnership for his own purposes, *e.g.* where he proposes to set up a new business. The duty of good faith continues in this respect even though the partnership is, in Megarry J.'s words,[91] " marching to its doom " after the giving of notice of dissolution by a partner, a state of affairs which does not justify " a surreptitious free-for-all." The right of access to the books, and to take copies therefrom, may be exercised through an agent provided he is a person to whom no reasonable objection can be taken and the purpose of the inspection or copying is consistent with the objectives and well-being of the whole firm. The agent may be required to give an undertaking that he will not disclose information received to third persons.

Power to expel partner

" 25. No majority of the partners can expel any partner unless a power to do so has been conferred by express agreement between the partners."

In contrast to company law, which tolerates a circumscribed right in the majority to " pay off " a minority, the 1890 Act follows the pre-existing law when it sets its face against majority rule in the matter of expulsion, although here, as elsewhere, it concedes the right of the parties to make contractual provision on the matter. If the parties are not perspicacious enough, or indeed able, to reach agreement on expulsion in the articles, the only course open to them in the event of disagreement is to seek a dissolution, and this may not always be granted.[92] Lord Eldon, whilst accepting in *Crawshay* v. *Maule* [93] that a partnership at will is dissoluble at any time, castigated those who omit to protect themselves against the " inconveniences " of a fixed-term contract and who subsequently call upon courts of justice to redeem them " from the penalties of their imprudence," pointing out that, like those who enter into a marriage, they must abide by it for better and worse. If there is specific provision on expulsion in the articles or elsewhere, a distinction can be drawn between, (a) the determination of the partnership with regard to a particular partner, and (b) the entire dissolution of the firm.[94] Although from a strict point of view both work a dissolution of the firm (the continuing partners in (a) in effect reconstitute themselves as a fresh firm), some of the confusion in the cases is perhaps attributable to a failure to appreciate the nature of this distinction.

An express power of expulsion must be wielded in a bona fide manner for the benefit of the partnership as a whole. The court expressed its disapproval in *Blisset* v. *Daniel* [95] of a majority which exercises its power of expulsion *intempestive, e.g.* where the affairs of the partnership, after a period in the doldrums, have taken, or are likely to take, a turn for the better. Nor did the court like the clandestine manner in which the moving spirit in that case had gone round to secure the ear of the majority to a proposal for expulsion which he desired for his own purposes. The editorial note appended to *Crawshay* v. *Maule*,[96] drawing on the Digest, justifies the unilateral and immediate dissolution of a partnership at will provided it is seasonable (*tempestiva*). The same note states that no direct authority can be found to support the distinction between seasonable and unseasonable dissolutions. Sir W. Grant M.R. doubted the notion of unseasonable dissolution in *Featherstonhaugh* v. *Fenwick* [97] but Lord Watson in the *Neilson* case (see below at p. 104), whilst accepting that a partnership at will might be determined instantly, added that notice must be given in good faith " and not for the purpose of deriving an undue advantage from the state of the firm's engagements." A partner who has been improperly expelled, either because those expelling him lacked the necessary power or, having the power, have exercised it mala fide, cannot bring an action for damages because the purported expulsion is in law a nullity.[98] The proper remedy in such a case is a claim for reinstatement.

In construing expulsion clauses the courts have been called upon to show semantic skill and social realism. Fortune did not favour the brave in *Re Solicitors' Arbitration*,[99] in which a notice of expulsion served by a partner upon his two co-partners on the ground of misconduct was held to be invalid because the use of the plural in the phrase " other partners " (given the power to expel) did not in this context include the singular. In *Carmichael* v. *Evans*,[1] it was held that the expulsion of a partner in a firm of general drapers who had been convicted of travelling by train without a ticket was a valid exercise of the power conferred by the articles to expel for " scandalous conduct detrimental to the partnership business," or for " flagrant breach of the duties of a partner." Byrne J. conceived it to be one of the first duties of a partner to be " an honest man," not only in relation to his fellow-partners, but also in relation to third persons, and that this duty should, at the least, constrain him to keep clear of fraud bringing him within the arm of the criminal law. If it is clear that not every brush with the criminal law will attract the stigma of dishonesty, it is less clear, although possible, that the standard required of the honest man has declined with the advent of the so-called " permissive society."

There are indications in the cases,[2] and elsewhere,[3] that the partner to be expelled ought to be given notice of the charge and the opportunity to rebut it; rights which were accorded to Adam prior to his banishment from the Garden of Eden. Support for this view is to be found in *Wood* v. *Woad*, which concerned the expulsion of a member from a mutual insurance company and in which it was said that the *audi alteram partem* rule was not confined to strictly legal tribunals but was applicable " to every tribunal or body of persons invested with authority to adjudicate upon matters involving civil consequences to individuals." [4] In that case the committee had the power

to exclude a member whose conduct was *deemed* suspicious or un-
worthy, the word " deemed " (like the old word " deemster " or
" dempster " for a judge) importing an inquiry into a decision which
might attach some stigma to the person expelled. Later cases [5] lean
against any general requirement of a " hearing " (however loosely
construed) in respect of expulsion or dissolution clauses in subjective
terms, particularly where provision for arbitration is added. These
later cases distinguish clearly between good faith (which is an
invariable requirement) and the *audi alteram partem* rule. In the most
recent case (*Peyton* v. *Mindham*), Plowman J. interpreting a clause
which empowered a partner to dissolve the partnership should his
co-partner become incapacitated from discharging his " fair share of
the work of the practice " considered that to speak of a requirement
of notice or of any opportunity to demonstrate capacity was to
misconceive the legal position, saying " No judicial or quasi-judicial
function is cast on the defendant . . . . The clause merely gives him
the right to initiate certain action whereby the matter would ultimately be decided either by an arbitrator under the arbitration clause,
or by the court." [6] Natural justice does not appear to have found
favour in the present context, although clearly much will depend
upon the wording of the clause in question.

Retirement from " partnership at will "

Except in the case of a fixed-term partnership, and possibly a
joint venture, any partner (seemingly even a dormant partner) may
determine the partnership by giving notice to that effect to all the
other partners. Section 26 declares the pre-existing common law:

" (1) Where no fixed term has been agreed upon for the
duration of the partnership, any partner may determine the
partnership at any time on giving notice of his intention so to do
to all the other partners.

(2) Where the partnership has originally been constituted by
deed, a notice in writing, signed by the partner giving it shall be
sufficient for this purpose."

Moss v. *Elphick* [7] shows that subsection (1) does not mean that
notice can be given in all those cases in which a definite period of time
has not been agreed on as the duration of the partnership. In that
case a provision in the partnership agreement for *solutio* " by mutual
arrangement only " was construed to mean that the partnership was
to last during the joint lives of the parties, neither of whom could

terminate the relationship unilaterally. Lord Eldon L.C. had, however, declined in 1818 to accede to the argument that the existence of unpaid debts or the taking of a fixed-term lease were probative facts with regard to the duration of the partnership; taking the argument to its *reductio ad absurdum* he pointed out that a partnership taking a fee simple must therefore, according to this argument, last for ever.[8]

The notice to dissolve must be unequivocal, be communicated to all the partners and have effect either immediately or prospectively; once given, it cannot be withdrawn save with the consent of the co-partners.[9] Formerly it was difficult, or even impossible, to communicate with all the partners in large unincorporated associations. The problem is likely to recur with the growth of large professional partnerships liberated from the restriction on numbers by the Companies Act 1967 and, *a fortiori* would become even more acute if mixed professional practices were adopted. Under subsection (2), a written and signed notice is sufficient to determine a partnership constituted by deed,[10] and the same rule applies if the original partnership has been transmuted into a partnership at will by continuance over after the expiration of the term fixed by the initial deed or agreement (see following section).

The retirement of a partner does not necessarily work a " dissolution " of the firm in the sense that realisation and distribution of the firm's assets must take place. The partnership agreement may (and, normally, should) provide against such a consequence and even if it does not make such provision the inference may be that the retiring partner envisaged the continuance of the business by the remaining partners, subject to a proper financial settlement, as in *Sobell* v. *Boston*,[11] where the retirement of a solicitor from his firm, following upon criminal convictions, was held on the facts not to entitle him to a sale of the firm's assets, including goodwill, or to the appointment of a receiver and manager. The evidence in that case pointed not to a dissolution involving a sale of the assets, including goodwill, but to a continuance by the remaining partners subject to a proper settlement.

Continuance over a fixed term partnership

Section 27 anticipates human inertia in those cases in which partners continue the partnership without a new agreement after the expiration of an original fixed term.

" (1) Where a partnership entered into for a fixed term is continued after the term has expired, and without any express agreement, the rights and duties of the partners remain the same as they were at the expiration of the term so far as is consistent with the incidents of a partnership at will.

(2) A continuance of the business by the partners or such of them as habitually acted therein during the term, without any settlement or liquidation of the partnership affairs, is presumed to be a continuance of the partnership."

In *Essex* v. *Essex*,[12] a provision in a fixed-term partnership that a surviving partner must acquire the share of a co-partner who had died before the end of the fixed term was held to remain in operation after the efflux of the set term so as to bind the surviving partner. But the statement in an Irish case (also made in the *Essex* case) that the original partnership was varied only as to the term of its duration, all other stipulations remaining in effect, was criticised in *Cox* v. *Willoughby*,[13] as being too widely expressed, the correct formulation (now adopted by the Act) being that the terms of the old partnership continue save for those stipulations which are incompatible with the new partnership at will. In that case, the obligation to pay a sum of money as the purchase-money of a deceased partner's interest in the goodwill was held to bind the surviving partner notwithstanding the continuation of the original fixed-term partnership. In the same way, an arbitration clause,[14] and the right of a sleeping partner to participate in profits,[15] have been held to remain unaffected by the expiry of the original term. The same principle has been applied in the case of a business continued by the surviving partners after the death of a member of the original firm, the court inferring as a fact from their conduct that the business was continued on the old terms [16]; but it is probably safe to assume that here also, if there were nothing more than a want of evidence to the contrary, a continuance on the old terms would be presumed.

Per contra, a term in the original agreement permitting one partner to dissolve the firm by reason of a co-partner's neglect of the business,[17] a term providing for the expulsion of a partner,[18] and a term laying down a period of notice to terminate the partnership,[19] exemplify terms which are repugnant to a partnership at will and which, on that account, do not survive the original term. In the Scottish case of *Neilson* v. *Mossend Iron Co.*, the House of Lords held that a clause making provision for the optional retirement of any

partner on special terms " three months before the termination of
this contract " did not apply to the partnership as continued beyond
the original term. Although the decision was based upon the construction of " a strangely and singularly worded article," which made
time of the essence, Lord Watson affirmed the general rule that
" when the members of a mercantile firm continue to trade as
partners after the expiry of their original contract without making
any new agreement, that contract is held in law to be prolonged or
renewed by tacit consent, or, as it is termed in the law of Scotland, by
' tacit relocation.' " [20] In a later case, a clause giving one partner the
option of buying out the other's share within three months " after
the expiration or determination of the partnership by effluxion of
time " was held to apply to the partnership as continued beyond the
original term, Stirling J. commented that, " The question is not, as I
read Lord Watson's observations [see above] ... whether the language
of the partnership originally constituted is strictly appropriate to the
termination of a partnership at will, but whether the provisions as to
the term of the original partnership are in their essence applicable or
inapplicable to a partnership at will." [21]

A relationship uberrimae fidei

As stated at the commencement of this chapter, the relationship
between partners is one of the utmost good faith. It is uncertain
whether the duty of full and frank disclosure is (as it is normally) a
pre-contractual obligation in relation to intended partnerships.[22]
The cases cited to support the existence of such an obligation involved
the issue of prospectuses by promoters of the former unincorporated
companies. It is doubtful whether such cases should govern modern
partnerships which appeal rarely to " the Publick " for funds and
which, because of the general restriction on numbers, are usually
more intimate associations than the old unincorporated companies
which often had hundreds of shareholders or " partners." [23] Some of
the cases are explicable on the basis that a *suppressio veri* can amount
to a *suggestio falsi*,[24] whilst others reveal that an agent for an
intended firm has departed from the path of fiducial rectitude.
Section 28 puts disclosure between partners on a statutory footing:

> " Partners are bound to render true accounts and full informa-
> tion of all things affecting the partnership to any partner or his
> legal representative."

A partner with superior knowledge of the affairs of the firm, such as a managing partner or a partner who superintends the finances and accounts of the firm, must put a partner whose share in the firm he proposes to acquire in full possession of all material facts and circumstances.[25] Unless the parties stand upon an equal footing, a failure to make full and frank disclosures of material facts entitles the " innocent " party to avoid the sale or other transaction, although the right of avoidance is lost if such party elects to waive the failure to disclose or, when put on inquiry by certain facts, decides to pursue the matter no further.[26]

The partner as fiduciary

If, as would appear, partners are not in general trustees for one another or for the firm,[27] at least during the currency of the partnership, there is certainly no lack of dicta to show that partners are fiduciaries in respect of their dealings with co-partners not only during the existence of the firm but also after its dissolution and until such time as it is wound up. That the fiduciary duty of good faith may survive a dissolution is shown by *Thompson's trustee in bankruptcy* v. *Heaton* [28] where it was held that a partner or his successor who acquires the reversion of a leasehold which has remained an undistributed partnership asset must account for the benefit received to his former co-partner. The fiduciary duty arose not from a trust of property but from the duty of good faith which each partner owes to the other. In *Gordon* v. *Gonda*,[29] Evershed M.R. referred to situations in which he found it impossible to resist the view that the partner is a *trustee* when partnership moneys or assets are used to acquire assets in his own name, the facts of this case, in which a partner had exchanged partnership assets for other assets which were then vested in his name alone, providing an example of one of those situations. Fundamental to the implied *fiducia* incumbent upon each partner is the duty to have regard for the interest of the firm and the avoidance of those occasions which create a conflict between that duty and the partner's private interests. " If fiduciary relationship means anything," said Bacon V.-C. in *Helmore* v. *Smith*,[30] " I cannot conceive a stronger case of fiduciary relations than that which exists between partners. Their mutual confidence is the life blood of the concern. It is because they trust one another that they are partners in the first place; it is because they continue to trust one another that the business goes on."

Three aspects of the partner's fiduciary duty were discussed in

Dean v. *MacDowell.*[31] (1) A partner is not permitted to receive an exclusive advantage for himself by reason of the use of partnership property or partnership information. This principle is illustrated by *Gardner* v. *M'Cutcheon*[32] in which one of two part-owners of a ship who were trading with it for their common benefit used it for private trading and was held accountable for profits so made. (2) He must not derive any exclusive advantage by engaging in transactions in rivalry with the firm. This principle is illustrated by *Somerville* v. *Mackay.*[33] There the partnership had been founded to supply goods to a firm in Russia and one partner supplied similar goods to this firm himself. (3) He is not allowed, in transacting the partnership affairs, to carry on for his own benefit any separate trade or business which, were it not for his connection with the partnership, he would not have been in a position to carry on. This third principle is illustrated by *Russell* v. *Austwick.*[34] In this case a partner who had obtained a contract from the Mint to carry silver by a route other than the route on which he and another had already received a contract to carry bullion for the Mint was held accountable for the profits of the contract awarded to him personally. These aspects of the fiduciary relationship [35] are now set out in sections 29 and 30:

" 29.—(1) Every partner must account to the firm for any benefit derived by him without the consent of the other partners from any transaction concerning the partnership, or from any use by him of the partnership property name or business connection.

(2) This section applies also to transactions undertaken after a partnership has been dissolved by the death of a partner, and before the affairs thereof have been completely wound up, either by any surviving partner or by the representatives of the deceased partner.

30. If a partner without the consent of the other partners, carries on any business of the same nature as and competing with that of the firm, he must account for and pay over to the firm all profits made by him in that business."

Accountability for private profits

Transactions concerning the partnership

An example of the duty of the partner not to derive a profit from a partnership transaction, without the consent of co-partners, is the old case of *Burton* v. *Wookey,*[36] in which one of two partners (who *(1455)* were in partnership to deal in *lapis calaminaris*) allowed the miners who bought goods in his shop to pay for those goods with the ore, but charged the partnership with the full selling price of the goods. Sir John Leach V.-C. held that the partner holding a position of trust or confidence had placed himself in a situation in which he had a bias against the due discharge of that trust or confidence in the pursuit of his own private advantage. Similarly, a partner who receives a premium in consideration of his work in negotiating the assignment of a lease to an intended partnership which is to include himself is accountable to his co-partners for the money so received.[37] In *Piddocke* v. *Burt*, a partner who held money belonging to the firm or its clients was held not to be subject to committal or attachment for non-payment of the money on the ground that in receiving such money the partner was acting as agent, Chitty J. saying that " it is not every agent who is fiduciary." [38]

Use of partnership property, name or business connection

If, on the expiry of a lease granted to the partnership, a partner renews the lease in his own name for his own advantage, his co-partners (including the personal representatives of a deceased partner) have the option of treating the lease as partnership property; it matters not that the renewal is effected in a clandestine manner, as in the leading case of *Featherstonhaugh* v. *Fenwick*,[39] or openly and after notification of intention to do so to the other partners, as in *Clegg* v. *Fishwick*.[40] The renewal is seen as a graft or addition to something which is partnership property. The position is less clear with regard to the purchase by a partner of the reversion on a lease in which the partnership has an interest. We have already seen from *Thompson's trustee in bankruptcy* v. *Heaton* (above, p. 106) that a partner who purchased the freehold reversion of a lease to the partnership, which had remained as an undistributed partnership asset following the dissolution of the partnership, was obliged to account as a fiduciary for the benefit which he had received. A different conclusion had, however, been reached on the facts of *Bevan* v. *Webb*,[41] in which it was held that a partner might take the reversion on a lease to himself without breach of fiduciary duty in the absence of fraud or of evidence that the lease was renewable by custom or contract, a case which was followed in *Brenner* v. *Rose* [42] where it was held that there was no equity which would prevent such a partner from exercising rights, such as forfeiture, which he might have exercised had he been a stranger to the partnership, although it is perhaps relevant to note that the firm in that case was being dissolved and put under a receiver at the time when the partner acquired the reversion expectant on the underlease held by the partnership. Although prima facie it cannot be said that a partner who buys the reversion on a lease held by the partnership does so by virtue of any interest in the leasehold, the purchase might place him a situation where his duty and interest conflict, e.g. where it falls to him to decide whether or not to renew the lease. The fiduciary would appear to be treated with greater leniency than the trustee with regard to the purchase of a reversion on a lease and is allowed to demonstrate that the purchase is not necessarily inequitable.

The equitable doctrine of laches is a spur to those who assert breach of fiduciary duty, particularly in cases of renewal of a lease of property of a speculative nature, such as a mine, in relation to which it would be inequitable to allow the co-partners to follow a dilatory policy of " wait and see," in order that it might be ascertained whether a profit or loss is likely to result.[43] A partners' share is his own property and not the property of the firm, so that if it is bought by a co-partner without the knowledge of the other partners, no breach of faith occurs, unless, of course, there is some special provision in the articles regulating the disposition of such a share.[44]

Competing business

Unless he has the consent of his co-partners (which consent will be narrowly construed), a partner cannot carry on a business which is of the same nature as, and competes with, the partnership business. So, where A, B, C and D are proprietors of a morning newspaper and A, B and C are proprietors of an evening newspaper, D may restrain A, B and C from first publishing in the evening paper intelligence obtained by the agency of the morning paper and obtained at the expense of the firm consisting of A, B, C and D.[45] A distinction must, however, be drawn between straight competition and participation in another business unrelated to the first, even though knowledge of, or opportunity to engage in, the other business was gained by reason of membership of the partnership. In the leading case of *Aas* v. *Benham*, a member of a firm of shipbrokers assisted in the formation of a joint-stock company to build ships, using information derived from his membership of the ship-broking firm. " It is not the source of the information, but the use to which it is applied which is important in such matters," said Lindley L.J., who,

with the other members of the Court of Appeal, held that the information in question had been used for purposes which were " wholly
without the scope of the firm's business." [46] This case was distinguished in *Boardman* v. *Phipps* [47] by Lord Hodson on the ground
that the solicitor acting for the trustees in the latter case was subject to
a constructive trust wider in nature than a partner's fiduciary obligation which relates to the partnership business. A partner who
engages in another business may well commit a breach of the partnership articles, as, for example, where these stipulate for full-time
service or forbid any participation, direct or indirect, in any other
business except upon the account and for the benefit of the partnership, but provided the business does not trench upon the partnership
sphere of business, the partner so breaking his contract is not liable
to account for profits arising from his breach of covenant, although
he may be restrained by injunction (unless the covenant is excessively
wide) and may have to pay damages (if loss to the partnership can
be made out), with the further possibility that his breach may found
an action for the dissolution of the partnership.

Rights of an assignee of share in partnership

Section 31 clarifies, both negatively and positively, the rights of
the assignee of a partner's share in the partnership:

" (1) An assignment by any partner of his share in the
partnership, either absolute or by way of mortgage or redeemable charge, does not, as against the other partners, entitle the
assignee, during the continuance of the partnership, to interfere
in the management or administration of the partnership business
or affairs, or to require any accounts of the partnership transactions, or to inspect the partnership books, but entitles the
assignee only to receive the share of profits to which the assigning
partner would otherwise be entitled, and the assignee must accept
the account of profits agreed to by the partners."

The vulnerability of the assignee's interest during the currency of
the partnership is demonstrated in *Re Garwood's Trusts*, where it
was held that the assignee of a partner's share could not validly
complain of a later bona fide agreement between the partners
providing salaries for necessary work by the partners and thus
reducing the share of profits to which the assignee would otherwise
have been entitled. Buckley J. accepted that it was the intention of
the Act to substitute the assignee for the assignor as the person

entitled to such profits as would have come to the latter, but added that the assignee had no right to interfere at all in bona fide acts of management and administration of which the payment of salaries in the present case was an example.[48] " It would hardly be possible to express more clearly the essential non-assignability in a subsisting partnership of the position and rights of one partner in relation to the other partners," said Sargant L.J. in another case.[49]

Section 31 (1) clarifies the distinction between assignment of a partner's *position* as partner and assignment of his *share in the business*, the former involving a change of partners whereas the latter leaves the composition of the firm unaffected. It is interesting to note that in *Dodson* v. *Downey*[50] the advisers of a partner who had contracted to sell his share in the business were under the misapprehension that they were assigning the partner's *position* as partner, a misapprehension which was cleared up by the refusal of the other partners to accept the assignee as partner. Farwell J. agreed that there had been no assignment or transfer of the partner's position in the firm as such and treated the case as one of assignment under section 31 (1), finding the contract to assign to be specifically performable, subject to an obligation on the assignee to indemnify the assignor against partnership liabilities on the analogy of the purchaser of real property who, as *cestui que trust*, is bound to indemnify the vendor as trustee from liabilities. To take Farwell J.'s example, the assignee who takes an assignment of a partner's share is entitled to the latter's share of profits during four years of lucrative profits, but, if these are succeeded by two " disastrous years " in which the liabilities exceed the assets, he cannot stand aside from the losses, but must indemnify his assignor, who has continued as " nominal partner," against the latter's share of the loss. The case underlines the vulnerability of the assignee referred to above.

On dissolution the position is different in that the rights of the assignee " crystallise " to the extent that he thereupon becomes entitled to the assigning partner's share of assets and to an account to enable that share to be ascertained.

> " (2) In case of a dissolution of the partnership, whether as respects all the partners or as respects the assigning partner, the assignee is entitled to receive the share of the partnership assets to which the assigning partner is entitled as between himself and the other partners, and, for the purpose of ascertaining that share, to an account as from the date of the dissolution."

The assignee is entitled to an account " once and for all in the presence of all the persons interested "[51] from the date of the dissolution.[52] Because the assignee's right is conferred upon him by statute, it cannot be taken away or abridged by an arbitration clause providing for the settlement of differences between partners, including differences concerning the settlement of account, unless, possibly, the arbitration clause is expressed to include the assignee within its terms.[53] Nor is the assignee affected by an agreement between the assignor-partner and his co-partner by virtue of which the former agrees to sell his share to the latter at a value agreed by the partners. Admittedly the assignee takes subject to equities, but to allow such an arrangement would be tantamount to saying to the assignee: " You are not entitled to any account as from the date of the dissolution, because we have already agreed with the mortgagor that, when dissolution comes, his share is to be so much." [54]

[1] (1844) 8 Beav. 129 at p. 133.
[2] (1824) T. & R. 496 at p. 523.
[3] (1820) 2 Bligh 270.
[4] (1870) L.R. 5 Ch. 687.
[5] (1923) 92 L.J. Ch. 136 at p. 138.
[6] (1875) L.R. 20 Eq. 25.
[7] 1965 S.L.T. 415, Ct. of Session.
[8] *Cf. Re Sterenchuk Estate* (1958) 16 D.L.R. (2d) 505.
[9] [1967] 1 A.C. 233.
[10] [1894] 1 Ch. 393 at p. 401.
[11] (1824) 2 Bing. 170.
[12] (1869) 4 Ch.App. 603, affirming (1868) L.R. 6 Eq. 479.
[13] [1912] 1 Ch. 663.
[14] (1881) 1 Ch.D. 698.
[15] [1953] 1 W.L.R. 537.
[16] [1965] 1 W.L.R. 412: *Eardley* v. *Broad* 120, N.L.J. No. 5441, pp. 432–433.
[17] S.C. at p. 416.
[18] [1964] 1 W.L.R. 456.
[19] On a lease to oneself, see *Rye* v. *Rye, infra*, at p. 85.
[20] *Ex p. M'Kenna* (1861) 3 De G.F. & J. 645, at pp. 658–659.
[21] (1849) 3 De G. & Sm. 613.
[22] [1954] 1 W.L.R. 366.
[23] (1873) L.R. 15 Eq. 402.
[24] S.C. at p. 406.
[25] (1879) 12 Ch.D. 813.
[26] (1820) 3 Y. & J. 384.
[27] *Crawshay* v. *Maule* (1818) 1 Swanst. 495 at pp. 518, 523; *cf. Jackson* v. *Jackson* (1804) 9 Ves. 591.
[28] (1818) 1 Swanst. 495 at p. 523.
[29] *Burdon* v. *Barkus* (1862) 4 De G.F. & J. 42: see 35 Conv.(N.S.) 17.

[30] See 46 L.Q.R. 77 *et seq.* for the view that there is neither a tenancy in common nor a joint tenancy but rather a beneficial interest in proportion to what is coming to the partners on the final taking of accounts: see also 50 L.Q.R. 19.

[31] [1933] Ch. 652.

[32] *Lake* v. *Craddock* (1723) 3 P.Wms. 158; *Buckley* v. *Barber* (1851) 6 Ex. 164 at p. 179.

[33] [1933] Ch. 652 at p. 656, *per* Luxmoore J. clarifying *Re Bourne.*

[34] [1962] A.C. 496 at p. 514.

[35] [1970] 1 W.L.R. 838.

[36] [1955] 1 W.L.R. 822.

[37] *Re Nicols* [1900] 2 Ch. 410 at p. 417.

[38] 1961 S.C. 362.

[39] *Campbell* v. *Mullett* (1818–19) 2 Swanst. 551 at p. 584.

[40] *Pearce* v. *Bulteel* [1916] 2 Ch. 544.

[41] See *Green* v. *Whitehead* [1930] 1 Ch. 38; *Re Holland* [1907] 2 Ch. 88; *Farquhar* v. *Hadden* (1871) L.R. 7 Ch. 1.

[42] *Op. cit.* p. 366.

[43] *Re Kempthorne* [1930] 1 Ch. 268.

[44] (*No.* 1) [1895] 1 Q.B. 737 at pp. 738–739.

[45] *Brown, Janson & Co.* v. *Hutchinson* (*No.* 1) 1 [1895] 1 Q.B. 737.

[46] *Brown, Janson & Co.* v. *Hutchinson* (*No.* 2) [1895] 2 Q.B. 126.

[47] *Re Hutchinson* (1885) 16 Q.B.D. 515.

[48] (*No.* 1) (1887) 35 Ch.D. 436 as clarified in *Newport* v. *Pougher* [1937] Ch. 214.

[49] (1886) 14 Ch.D. 345.

[50] Lindley, p. 381.

[51] (1849) 1 Mac. & G. 136.

[52] (1863) 1 De G.J. & Sm. 337.

[53] (1855) 20 Beav. 98.

[54] (1849) 7 Hare 159.

[55] (1869) L.R. 7 Eq. 538 at p. 541.

[56] (1880) 16 Ch.D. 83 at p. 87.

[57] *Op. cit.* p. 75.

[58] Report of Company Law Committee (1962), Cmnd. 1749, para. 335.

[59] (1865) 3 De G.J. & Sm. 1.

[60] *Dinham* v. *Bradford* (1869) 5 Ch.App. 519. On interest, see p. 94.

[61] [1974] 1 W.L.R. 9.

[62] *Per* Lord Justice Turner in *Ex p. Chippendale, Re German Mining Company, Ball's Case* (1853) 4 De G.M. & G. 19 at p. 41.

[63] *Thomas* v. *Atherton* (1878) 10 Ch.D. 185. The rule concerning contribution between joint tortfeasors, *per Merryweather* v. *Nixan* (1799) 8 T.R. 186, is now altered by Law Reform (Married Women and Joint Tortfeasors) Act 1935.

[64] *Boulter* v. *Peplow* (1850) 9 C.B. 493.

[65] *Sedgwick* v. *Daniell* (1857) 2 H. & N. 319.

[66] *Lowe* v. *Fixon* (1885) 16 Q.B.D. 445.

[67] (1856) 6 De G.M. & G. 572 at p. 588; *Re German Mining Company, Ball's case,* n. 62 *supra; Re Norwich Yarn Co., ex p. Bignold* (1856) 22 Beav. 143.

[68] *Re Worcester Corn Exchange Company* (1853) 3 De G.M. & G. 180.

[69] See *Re Norwich,* n. 67, *supra.*

[70] *Op. cit.* p. 419.

[71] *Watney* v. *Wells* (1867) L.R. 2 Ch.App. 250.

[72] (1872) 8 Ch.App. 1.

[73] *Rowe* v. *Wood* (1882) 2 Jac. & W. 553, 558.

[74] [1970] A.C. 1099.

75 [1973] A.C. 360.
76 See further, D. D. Prentice (1973) 89 L.Q.R. 107.
77 (1963) 107 S.J. 512.
78 *Airey* v. *Borham* (1861) 29 Beav. 620.
79 *Infra*, p. 110.
80 *Infra*, p. 117.
81 *Brown* v. *De Tastet* (1821) Jac. 284; *Ex p. Barrow* (1815) 2 Rose 252.
82 (1834) 3 M. & K. 1 at p. 20, cited in *Byrne* v. *Reid* [1902] 2 Ch. 735, 742–743.
83 (1878) 8 Ch.D. 129.
84 *Op. cit.* p. 332.
85 *Highley* v. *Walker* (1910) 26 T.L.R. 685.
86 (1824) T. & R. 496 at p. 525.
87 *Blisset* v. *Daniel* (1853) 10 Hare 493.
88 (1833) 1 Cr. & M. 345.
89 *Trego* v. *Hunt* [1896] A.C. 7.
90 (1847) 1 De G. & Sm. 692.
91 *Floydd* v. *Cheney* [1970] 1 Ch. 603 at p. 608.
92 See *Moss* v. *Elphick*, discussed *infra*.
93 (1818) 1 Swans. 495.
94 *Steuart* v. *Gladstone* (1879) 10 Ch.D. 626.
95 (1853) 10 Hare 493, 530.
96 See n. 93, *supra*.
97 (1810) 17 Ves. 289 at p. 309.
98 *Wood* v. *Woad* (1874) L.R. 9 Ex. 190.
99 [1962] 1 W.L.R. 353.
1 [1904] 1 Ch. 486.
2 *Barnes* v. *Youngs* (1898) 1 Ch. 414; *Blisset* v. *Daniel* (1853) 10 Hare 493.
3 Bernard J. Davies (1969) 33 Conv.(N.S.) 32.
4 (1874) L.R. 9 Ex. 190 at p. 196.
5 *Russell* v. *Russell* (1880) 14 Ch.D. 471 (Jessel M.R., leaving open the question of several partners exercising a power, was clear that " the moment you give the power to a single partner in terms which show that he is to be sole judge for himself, not to acquire a benefit, but to dissolve the partnership, then he may exercise that discretion capriciously and there is no obligation upon him to act as a tribunal, or to state the grounds on which he decides for himself "—p. 480); *Green* v. *Howell* [1910] 1 Ch. 495.
6 [1972] 1 W.L.R. 8 at p. 14.
7 [1910] 1 K.B.; *Abbott* v. *Abbott* [1936] 3 All E.R. 823; *Firth* v. *Armslake* (1964) 108 S.J. 198. See further s. 32 (*c*).
8 *Crawshay* v. *Maule* (1818) 1 Swans. 495 at p. 508.
9 *Jones* v. *Lloyd* (1874) 18 Eq. 265.
10 *Doe* v. *Miles* (1816) 1 Stark. 181.
11 [1975] 1 W.L.R. 1587.
12 (1855) 20 Beav. 442. *Cookson* v. *Cookson* (1837) 8 Sim. 529, is of doubtful authority on this point and *Yates* v. *Finn* (1880) 13 Ch.D. 839, has been distinguished; see *Daw* v. *Herring* [1892] 1 Ch. 284 at p. 289.
13 (1880) 13 Ch.D. 863 at p. 871.
14 *Gillett* v. *Thornton* (1875) L.R. 19 Eq. 599.
15 *Parsons* v. *Hayward* (1862) 4 De G.F. & J. 474.
16 *King* v. *Chuck* (1853) 17 Beav. 325.
17 *Clark* v. *Leach* (1862) 32 Beav. 14.
18 *Daw* v. *Herring* [1892] 1 Ch. 284 at p. 290, *per* Stirling J.
19 *Featherstonhaugh* v. *Fenwick* (1810) 17 Ves. 298.

[20] (1886) 11 App.Cas. 298 at p. 308.

[21] *Daw* v. *Herring* [1892] 1 Ch. 284, 288.

[22] For the view that a pre-contractual duty of disclosure exists, see Lindley (13th ed.), pp. 335–336; *Bell* v. *Lever Bros.* [1932] A.C. 161 at p. 227, *per* Lord Atkin.

[23] *Cf.* Lord Romilly's opinion in *Central Railway of Venezuela* v. *Kisch* (1867) L.R. 2 H.L. 99 at p. 125. The duty to disclose to an incoming partner is not the same thing as imposing a duty to disclose upon persons about to form a partnership *de novo*.

[24] *Hichens* v. *Congreve* (1828) 1 Russ. & M. 150n.

[25] *Law* v. *Law* [1905] 1 Ch. 140 (C.A.), following *Maddeford* v. *Austwick* (1826) 1 Sim. 89; both cases concerned the purchase of a partner's share at undervalue.

[26] As in *Law* v. *Law*, above.

[27] *Knox* v. *Gye* (1872) L.R. 5 H.L. 656.

[28] [1974] 1 W.L.R. 605.

[29] [1955] 1 W.L.R. 885.

[30] (*No.* 1) (1886) 35 Ch.D. 436 at p. 444.

[31] (1878) 8 Ch.D. 345 at p. 354.

[32] (1842) 4 Beav. 534.

[33] (1810) 16 Ves. 382.

[34] (1826) 1 Sim. 52.

[35] *Clements* v. *Hall* (1857) 2 De G. & J. 173.

[36] (1822) 6 Madd. 367.

[37] *Fawcett* v. *Whitehouse* (1829) 1 Russ. & M. 132.

[38] [1894] 1 Ch. 343 at p. 346. The criticism of this decision in Waters, *Constructive Trust*, pp. 326–328, seems well founded.

[39] (1810) 17 Ves. 298.

[40] (1849) 1 Mac. & G. 294.

[41] [1905] 1 Ch. 620.

[42] [1973] 1 W.L.R. 443.

[43] *Clements* v. *Hall* (1857) 2 De G. & J. 173.

[44] *Cassels* v. *Stewart* (1881) 6 App.Cas. 64. S. 42 deals with the continuation of the business after the death or retirement of a partner without final settlement of accounts and overlaps to some extent with s. 29 (1): *Pathirana* v. *Pathirana* [1967] 1 A.C. 233.

[45] *Glassington* v. *Thwaites* (1822–23) 1 Sim. & St. 124.

[46] [1891] 2 Ch. 244 at p. 256.

[47] [1967] 2 A.C. 46 at p. 108.

[48] [1903] 1 Ch. 236 at p. 239.

[49] *Public Trustee* v. *Elder* [1926] Ch. 776 at p. 790.

[50] [1901] 2 Ch. 620.

[51] *Per* Fry J. in *Bergmann* v. *Macmillan* (1881) 17 Ch.D. 423 at p. 427, cited in the *Elder* case n. 49, *supra*.

[52] In the *Elder* case, at p. 787, Warrington L.J. left open the question of a final settlement of accounts before dissolution.

[53] *Bonnin* v. *Neame* [1910] 1 Ch. 732.

[54] *Watts* v. *Driscoll* [1901] 1 Ch. 294 at p. 301, *per* Farwell J.

CHAPTER FIVE

DISSOLUTION OF PARTNERSHIP

IT is convenient to treat dissolution of partnership according to whether or not the assistance of the court is required for that purpose.

I. DISSOLUTION WITHOUT THE AID OF THE COURT

The types of dissolution falling under this head and dealt with by the 1890 Act are as follows:

" 32. Subject to any agreement between the partners, a partnership is dissolved:

 (*a*) If entered into for a fixed term, by the expiration of that term:

 (*b*) If entered into for a single adventure or undertaking, by the termination of that adventure or undertaking:

 (*c*) If entered into for an undefined time, by any partner giving notice to the other or others of his intention to dissolve the partnership.

In the last-mentioned case the partnership is dissolved as from the date mentioned in the notice as the date of dissolution, or, if no date is so mentioned, as from the date of the communication of the notice."

(*a*) *Expiration of fixed term*

If a fixed term has been agreed upon, the partnership will end *proprio motu* on the expiration of that term without any positive or formal act by any of the partners, although it may end sooner if one of the partners dies before the efflux of the set term, or if there is provision for prior termination, *e.g.* on one of the partners giving notice to terminate. We have already seen that partners who continue in business together after the expiration of a fixed term are partners at will and each may give notice to terminate at any time.[1]

(*b*) *Termination of adventure*

A joint adventure resembles a fixed-term contract to the extent that the parties thereto are expected to persevere " for better or worse " to the end. However, in *Reade* v. *Bentley*,[2] a joint adventure between a publisher (who was to bear the risks and the expenses) and an author to share equally the net profits of a book was held to be terminable by the author after the publication of a given edition, the publisher's claim to hold an irrevocable licence to publish the book being considered unreasonable in the circumstances.

(c) Notice to dissolve

If the partnership is one of indefinite duration, any partner may give notice of intention to dissolve the partnership at any time. " By that notice," said Lord Eldon L.C., " the partnership is dissolved, to this extent, that the court will compel the parties to act as partners in a partnership existing only for the purpose of winding up the affairs." [3] That a termination of a partnership of the kind under discussion is lawful between partners *inter se*, does not absolve the partnership from liability for breach of contract as regards third persons.[4] Dissolution may end a partner's licence to go upon premises used (but not owned) by the partnership so that a subsequent entry may constitute a trespass. The notice to dissolve is effective when communicated,[5] subject to which it takes effect from the date of the notice.[6] Express notice is not essential; conduct may be sufficient. In *Griffiths* v. *Bracewell*, six months' notice of dissolution given by a partner under the terms of the partnership agreement was held to dissolve the partnership at the expiration of the six months, a further provision that the assets should be valued and that the partnership should then " cease and determine " being held to relate to the quasi and qualified partnership which continued for that purpose.[7] If there is provision for notice in addition to provision for summary determination for breach of covenants or for other reasons, notice once given under the former provision will normally preclude the party giving it from falling back on the summary procedure.[8]

" 33. (1) Subject to any agreement between the partners, every partnership is dissolved as regards all the partners by the death or bankruptcy of any partner.

(2) A partnership may, at the option of the partners, be dissolved if any partner suffers his share of the partnership property to be charged under this Act for his separate debt."

(d) Death

Although the effect of the death of a partner is expressed to be subject to any agreement between the partners, it seems clear that the partnership is ended by a partner's demise whatever the agreement may say; any partnership which continues being a new partnership. If there is provision in the articles of a fixed-term partnership that the personal representatives of a deceased partner shall succeed to his share and become partners in his place, the surviving partners have no option to refuse admission in such a case, although the court will not compel such personal representatives to come in against their will. If the personal representatives refuse to come in, the partnership must be treated as dissolved from the death of the partner and wound up on that footing.

Death of a partner works a premature dissolution of a fixed-term partnership and, indeed, may end a partnership which has not been effectively terminated by notice. The latter point is graphically illustrated by *McLeod* v. *Dowling* [9] in which it was held that a partnership had been ended by death, and not by notice, where a partner who had sent a notice of dissolution died before such notice was received by his co-partner, with the result that the surviving partner was able to acquire the business and goodwill on the terms laid down in the articles, instead of being confined to a claim for an equal share on dissolution which would have been the case had the firm been ended by notice.

(e) Bankruptcy

The bankruptcy of a partner ends the partnership and vests his share therein in his trustee in bankruptcy, whose rights cannot be affected by any agreement amongst the partners, *e.g.* that the partnership is to continue notwithstanding the bankruptcy of one of its number.[10] Lord Loughborough's statement [11] that " The issuing of the commission does nothing, unless he is found a bankrupt. The adjudication, that he is a bankrupt, is what severs the partnership," is still true, but must be taken subject to the operation of the doctrine of " relation-back " under which the partnership will end at the commencement of the bankruptcy (normally the act of bankruptcy upon which the petition is founded),[12] from which date the trustee will be able to claim the bankrupt's share in profits until such time as the final winding-up occurs (see s. 42, *infra*).

(f) Charging order

Former doubt on the effect of a charging order (see s. 23, *supra*) is removed by subsection (2) which makes clear that the effect of such an order on a partner's share is not to dissolve the partnership automatically, but that the co-partners are given an option to dissolve.[13] This they must exercise without undue delay and in an unequivocal manner, *i.e.* either expressly, or by some unambiguous act demonstrating a clear intention to dissolve the partnership. It is unclear if all the other partners must concur in the exercise of the option, or if each is at liberty to exercise a personal option. The former seems the more acceptable view.

(g) *Illegality*

" 34. A partnership is in every case dissolved by the happening of any event which makes it unlawful for the business of the firm to be carried on or for the members of the firm to carry it on in partnership."

A partnership cannot be formed, or continued, if, (a) it is illegal to carry on the business of the firm, or (b) it is illegal for the members of the firm to carry on that business. (a) is typified by the outbreak of war which renders unlawful a partnership between A, an Englishman resident in England, and B, who is resident in the country with which this country is at war. Such an outbreak dissolves the partnership without more ado.[14] It may be noted that, in the example given, B need not be a national of the state in which he is resident, inasmuch as the term " enemy alien " includes persons of any nationality who are voluntarily resident in the hostile country. Although supervening illegality is but a form of frustration, the view has been expressed that the latter has no application to partnership cases in view of the plenitude of remedies, both judicial and extra-judicial, provided by the Act.[15]

Under (b), the business may be lawful in itself but those who perform it may be required to comply with certain requirements [16] or possess certain qualifications. So, for example, solicitors, medical practitioners, dental surgeons, bookmakers, insurers, moneylenders and many others cannot conduct business unless they possess certain qualifications or register. In *Dungate* v. *Lee*,[17] the court declined to brand a bookmaking partnership with illegality because one of the two partners had not obtained a bookmaker's permit, even though there was evidence that the unqualified partner had occasionally taken bets on the telephone and thus broken the law. The purpose of the partnership was not illegal, nor did the parties set out with the intention of achieving the partnership's legal purpose by illegal means.

II. DISSOLUTION BY THE COURT

Before treating of the grounds upon which the court may decree a dissolution of partnership, it is well to remember at the outset that partners, with the exception of those linked by a partnership at will, are expected (like those who are parties to another kind of relationship) to put up with each other for better and worse and not to harass the court with " trifling circumstances of conduct," as, for example, that " one is more sullen, or less good tempered than the other." [18] However, in six situations (of which one, that relating to insanity, has been replaced by the Mental Health Act 1959, s. 149 (2) and Sched. 8), section 35 of the Act permits a partner, but not a creditor, to seek a court decree dissolving the partnership. Several of the cases turn upon the construction of articles which provide for dissolution for certain reasons, such as misconduct by a partner, but nevertheless afford valuable guidance on the position where the articles, if any, are silent. There is no doubt that occasionally the various grounds for dissolution run into one another, but care is still needed in distinguishing between them in that some cannot be invoked by the partner suing. Where the grounds of dissolution are insanity, the Court of Protection has jurisdiction [19]; otherwise the High Court has jurisdiction which is exercised by the County Court where the partnership assets are less than £5,000. [20]

(a) Insanity

A judge nominated under the Mental Health Act 1959 may by virtue of section 103 (1) (f) of that Act make an order for the dissolution of a partnership of which the patient is a member. For the purposes of that Act, a " patient " is a person as to whom the judge is satisfied on consideration of medical evidence that he is incapable by reason of mental disorder of managing and administering his property and affairs. Although the power conferred upon the judge by section 103 is to be exercised for the benefit of the patient, it is clear from the old law [21] that a decree of dissolution is equally available in a proper case for the benefit of the other partners for the reason that the complete incapacity of a party strikes at a condition of the agreement. Of this incapacity the court must judge. Because there is no automatic dissolution by reason of a partner's mental infirmity, the partnership continues; this may accord with the wishes of a co-partner who hopes that his partner's malady is transient, but even if it does not, the partnership still continues. In any case, the partner continuing the business is accountable for the share of profits belonging to his afflicted co-partner, although the court may grant an injunction to restrain the latter partner from interfering in the business pending a dissolution so that injury to the business and the assets may be avoided.[22] Because of the likely harm to creditors, the court will rarely make a decree for retrospective dissolution,[23] and this is true whatever the reason for dissolution, unless a partner has been guilty of misconduct or breach of the partnership agreement.[24] It is curious (bearing in mind the central part played by agency in partnership law) that the agency rule, that insanity of a principal *ipso facto* terminates the agent's authority, has no application to partnerships. *Semble* the insanity of a dormant partner would not constitute a ground for dissolution.[25]

(b) Permanent incapacity

" 35. (b) When a partner, other than the partner suing, becomes in any other way permanently incapable of performing his part of the partnership contract."

Whether a partner has become permanently incapable is a question of fact so that, for example, the gradual and imperceptible diminution in powers which is man's lot, that is to say, normal senescence as opposed to senility, would not ordinarily provide a ground for dissolution in the same way as would confirmed and incurable insanity.[26] Whilst there is little doubt that the six cases overlap to some degree, it should be noted that a claim under the present head (unlike (a), *supra*) may only be brought by a partner other than the partner afflicted with incapacity.

(c) Prejudicial conduct

" 35. (c) When a partner, other than the partner suing, has been guilty of such conduct as, in the opinion of the Court, regard being had to the nature of the business, is calculated to prejudicially affect the carrying on of the business."

The conduct complained of may either (1) relate to the business of the firm, as where a solicitor-partner embezzles trust moneys,[27] or (2) have no direct connection with the firm's business yet have an effect on it. " This Court is not a *censor morum* " said Lord Romilly M.R., refusing a dissolution in *Snow* v. *Milford*[28] based upon a banker's adultery with various persons in Exeter. The articles of the banking partnership referred to acts " to the discredit or injury " of the firm, words which were construed to mean acts affecting the pecuniary credit of the firm. In the absence of evidence to show injury or likely injury to the firm, the partner's conduct (resulting in his divorce) was not such as to justify dissolution either under the articles or under the " general law." If the Court is spared the task of delivering moral or ethical judgments, it must still assess the impact of a partner's misconduct on the firm's business, an exercise which may on occasions involve value judgments concerning the current state of morality. The conduct of a partner may have a prejudicial effect upon the firm's business, either because it relates directly to that business, as where a solicitor-partner embezzles trust moneys of the firm, or an accoucheur behaves immorally in his medical work, or because it has an indirect influence upon the firm's business, as where a partner suffers a criminal conviction unrelated to the business of the firm but rendering his continuance in the firm either impossible or undesirable, or engages in unprofessional conduct, like the medical practitioner who advertises that his medical brethren are " professional poisoners " or the dental surgeon who suggests in advertisements that other dental surgeons are indifferent to the sterilising of instruments or, worse still, the honour of unattended female patients.[29] Misconduct which indirectly affects the partnership business is likely to be the more difficult type of misconduct to evaluate for its effect on the firm. It is possible that what ranks as misconduct in one's profession or to the world at large may not rank as misconduct under section 35 (c) or the relevant clause, if any, in the partnership agreement. The converse of this statement is also possible.

(d) *Persistent or wilful breach of partnership agreement, etc.*
"When a partner, other than the partner suing, wilfully or persistently commits a breach of the partnership agreement, or otherwise so conducts himself in matters relating to the partnership business that it is not reasonably practicable for the other partner or partners to carry on the business in partnership with him."

Whether it is persistent breach of the partnership agreement or the conduct of the other partner which is complained of, case (d) covers a situation in which one partner has come to feel a justifiable lack of confidence in the others, with the result that it has become impossible to carry on the business without injury to the parties. Nevertheless, one should remember the reminder given by Sir L. Shadwell V.-C. in *Loscombe* v. *Russell* [30] that: "With respect to occasional breaches of agreements between partners, when they are not of so grievous a nature as to make it impossible that the partnership should continue, the Court stands neuter." The keeping of erroneous accounts and the failure to enter receipts into the partnership books [31] and a father's treatment of his partner-son [32] (opening his private letters and, like some parents, failing to realise that his son is now a grown man) have been held to justify a dissolution.

7. 10 pm.

(e) *Loss*

"When the business of the partnership can only be carried on at a loss."

Here, the court acts on the rationale that expectation of profit must be implied into every partnership, so that where it is demonstrated that there is to all effects and purposes a practical impossibility of profits, as opposed to those vagaries of profit and loss often inseparable from business, the partners will be relieved from what is more or less a certain loss. [33] The circumstance that one of the partners is rich and happens to be well equipped to suffer the loss is no answer to an action for dissolution; asking the court to take such a circumstance into account is tantamount to saying that the fortunes of a rich realist should be placed at the mercy of a Micawberish optimist.

The present provision is wider than section 222 (*e*) of the Companies Act 1948, which permits the court to wind up a company which "is unable to pay its debts." It is not necessary to show that the partnership has reached the low ebb of present insolvency. In *Re Expanded Plugs Ltd.*,[34] Plowman J., confronted with a contributory's petition for the winding up of a registered company on the just and equitable ground, warned against pressing the quasi-partnership concept too far, saying that, "there seems to me to be no *a priori* reason why a quasi-partner should be entitled to petition the court to wind up an insolvent company (if grounds of dissolution otherwise exist) merely because the insolvency of the partnership would be no answer to an ordinary partner's action to have it wound up." His Lordship felt that the analogy with partnership broke down in at least two important respects: (1) because of his unlimited legal liability a partner has a financial interest in bringing a failing partnership to an end; (2) an insolvent partnership cannot be dissolved at the instance of creditors who, in the case of a company, have a financial interest in a winding-up.

(f) Just and equitable

"Whenever in any case circumstances have arisen which in the opinion of the Court render it just and equitable that the partnership be dissolved."

This ground of dissolution is the widest of the six cases in that it leaves it to the court to consider in the widest possible terms what justice and equity require, unconstrained by any *ejusdem generis* rule (which would limit this ground to the same genus as the other grounds in s. 35) or by any categorisation of circumstances into which a particular case must fit.

Although the court can act on the application of a party who would otherwise be barred from applying (see grounds (b), (c) and (d), *supra*), it is unlikely that the court would act on the application of a partner who, for example, is guilty of misconduct under (c), except where, as is not uncommon, both he and his co-partner are *in pari delicto*. In the leading case of *Re Yenidje Tobacco Co. Ltd.*,[35] dissolution of a private limited company (in substance a quasi-partnership company and therefore governed by the legal régime of the partnership) was ordered despite the company's flourishing business, because of deadlock between the " partners " who only communicated with each other through the company secretary, who seems to have acted as a sort of conduit or *nuntius*. The following passage from Lindley was approved: " Refusal to meet on matters of business, continued quarrelling, and such a state of animosity [36] as precludes all reasonable hope of reconciliation and friendly co-operation have been held to justify a dissolution. It is not necessary, in order to induce the court to interfere, to show personal rudeness on the part of one partner to another,[37] or even gross misconduct as a partner. All that is necessary is to satisfy the court that it is impossible for the partners to place that confidence in each other which each has a right to expect, and that such impossibility has not been caused by the person seeking to take advantage of it. . . ."

In *Re Lundie Bros. Ltd.*,[38] Plowman J. took these last words in the extract from Lindley to mean that the impossibility there referred to has not been caused *exclusively* by the person wishing to take advantage of it. The petitioner in *Ebrahimi* v. *Westbourne Galleries Ltd.* [39] (a case on the " incorporated partnership," but relevant in the present context) came to court " with clean hands," notwithstanding that he may have been " perpetually complaining," since all that had happened was, in the words of Lord Cross, " that *without one being more to blame than the other* the two could no longer work together in harmony." Whatever his failings the petitioner had not committed misconduct justifying his expulsion from the management of the company. Conversely, the petitioner was not obliged to prove *mala fides* on the part of his co-directors or that they had acted against the interests of the company. The co-directors may have genuinely considered themselves to have acted in good faith in the interests of the company but, as Lord Wilberforce somewhat acidly commented, this may mean little more than " the interests of the majority." It is significant that although the petitioner in this case succeeded on the " just and equitable " ground, he failed to make out a case of oppressive conduct by his co-directors sufficient to found an order under section 210 of the Companies Act 1948 (the " alternative remedy " for which no counterpart exists in partnership law).

For a registered company, the facts founding a dissolution on the just and equitable ground are those which obtain at the time of the hearing and not when the petition is presented (*per* Megarry J. in *Re Fildes Bros. Ltd.* [1970] [40]). A similar rule would appear to be applicable to partnership cases where circumstances " have arisen " which " render it just and equitable " to dissolve.

Whilst doubtless the court will have regard to the partnership agreement, it is not tied by the terms of that agreement in ordering a winding-up on the just and equitable ground, *e.g.* it may wind up a partnership for a fixed term not yet expired.

Arbitration

Although the courts will disregard a provision in an arbitration agreement which purports to exclude their jurisdiction, they have shown themselves to be sympathetic towards arbitration as a method of settling disputes without the publicity of open court proceedings and the possible injury which may flow from such publicity. A party to an arbitration agreement is therefore at liberty to bring an action concerning a dispute covered by the agreement only to find that the court stays the action under section 4 of the Arbitration Act 1950. It is dangerous to generalise as to the manner in which the courts exercise their discretion. Since *Joplin* v. *Postlethwaite* [41] there would appear to have been a trend to refuse stays in disputes concerning dissolution, typified by *Oliver* v. *Hillier* [42] in which Roxburgh J. allowed the action to proceed on the footing that dissolution on grounds (*d*) and (*f*) of section 35, and the question of the appointment of a receiver and manager, were matters better dealt with by the court than by arbitration. More recently, the tendency has been to revert to the attitude exemplified in *Russell* v. *Russell* [43] where it was envisaged that the cases in which the court itself would take up an arbitrable issue were " few and exceptional." Thus, in *Phoenix* v. *Pope*,[44] it was held that an arbitration agreement extended to cover dissolution by the arbitrator notwithstanding the absence of any reference, express or implied, to dissolution in the arbitration agreement and, further, that the court need not be deterred from allowing an arbitration to proceed because it involves the statutory application of section 35 or the appointment of a receiver. The party opposing a stay by the court of arbitration proceedings covering a dispute within the provenance of a valid and subsisting arbitration agreement takes upon himself the burden of showing to the satisfaction of the court a sufficient reason why effect should not be given to that agreement. Despite the reference made above to trends in court attitudes, it is impossible to formulate the exceptional circumstances in which the court will exercise discretion to stay proceedings, although one of the factors influencing the court will be the suitability of the arbitration machinery to deal adequately with the matter at issue. In *Radford* v. *Hair*,[45] the application for a stay of proceedings by the defendants was refused because of allegations which they had made imputing actual dishonesty to the plaintiff, which, if made out, would damage his professional reputation—allegations better tried by a judge in open court than behind the locked doors of an arbitration. Jessel M.R. in the *Russell* case (*above*) considered that in cases of charges of fraud against the party who has commenced legal proceedings it would be almost a matter of course not to refer those charges to a private arbitrator, different considerations applying to the party who makes the charges of fraud who, if a stay were to be refused as of course, could prevent a dispute going to arbitration by the simple device of " throwing plenty of mud."

OTHER CAUSES OF DISSOLUTION

In common with contracts generally, the contract of partnership may be rescinded for duress, fraud or misrepresentation (including

innocent misrepresentation).[46] Section 41, which is discussed below
(p. 144 *et seq.*), gives the party entitled to rescind certain rights
which can be exercised without prejudice to any other rights which
he may have. Both as regards the right to recind itself and the special
rights conferred by that section, the fact that a contract of partnership resulting from an innocent misrepresentation has been executed
does not, and did not, prevent the representee from seeking rescission,
notwithstanding the rule in *Seddon's* case, which itself was repealed
by section 1 of the Misrepresentation Act 1967.

A partnership consisting of not less than eight members and which
is not a foreign partnership may be wound up (other than voluntarily
or subject to supervision) as an " unregistered company " under
section 399 of the Companies Act 1948. There must be at least eight
members ignoring past members, the personal representatives of
deceased members or the trustee of a bankrupt member. The grounds
on which such a " company " may be wound up under this section
are that (a) it is dissolved, or has ceased to carry on business, or is
carrying on business only for the purpose of winding up its affairs;
(b) it is unable to pay its debts; (c) the court is of the opinion that it is
just and equitable that it should be wound up. A partnership of less
than eight members can, of course, be wound up in an ordinary
partnership action.

Rights of persons dealing with firm against apparent members of firm

Both section 14 (discussed above at p. 59 *et seq.*) and section 36
show that a person who is not a partner may nevertheless incur
liability to third persons as a partner. Section 36 indicates the
circumstances in which third persons can or cannot sue such a
person:

" (1) Where a person deals with a firm after a change in its
constitution he is entitled to treat all apparent members of the
old firm as still being members of the firm until he has notice of
the change.

(2) An advertisement in *The London Gazette* as to a firm
whose principal place of business is in England or Wales, in
The Edinburgh Gazette as to a firm whose principal place of
business is in Scotland, and in *The Dublin Gazette* [47] as to a firm
whose principal place of business is in Ireland, shall be notice
as to persons who had no dealings with the firm before the date
of the dissolution or changes so advertised.

(3) The estate of a partner who dies, or who becomes bankrupt, or of a partner who, not having been known to the person dealing with the firm to be a partner, retires from the firm, is not liable for partnership debts contracted after the date of the death, bankruptcy, or retirement respectively." [48]

In order that a person, no longer a member of a firm, should be made liable at the suit of a third person, it was settled long before the Act that he must have been known by the third person to have been a member of the firm, either because of direct dealings with the firm or because of " public notoriety." [49] It was also necessary that the persons should not have received adequate notice of the partner's withdrawal. Subsection (1) subjects " apparent members " to liability unless they give adequate notice of the change. In the leading (and indeed, on this section, the only reported) case of *Tower Cabinet Co.* v. *Ingram*,[50] Lynskey J. rejected the contention that " apparent members " meant members who were apparent to the whole world (or notorious), saying that the term " means members who are apparently members to the person who is dealing with the firm . . . either by the fact that the customer has had dealings with them before, or because of the use of their names on the notepaper, or from some sign outside the door, or because the customer has had some indirect information about them." All three subsections were concerned with particular individuals and not the public at large. In the case itself, A and B had dissolved partnership, A continuing the business under the firm-name of " Merry's " and agreeing to notify those dealing with the firm that B had ceased to be connected with it. No notice was inserted in *The London Gazette* and no alteration was made in the Register of Business Names, but new notepaper omitting B's name was printed for future use in the business. Some months after B's retirement, The T Co., which had had no previous knowledge of Merry's, obtained an order from it for furniture which, by mistake, was written on old notepaper showing B as a member of the firm. It was held that B could not be held liable for the following reasons: (a) He was not known to the T Co. as a partner, so that when he retired he ceased to be liable for subsequent debts under subsection (3) (which Lynskey J. considered applied equally to a dormant partner and an ostensible partner). He was not known by T Co. to have been a partner prior to his retirement, and was accordingly under no obligation to give notice in any form to those who might learn after his retirement that he had been a member of the firm. (b) He had not knowingly allowed A to hold him out as a partner under section 14 (see above, p. 59 *et seq.*). (c) The fact that his name still appeared in the Business Names Register was irrelevant because the T Co. had not searched the Register.

In the light of the *Tower Cabinet* case, it is now necessary to distinguish between three classes of creditors.

(1) A creditor who has had previous dealings with the firm is entitled to treat all those whom he knew to be members of it as remaining members until he has actual notice to the contrary. Once notice in fact is proved, it is immaterial how the creditor came by it, so that if, for example, it can be shown that the creditor was aware of the deletion of the partner's name from the letterhead, this will suffice. The filing of amended particulars deleting the name of the retiring partner in the Register of Business Names, will not suffice unless it can be shown that the creditor in fact knew of it.

(2) A creditor who has had no previous dealings with the firm, but who knew who the partners were, *i.e.* the " apparent members " as defined by Lynskey J. above, is entitled to treat such partners as members of the firm until either he receives actual notice to the contrary, or the retirement is published in *The London Gazette*. The creditor must prove that he obtained knowledge of the constitution of the firm prior to the retirement of the partner whom he seeks to hold liable. Publication in the *Gazette*, whether seen by the creditor or not, is sufficient notice.

(3) A creditor who has not had previous dealings with the firm or knowledge of its constitution is not entitled to hold a retired partner liable for debts incurred by the firm subsequently to his retirement, *notwithstanding that no notice of any sort is given*, unless it can be shown that the retired partner represents himself or knowingly suffers himself to be represented as a partner under section 14 of the Act (*q.v.*).

Moreover, if the partnership is dissolved by death or bankruptcy, the estate of the deceased or bankrupt partner is not liable for subsequent debts, notwithstanding that no notice of any sort is given (subs. (3)).

Right of partners to notify dissolution

Quite apart from a partner's right to notify those dealing with the firm that he or another partner has ceased to be a member thereof, section 37 confers upon each partner the right to make a public notification.

> " On the dissolution of a partnership or retirement of a partner any partner may publicly notify the same, and may require the other partner or partners to concur for that purpose in all necessary or proper acts, if any, which cannot be done without his or their concurrence.

This section puts into statutory form earlier decisions which had recognised a partner's right to notify a dissolution or retirement and to call upon the co-operation of his co-partners where this is necessary for that purpose, *e.g.* by signing notices. The notice must be factual, unlike that given by Charles Dickens when he announced his withdrawal from the editorship of the magazine *Household Words* and the discontinuance of that magazine. The former was a factual statement; the latter something which could only be determined as a consequence, although there was little doubt that his withdrawal would " *de facto* annihilate *Household Words.*" [51]

Continuing authority of partners for purposes of winding up

On a winding up, a registered company ceases to exist as a corporate *persona*. The term " dissolving the partnership " is, in contrast, somewhat ambiguous in that it may denote (a) the termination of the mutual authority of the partner to bind each other in future dealings, or (b) the dissolution of any joint ownership of property, its realisation and distribution.[52] Ordinarily, the term " dissolution " will carry the first of these meanings and be followed in point of time by a distribution of assets. Construing articles providing for a dissolution and a subsequent valuation of assets (upon which latter event the partnership was to cease and determine), Sir John Romilly M.R. drew a distinction between dissolution proper and the " quasi and qualified partnership " which continued to enable the interests of the partners to be ascertained.[53]

In the case of a partnership dissolved by death, the surviving partner has both a right, and a duty co-extensive with that right, to wind up the partnership and to do all such acts as are necessary for that purpose, *e.g.* to continue the business, to borrow money and to sell assets whether consisting of real or personal property.[54] If they wish, former partners may give express authority to a continuing partner to enable the business to be wound up,[55] or they may permit a continuing partner to continue the business on agreed terms.

Express authority apart, the law endows each partner with apparent authority to perform such acts as may be necessary to wind up the partnership. In certain circumstances, the court will appoint a receiver to wind up the partnership affairs, or, more rarely, a receiver and manager to carry on the partnership business until such time as it can be wound up, the courts understandably showing little enthusiasm for appointments other than to wind up the business. The grounds on which appointments of either sort will be made by the court are diverse—the partners themselves may agree that an appointment is desirable, there may be disagreement amongst the partners, possibly because of the misconduct of one partner, or the partnership assets might otherwise be in jeopardy. The effect of an appointment of a receiver is to interdict the partners from control of the partnership assets, except where a partner is appointed receiver, in which event he acts as an officer of the court. The continuing authority of the partners is now set out in section 38:

" After the dissolution of a partnership the authority of each partner to bind the firm, and the other rights and obligations of the partners, continue notwithstanding the dissolution so far as may be necessary to wind up the affairs of the partnership, and to complete transactions begun but unfinished at the time of the dissolution, but not otherwise.

Provided that the firm is in no case bound by the acts of a partner who has become bankrupt; but this proviso does not affect the liability of any person who has after the bankruptcy represented himself or knowingly suffered himself to be represented as a partner of the bankrupt."

The cases show that a partner acting for the purposes of winding up the affairs of the firm, or to complete unfinished transactions, may perform the following acts—sell the whole or part of the partnership property in order to pay off partnership debts [56]; draw upon the partnership bank account [57]; indorse a bill previously drawn and accepted during the partnership to an indorsee who knows of the dissolution but who is unaware that the indorsement in the firm's name is for the private purposes of the partner indorsing the bill [58]; receive debts due on behalf of the firm [59]; pledge shares, bought but not paid for before the dissolution, with the firm's bankers to raise the purchase price thereon, with an authority to the bank to sell the same by way of indemnity [60]; issue a bankruptcy notice in connection with a judgment given in favour of the firm prior to dissolution [61];

and receive notice of the dishonour of a bill drawn by the firm but dishonoured after dissolution.[62] The continuance of the rights and obligations of the partners may involve them in liabilities in respect of transactions begun but not finished before the dissolution of the firm. We have already referred to *Welsh* v. *Knarston* (p. 69, above) where section 38 was seen to lay upon all the partners an obligation to complete the transactions undertaken by them before the dissolution of the firm with a corresponding liability for the negligent non-performance of that obligation.

The bankruptcy of a partner automatically causes a dissolution of the partnership, as we have seen from section 33, but the bankrupt partner cannot by virtue of the proviso bind the firm. Where two of the three partners indorsed a bill belonging to the firm in the firm's name it was held in *Thomason* v. *Frere* [63] that the indorsee acquired no title to the bill because the two partners had previously committed acts of bankruptcy. However, third parties without notice of an act of bankruptcy may be " protected " under the Bankruptcy Act 1914, s. 45. The proviso does not apply to any person who, after the bankruptcy, has represented himself or knowingly suffered himself to be represented as a partner of the bankrupt. On this footing, it was held in *Lacy* v. *Woolcott* that a bill, accepted for his own purposes in the name of the firm by a partner who had committed an act of bankruptcy, could be enforced against the latter's co-partner by a holder in good faith and for value into whose hands the bill had come. The court refused to accept that the firm could turn round and say " true it is, that we drew the bill, we received the amount of it from the drawer, but one of us was bankrupt at the time it was drawn, and therefore it is not to be paid." [64] The *Thomason* case was confined to the situation in which the bankrupt purports to dispose of property belonging to the firm, which disposition, were it to be held effective, would prejudice creditors. A partner may still get in partnership assets, notwithstanding the appointment of a receiver to his co-partner's property following upon a bankruptcy petition filed by the co-partner, and may use the name of his co-partner's trustee in bankruptcy upon giving him an indemnity.[65]

Rights of partners as to application of partnership property

" 39. On the dissolution of a partnership every partner is entitled, as against the other partners in the firm, and all persons claiming through them in respect of their interests as partners, to have the property of the partnership applied in payment of the debts and liabilities of the firm, and to have the surplus assets after such payment applied in payment of what may be due to the partners respectively [66] after deducting what may be due from them as partners to the firm [67]; and for that purpose any partner or his representative may on the termination of the partnership apply to the Court to wind up the business and affairs of the firm.

It would appear from *Stekel* v. *Ellice* that a partner lacking a sufficient proprietary interest in the partnership assets may not be able to invoke this section, notwithstanding the references therein to " every partner " and " any partner," Megarry J. expressing the view in that case that it would not surprise him if the majority of salaried partners had no real claims to an order for winding up. The *Stekel* v. *Ellice* type of case apart, the right of each partner to have the partnership assets applied to (a) the payment of partnership debts and liabilities, and then (if any remain), to (b) repayments to the partners according to what is due to them, after deducting what may be due from them as partners to the firm, has been classified as a type of equitable lien which differs from a possessory lien in that it is not dependent upon the retention of possession of chattels until some claim against the owner thereof has been met. As Lindley says, " The right, lien, quasi-lien or whatever else it may be called, does not exist for any practical purpose until the affairs of the partnership have to be wound up, or the share of a partner has to be ascertained." [68] In *Re Bourne*,[69] Fletcher-Moulton L.J. could " not help thinking that a great deal of confusion in this case has arisen from the phrase that the deceased partner has a lien on the surplus assets of the firm. I doubt whether a ' lien ' is the word which best describes his right. It is not a lien on any specific property existing at the date of death such as would fetter its realisation or conversion into money, but the right is really a claim against the surplus assets after the realization. . . As soon as you get your surplus assets the lien attaches. Until you get your surplus there is no claim or lien which in any way affects the power and duty of the surviving partner to realize the property of the partnership, and to discharge its liabilities."

The rights conferred by section 39 attach only to partnership property existing as such at the date of dissolution, so that if one of two partners dies, and the executors of the deceased partner allow the survivor to continue the business of the firm, their general lien on surplus assets will not extend to stock-in-trade acquired after the dissolution worked by the death of the partner; if the surviving partner is later adjudicated bankrupt, the stock-in-trade in question will belong to his creditors and not to the creditors of the former partnership.[70] Sir John Romilly M.R. drew a contrast between a lien or mortgage on stock-in-trade (which would now be termed a floating charge) and the right of a totally separate and distinct character arising on the death of a partner which he termed " a quasi-lien." If, as in *Stocken* v. *Dawson*, the surviving partner continues without authority to use the deceased partner's share, the personal representatives of the latter are entitled not only to their entitlement to a moiety of the property of the partnership but also to a lien upon the other moiety for the share of profits due to his estate; Lord Langdale considered that " it would reduce the jurisdiction of this court to a very low ebb, if we were told that no person could ever demand an account of the profits coming from an improper use of his money, without making himself and his property liable to the debts incurred by those who were making an improper use of his capital.[71]

Against whom available

The rights bestowed on each partner by section 3 9 are exigible not only against the other partners, but also against those who claim an interest in a partner's share, such as the assignee of a share (see s. 31 above) or the personal representative of a deceased partner. A partner who continues the business for the purposes of winding up may alienate, mortgage or pledge partnership property, notwithstanding the partners' " lien," provided the third party has no notice of an actual want of authority on that partner's part.[72] The third party may be compared with the purchaser from trustees for sale who can overreach equitable interests. Thus, in *Re Bourne*,[73] a surviving partner carried on the business after the death of his co-partner and granted an equitable mortgage by deposit of title deeds with the bank in order to secure the partnership overdraft. The Court of Appeal, affirming the decision of Farwell J. at first instance, held that the surviving partner was entitled to carry on the business in order to wind up the affairs of the partners, and that the mortgage was valid and took priority over the general lien held by the personal representatives of the deceased partner. It was also held that no distinction existed between dispositions of real, as opposed to personal, property (partnership realty being in any case subject to the doctrine of conversion, see s. 22, above), and that the rule in *Clayton's Case* (whereby subsequent payments into the joint account would go to liquidate the indebtedness of the partnership at the time of the deceased partner's death), had no application, inasmuch as the account must be deemed to continue for the purpose of winding up. In *Lingen* v. *Simpson* [74] it was agreed on dissolution that certain articles should become the exclusive property of one of the partners and that a certain fund should be set aside for debts. The other partner lost his lien over these articles despite the fact that the latter fund proved to be insufficient.

Likewise, the individual partners cannot require a judgment creditor of the firm to pursue his remedy against the partnership property before having recourse to the separate property of the partners; a judgment against the firm is nothing more than a judgment against the partners as joint debtors and is treated like any other judgment of that nature. Creditors on the other hand have no specific rights against partnership property (the debenture, whether fixed or floating, having no application to partnerships), except such as they acquire, *e.g.* by taking property in execution. Some of the older cases cited in Pollock, in which creditors levied execution on partnership property for the separate debts of partners, have now been overtaken by section 23 of the Act, but the charging order which must now be made on a partner's interest must take account of sums due to the firm by the partner whose interest is charged. [75]

Goodwill

Well understood in business, the term " goodwill " as a legal term of art is " A thing very easy to describe, very difficult to define. It is the benefit and advantage and connection of business. It is the attractive force which brings in custom. It is the one thing which distinguishes an old-established business from a business at its start." [76] Lord Eldon's oft-quoted definition of the term as " nothing more than the probability that the old customers will return to the old place " [77] is too narrow. Scrutton L.J. referred in *Whiteman Smith Motor Company* v. *Chaplin* to the " cat and dog " bases of goodwill; the cat stays in the old home even though the person who keeps the house departs, whereas the dog follows the person. Those who are attached to neither place nor person he termed " the rat." [78] Maugham L.J. felt that this incursion into the animal kingdom might

produce misleading results, but was not averse to adding a fourth
animal to the menagerie in the shape of " the rabbit," who comes
because of propinquity to the premises, unlike the cat, who may be
enticed away with a gentle stroke on the back and the promise of a
bowl of milk.[79] The " rabbit " is attached to what Maugham L.J.
termed " site goodwill," which may be exploited at the inception of a
business, in contrast to " net adherent goodwill " which attaches to
the business. Goodwill may inhere in the premises and pass with a
conveyance or devise thereof, for which reason partnership premises
should be sold with the rest of the undertaking and not separately.
If goodwill attaches to the persons it would appear not to be transferable, as is the case with solicitors and others who belong to a profession which is dependent upon personal and confidential relationships in which goodwill in the ordinary sense can scarcely be said to
exist.[80] Even so, some advantage may well attach to the continued
use of the firm-name, particularly if the vendor of the business does
not compete. Under the socialised medical system introduced in
1948, the sale or purchase of goodwill in medical practices providing
general medical services is, with certain exceptions, forbidden and
subjected to penalties. Nevertheless, goodwill in such practices is not
destroyed and there is nothing in the national health legislation
which precludes goodwill from being treated as an asset which, as we
shall see below, may be protected by a suitably drawn covenant.

Rights of partners to goodwill

Goodwill is a partnership asset and, like other assets, must be
sold so that the proceeds may be applied to the liquidation of the
firm's debts and liabilities and then to the partners according to
what may be due to them.[81]

It is open to partners to dissolve partnership and close down the
business completely. If, as is more usually the case, the business is
sold, the following rules apply in so far as they are not excluded or
modified by agreement:

(a) The purchaser alone may represent himself as continuing or
succeeding to the business of the vendor.[82] *Chintan V Douglas*

(b) The vendor may nevertheless carry on a similar business in
competition with the purchaser, if needs be, next door to the business
transferred. This right is subject to (a), above, and it is possible that
the purchaser of the business may be able to object successfully if the
vendor carries on competing business under his own name if such

name has been used as the name of the erstwhile firm so as to be part of its goodwill.

(c) The vendor may publicly advertise his business. In this context the term vendor does not include an expelled partner, a bankrupt or a debtor who has assigned his business for the benefit of creditors and even a vendor is restricted by the rule that he cannot canvass customers of the old firm, a rule which applies to a vendor's executor carrying out a contract for the sale of goodwill on which he may have no choice.[83] Lord Herschell drew a distinction in *Trego* v. *Hunt* [84] between the former partner who " sets up in business on his own account and appeals generally for custom " and such a partner who " specifically and directly appeals to those who were customers of the previous firm "; to sanction the latter would, in Lord Macnaghten's words in the same case, allow him to " sell the custom and steal away the customers." [85] In this latter connection, it makes no difference that the former customers have of their own volition continued to deal with the vendor of goodwill,[86] or that there is an express provision in the articles allowing the outgoing partner to start a similar business in the neighbourhood (which, after all, is only declaratory of the legal position). *Levy v Walker*

(d) The sale carries the exclusive right to use the name of the former firm.[87] This is subject to the qualification that the vendor is not thereby exposed to liability, but provided that the rules laid down in section 38 are complied with, it is difficult to see how the continued use of the vendor's name could expose him to any liability. The purchaser has the right to trade as the vendor's successor, but not to hold out the vendor as still involved in the business and as personally answerable.[88] A sale of goodwill carries with it the benefit of any covenant by a partner not to carry on a competing business for a fixed term,[89] in which connection it may be noted that a purchase of " assets " without any restrictive terms (including the partner who retains " assets " on dissolution) is entitled to the goodwill with its incidental rights. Any special terms however must be considered in each case as they occur.[90]

Goodwill does not " survive "

Although it was formerly stated that the goodwill in a partnership survived for the benefit of continuing partners, even without any express agreement to that effect, it is now settled that this is not so.[91] There may be express agreement on goodwill, or an agreement that the surviving or continuing partners are to have the benefit of the goodwill may be inferred from conduct. " When a partner retires from a firm, assenting to or acquiescing in the retention by the other partners of possession of the old place of business and the future conduct of the business by them under the old name, the goodwill remains with the latter as of course." [92] But what this really amounts to is that the goodwill ceases to have any separate value in that even if the retiring partner expressly agrees to assign the goodwill he is not thereby compelled to abstain from business of the partnership kind in that neighbourhood (as we have already seen), whilst if a partner dies, there is no obligation on the surviving partner to retire from business in the neighbourhood in order that the goodwill may be realised as a valuable asset for the benefit of the deceased's estate. Indeed, *Burchell* v. *Wilde* [93] shows that after dissolution the former partners may use the old firm-name, provided they do not hold out the others as still in partnership with them.

None of the foregoing, however, undermines the validity of the proposition that on a dissolution, each partner, is in the absence of agreement to the contrary,[94] entitled to have the assets, including the goodwill for what that is worth, sold and applied in the manner specified in section 39. The corollary is that until such time as the partnership affairs are wound up, a partner (or his representative) who, without agreement to that end, carries on the same business under the partnership name may be restrained at the suit of his co-partners or their representatives.[95] *Scott* v. *Rowland* [96] is express authority for the rule that a partner must not use the name or property of the partnership to carry on business on his own account while a liquidation of partnership is pending inasmuch as it is his duty to do nothing to prejudice the saleable value of the partnership property until sale.

Valuation of goodwill

Because of its shadowy character, it is often a matter of some difficulty to know on what principle goodwill should be valued, either when it is sold with the business to a third party or, as is not unusual, when a surviving or continuing partner takes over, in which event it may well transpire that no payment at all in respect of good-will is needed. In *Hodern* v. *Hodern* [97] a clause in the articles stipulated that the surviving partner should pay the executors of the deceased partner for the latter's full share in the partnership,

" nothing being charged for goodwill " which was therefore excluded. Alternatively the sum payable may be purely nominal as in *Austen* v. *Boys*.[98] Each partner was entitled on retiring to the value of his share including goodwill. One partner retired two days before the expiration of the fixed term but he was held to be entitled to a nominal amount only since the goodwill must be measured by reference to the fixed term. Goodwill is almost invariably sold with the undertaking. Indeed Lord Eldon L.C. criticised the separate valuation of each article in *Cook* v. *Collingridge*, saying that what counted was the " value of the whole, every part being valued in connection with every other." [99] Dealing with partnership articles which, in effect, contained a contract for the sale of partnership assets to the surviving partner, Romer J. held that goodwill formed part of those assets and must be valued " on the consideration of what its value would have been to the partnership if there had been no contract between the partners that the surviving partner should purchase the share of the deceased partner in the partnership effects and securities, and therefore on the footing that, if it were sold, the surviving partner would be at liberty to carry on a rival business, but also I think on the footing that he could not use the name of the partnership firm of *Letricheux and David*, and would not have the right to solicit the old customers of the firm." [1] For the purpose of valuing goodwill there is therefore no difference between a sale to a partner and a sale to a stranger, the goodwill in either event falling to be included in the assets and sold therewith, if necessary, by a Chancery order.

It is not infrequently a nice question of construction whether or not the articles mean that goodwill must be paid for separately by a surviving or continuing partner. In *Jennings* v. *Jennings*, Stirling J. (whose judgments in partnership questions command respect), interpreting a compromise between two partners whereby one of them was to retain " the assets," concluded that that partner was entitled to an injunction to restrain the other partner from soliciting the old customers of the firm on the basis that " assets " was a compendious expression for the aggregate of the several items of property belonging to the partnership.[2] On the other hand, goodwill is not included in accounts employed for the purpose of ascertaining profits in a going concern, and this is so even where the partnership agreement provides for the inclusion of property " susceptible of valuation " in such accounts. Jessel M.R. in *Steuart* v. *Gladstone* [3] (in which the articles had provided for the inclusion of such property as is referred to in the preceding sentence) repudiated the notion that goodwill was susceptible of valuation in the sense that it could be drawn on or turned into money whilst the concern was still going. Hence, an agreement to pay a retiring partner his share *per* the last annual account confers upon such a partner no right to receive a payment for goodwill if an item under this head was omitted from the general account.[4]

Express agreements not to compete

We have seen that the freedom of the vendor of goodwill to carry on in the same neighbourhood a business similar to the one sold may constitute a serious defect in the goodwill sold.[5] Because of this, the purchaser of goodwill is well advised to take a covenant from the vendor restricting the latter's freedom to compete with the business sold, both spatially and temporarily; such a covenant, if reasonable in the interests of the parties and not inimical to the public interest, will be enforced by the court. Recognising that refusal to enforce covenants of this sort would have the effect of rendering goodwill unsaleable for all practical purposes, the court takes a view of these covenants which is markedly more benign than that shown to similar covenants by employees.[6] We have already seen that the socialised system of medicine introduced into this country in 1948 does not preclude the enforcement of restrictive covenants between medical practitioners who provide general medical services under that system. Such covenants were held to be enforceable in *Whitehill* v. *Bradford*[7] and, more recently, in *MacFarlane* v. *Kent*,[8] in which Stamp J., whilst doubting whether a covenant not to practise at all within a prescribed area, being designed to protect the goodwill of a medical practice, which cannot be sold and which has no significant number of paying patients, could ever be reasonable, was prepared to sever and enforce a reasonable covenant not to " professionally advise, attend, prescribe for or treat any person " who is or has been a patient of the partnership. That care is needed in drafting such covenants is shown by cases such as *Lyne-Pirkis* v. *Jones*[9] (where the covenant was wider than was reasonably necessary to protect the partnership in that it would have precluded practice as a consultant), and the recent case of *Peyton* v. *Mindham*[10] where, notwithstanding the use of the words quoted above from the *MacFarlane* case, the covenant was held to be too wide since it would extend beyond general medical practice to consultancy work, on which ground it was held to be unenforceable, a conclusion which, because it deprived the doctor, who had nurtured the medical practice through his partner's illness, of protection as to goodwill, has been criticised.[11]

Apportionment of premium when partnership is prematurely dissolved

A " premium " differs from a partner's capital contribution in important respects: (a) like a " fine " in conveyancing law,[12] it goes into the pocket of the person receiving it so that any claim for its return must be made against the receiver and not, as in the case of capital contributions to a partnership, against the assets of the firm remaining after debts and liabilities have been cleared; (b) whereas a capital contribution might be made in connection with any kind of partnership (and capital will nearly always be needed), there is obviously little point in paying a premium for the dubious privilege of admission into a relationship which can be ended at any time, as is the case with a partnership at will.

A premium may be returnable on the terms of some special agreement between the parties, or it may be recoverable because of fraud or other reason. Apart from such special cases, the court has a general equitable jurisdiction in the matter of returning the whole or part of any premium. This jurisdiction is now contained in section 40, which draws on and clarifies the pre-existing law:

" Where one partner has paid a premium to another on entering into a partnership for a fixed term, and the partnership is dissolved before the expiration of that term otherwise than by the death of a partner, the Court may order the repayment of the premium, or of such part thereof as it thinks just, having regard to the terms of the partnership contract and to the length of time during which the partnership has continued; unless

(a) the dissolution is, in the judgment of the Court, wholly or chiefly due to the misconduct of the partner who paid the premium, or

(b) the partnership has been dissolved by an agreement containing no provision for a return of any part of the premium."

The House of Lords decision in *Atwood* v. *Maude* [13] (upon which section 40 is thought to have been modelled) shows the width of the discretion possessed by the court. In that case it was evident that the court felt that a solicitor who had taken a premium of £800 from an inexperienced person and who now, after only two of the seven years agreed as the life of the partnership had run, was seeking a dissolution because of his co-partner's incompetence was hardly entitled to retain the whole premium. The Court of Appeal stated that an appellate court ought not to interfere with the exercise of a lower court's discretion " except upon very sufficient grounds." [14]

The section specifically excludes repayment in the case of the death of any partner, presumably on the basis that the partners must be understood to have considered such a possibility when agreeing upon a premium.[15] The position with regard to other, everyday risks is uncertain. Bankruptcy was treated on the same footing as death in *Akhurst* v. *Jackson*,[16] where a premium paid to a partner who had become bankrupt was held to be irrecoverable on the ground that an 18-year term could not be made proof against the vicissitudes of death and bankruptcy. Although not overtly given as part of the *ratio* in the case itself, Lord Cairns in the *Atwood* case [17] (*supra*) adverted to the circumstance that the partner receiving the premium in *Akhurst* was known by the payer of the premium to be in a financially embarrassed state (evocative of the dangers in accepting lifts from drivers who are patently drunk!). And in *Freeland* v. *Stansfield*,[18] which Pollock considered to represent the better view, the court ordered the return of part of a premium paid by one surgeon to another when the latter's bankruptcy, " not occasioned by any sudden or unexpected loss, but by a progressive course of expenditure beyond the amount of his receipts from his practice," [19] resulted in the dissolution of the partnership. Again, the receiver of the premium was not in flourishing circumstances at the time the premium was agreed, but unlike *Akhurst*, this fact was not known to the payer of the premium. The decision can be rationalised by reference to the *exclusio unius est exclusio alterius* rule of interpretation. The position may, perhaps, be summarised by saying that the bankruptcy of the firm cannot of itself be grounds for the return of a premium; nor can the bankruptcy of the recipient of the premium at least when his financial embarrassment, if any, was known to the payer (*secus* it would appear when such embarrassment was unknown to the payer) and possibly also when the receiver's bankruptcy stems from supervening causes which are wholly or largely outside his control. In this latter connection, a distinction can be observed in bankruptcy law between the bankrupt who is the author of his own misfortune and the bankrupt who is the victim of accidents and who may be entitled to a certificate of misfortune.

The effect of the payer's bankruptcy is no clearer. *Semble* a bankruptcy attributable wholly or chiefly to the payer's misconduct would bar a claim for the recovery of premium, and although it is arguable that a bankruptcy not so caused ought not to have the same effect, it would seem unlikely that a court would order a return of premium in view of the uncertainty which this would raise in all cases of premium payments and in view of the hardship which might result to recipients who had altered their positions on the strength of the premium.

Amount returnable

Unless there has been a total failure of consideration (covered in any case by the common law), the court ordering a repayment of premium will normally order the repayment of such part of the premium as bears the same proportion to the whole sum which the unexpired period of the term bears to the whole term.[20] The requirement in the section that the court will have regard to the " time formula " (" a mere arithmetical question "),[21] does not preclude the court from employing some other measure in those cases where the time formula would not produce a fair result, *e.g.* where the benefit conferred on the payer of the premium is greater in the early years.[22]

Misconduct

Proviso (*a*) to the section is obviously designed to prevent the injustice which might arise were the payer of the premium able to recover his premium notwithstanding the misconduct by him which has occasioned the dissolution. Fry J. refused to order a return of premium (in fact, ordering the payment of premium unpaid) on this ground in *Bluck* v. *Capstick*,[23] but drew a distinction between three cases in which the court might, *not* must, direct a return of premium, *viz.* (a) where there was no fault on either side; (b) where there was misconduct on both sides [24]; and (c) where the recipient of the premium had brought about the dissolution. (a) is illustrated by *Hamil* v. *Stokes*,[25] in which a partner who had stipulated for a premium of £1,050 as the price of admission into a partnership for five years, procured the suing out of a commission of bankruptcy against his co-partner upon which the latter was adjudicated bankrupt. By so doing, the court considered that he had committed such a grievous offence against morality as ought to bar a claim to retain the whole premium. The degree of misconduct must be " such a serious and deliberate breach of the partnership contract as might be considered equivalent to a repudiation of it altogether," [26] whilst misconduct by the payer must be such as, in the court's opinion, causes the dissolution of the partnership.

Dissolution by agreement without provision for premium

In line with the earlier case of *Lee* v. *Page*,[27] no order for the repayment of premium will be made where the partnership has been dissolved by an agreement which contains no provision for a return of premium. The omission may be deliberate. If it is not a deliberate omission, the court cannot cure the *casus omissus*. Furthermore, it is only on special grounds that relief as regards the return of premiums will be given when such relief was not asked for at the time when a decree of dissolution was granted; a rule which is justified by resort to the maxim *interest republicae ut sit finis litium*.[28] It may be added here that arbitrators acting under common-form arbitration clauses in partnership articles (which do not expressly provide for the reference of questions concerning the return of premiums) may, as part of their award on the terms of dissolution, include a provision for the return of the premium, in whole or in part.[29]

Rights where partnership dissolved for fraud or misrepresentation

"41. Where a partnership contract is rescinded on the ground of the fraud or misrepresentation of one of the parties thereto, the party entitled to rescind is, without prejudice to any other right, entitled:
  - (a) to a lien on, or right of retention of, the surplus of the partnership assets, after satisfying the partnership liabilities, for any sum of money paid by him for the purchase of a share in the partnership and for any capital contributed by him, and is
  - (b) to stand in the place of the creditors of the firm for any payments made by him in respect of the partnership liabilities and
  - (c) to be indemnified by the person guilty of the fraud or making the representation against all the debts and liabilities of the firm."

The rights of a partner induced to enter into a partnership contract by fraud or misrepresentation are contained in an unhappy *mélange* of common law and statute, for further information on which the reader is commended to monographs on contract. A partner may have the following rights:

(1) A claim for damages either for (a) fraud or (b) innocent misrepresentation, subject to the restriction, provided by the Misrepresentation Act 1967, s. 2 (1), that a person who has entered into a contract after a misrepresentation has been made to him by another party thereto, and has suffered loss as a result, will not be awarded damages if the other party can prove that he had reasonable grounds to believe, and did believe up to the time the contract was made, that the facts represented were true. Under section 2 (3) of the Misrepresentation Act the court or arbitrator may award damages in lieu of rescission. If damages are thus awarded section 41 is inapplicable and rights given thereunder may not be claimed. Although the section seems to envisage fraud or misrepresentation in the formation of a partnership contract, it should be remembered that these may arise in connection with the variation or dissolution of such a contract.

(2) A right of rescission for either (a) fraud, or (b) innocent misrepresentation whether or not the false statement has been incorporated into the contract. The so-called rule in *Seddon's* case [30] (which precluded rescission of an executed contract induced by innocent misrepresentation) was repealed by section 1 of the Misrepresentation Act 1967, but it is clear from section 41 that this rule had no application in partnership cases. Because a contract affected by actionable misrepresentation is voidable and not void *ab initio*, debts and liabilities incurred by a partner as such are, and remain, valid notwithstanding a later avoidance of the contract. The right to rescind is lost if the contract has, notwithstanding the false statement, been affirmed either expressly or impliedly by the representee. [31] In *Adam* v. *Newbigging*, [32] which was decided before the Act, a partner who had been induced to enter a firm as the result of a substantial misstatement (although not fraudulent) was held entitled to have the whole contract set aside even where the financial position of the firm had deteriorated to such an extent as to make the firm practically valueless at the time when rescission was sought.

(3) The special rights conferred by section 41, *viz.*:

    (a)   A lien on surplus assets for capital contributed;

    (b)   A right to be subrogated to the position of creditors of the firm in respect of payments made by the party entitled to rescind; and

(c) A right of indemnity against all the debts and liabilities of the firm. Apart from the Act, the person induced to enter a contract by an innocent misrepresentation not incorporated into the contract may claim an indemnity in respect of liabilities arising out of the contract even though damages could not (prior to 1967) be awarded. The present section gives a very wide indemnity against " all the debts and liabilities of the firm " which in strictness do not arise out of the contract of partnership but rather out of the firm's subsequent *negotia*. Although now of purely historical interest, it is interesting to note that Lord Watson declined to decide on the extent of the indemnity in *Adam* v. *Newbigging*,[33] although Bowen L.J. in the court below appeared to take a narrower view in the *obiter dictum* that the person entitled to an indemnity was not, like a person entitled to damages for deceit, entitled to be replaced as far as possible in his *status quo ante*, but only replaced in his former position " so far as regards the rights and obligations which have been created by the contract into which he has been induced to enter." [34]

Rights of outgoing partner to post-dissolution profits

It may be a precept in business that one should always endeavour to use other persons' money, but continuing partners who use the share of a deceased or former partner without any settlement of accounts are, in the absence of special agreement, liable to account not only for the share so utilised but also for profits (if any) attributable to the employment of the share, or, at the option of the former partner (or his representative), to interest on the share.

We have already seen that partners may, *inter alia*, continue the business for the purpose of winding up and that in so doing they exercise a power and, *uno flatu*, discharge a duty (see pp. 69 and 132 above). It has been suggested that the option about to be discussed cannot apply unless the business is carried on without authority, statutory or otherwise.[35] It is respectfully submitted that section 42 ought and probably does cover a lawful continuance of the business under section 38, for three main reasons. (a) The latter section deals with the *authority* of continuing partners, *i.e.* the extent to which they can bind the firm. (b) It would be unfair to debar a former partner (or his representative) from an *aliquot* share of profit (or interest) during this period. (c) It has been ruled that the liability to account under what is now section 42 does not proceed upon the ground of misconduct at all.[36] This preliminary hurdle cleared, section 42 can now be discussed in more general terms:

" 42–(1) Where any member of a firm has died or otherwise ceased to be a partner, and the surviving or continuing partners carry on the business of the firm with its capital or assets without any final settlement of accounts as between the firm and the outgoing partner or his estate, then, in the absence of any agreement to the contrary, the outgoing partner or his estate is entitled at the option of himself or his representatives to such share of the profits made since the dissolution as the Court may find to be attributable to the use of his share of the partnership assets, or to interest at the rate of 5 per cent. per annum on the amount of his share of the partnership assets.

(2) Provided that where by the partnership contract an option is given to surviving or continuing partners to purchase the interest of a deceased or outgoing partner, and that option is duly exercised, the estate of the deceased partner, or the outgoing partner or his estate, as the case may be, is not entitled to any further or other share of profits; but if any partner assuming to act in exercise of the option does not in all material respects comply with the terms thereof, he is liable to account under the foregoing provisions of this section."

The option

Where it exists, a claim for profits is an alternative to a claim for interest; but one or other must be distinctly chosen. Therefore, a double claim is inadmissible, as is a mixed claim. A claim for profits for part of the time, and for interest as to the rest of the time, or for profits against one or more partners and for interest against others, or, for profits against some capital and interest against others, are all equally exceptionable.

(*i*) *Share of profits*. A share of profits was awarded in *Manley* v. *Sartori* to the personal representatives of a deceased partner whose partner had continued to carry on the business of the partnership without a settlement of accounts and the share awarded was held to be proportionate to the deceased's share of assets less an allowance for the management of the business after dissolution. The broad principle was put by Romer J. in that case: " You must ascertain what profits have been earned by the utilisation of the assets of the partnership as a whole. Once you have found that, then having ascertained what the deceased partner's interest in those assets was, you can easily ascertain his share in the profits earned by them." [37] However, the principle is easier to state than to apply and needs to be taken *cum grano salis.*

At the outset, it needs to be recognised that the profits made since dissolution may not relate directly or indirectly to capital at all; something which, it is conceded, Romer J. accepted. If, as in *Wedderburn* v. *Wedderburn*,[38] the surviving partners, to whom the goodwill passes under the articles, do not attempt to realise the business at the time of their co-partner's death because of its perilous financial state, but by dint of skill and the infusion of extra funds into the business manage to make great profits so that the firm's liabilities may be met and the assets realised, it does not follow that the deceased partner's legatees have any claim beyond the interest already credited to them on the estimated value of the deceased partner's share. Several factors may have to be taken into account, such as the nature of the trade, the manner of carrying it on, the capital employed, the state of the account between the late partnership and the deceased or former partner at the time of dissolution, and the subsequent conduct of the parties, to draw on the examples given by Wigram V.-C. in *Willett* v. *Blanford.*[39] Indeed, the capital element may be chimerical, as the example chosen by the Vice-Chancellor in the last-named case shows, *viz.* a partnership between A and B who share equally in profits, A finding the capital and B the skill. If B dies before there has been time for his skill to produce any goodwill of appreciable value to the firm it would seem that B's estate will be entitled to little or no share of the profits made by A who continues the business. Indeed in certain partnerships, particularly those concerned with the professions or services, the element of capital may be small. On the other hand the example given by Wigram V.-C. does not mean that partners contributing skill or labour are *ergo* entitled to no share in the partnership assets (and it is to these that s. 42 refers); section 44 (*infra*) shows that such partners may well have claims upon assets in the event of winding up. One grain of comfort to those bent on prosecuting a claim for profits is contained in Romer J.'s statement in the *Manley* case (*supra*) that there is (a) a presumption that profits will prima facie be apportioned to the share of assets continued to be used in the business and, (b) that the onus is on the surviving partner (one must not say the burden " shifts ") to show that the profits have been earned wholly or partly by means other than the utilisation of the assets, including goodwill.

The determination of what constitutes a partner's " share " is a question of fact, e.g. whether profits which have been allowed to accrue to capital are to be treated as the capital of the partners [40] or not,[41] and also whether capital means capital contributed, capital agreed to be contributed or some notional capital yardstick which remains constant despite advances and withdrawals during the subsistence of the firm.[42] In the Irish case of Meagher v. Meagher,[43] (which proceeded on the basis that a partner cannot be forced to accept a valuation) it was held that the proper date for the valuation of the partnership assets, which in that case had risen in value after the death of a partner, was the date of realisation, on the ground that this was sound practice and obviated elaborate inquiries. The appreciation of partnership assets was held to be profit derived from the use of those assets, following the wide definition of profit given in Re Spanish Prospecting Co. Ltd.[44] It was found that " use " is not incompatible with passivity, as where whisky is locked away until such time as it can be realised at a greater profit.

Another difficulty has occurred in deciding how the profits are to be " attributed " to the respective shares of the partners, viz. should capital or profit-sharing ratios be used? Thus, in Yates v. Finn, A and B were partners sharing profits equally but contributing capital respectively in the ratio 3:1. Hall V.-C. felt unable to apply the equal profits rule to profits made after a partnership as such had ceased to exist, saying that it was " ordinarily just and right that the profits made by the business should be apportioned according to the capital employed in it." [45] In the light of Romer J.'s remarks in the Manley case (supra) it would appear that this method of apportioning profits is now more likely to be used.

Lindley [46] refers to the " fearfully oppressive " effect of judgments for an account of profits after dissolution and doubts whether there is any instance in which such a judgment has been worked out in a manner beneficial to the person in whose favour it has been made. In Pathirana v. Pathirana,[47] one of two partners who operated a tied garage as partners continued the business after the withdrawal of his co-partner but using the latter's capital. The partnership agreement provided for equality of both capital contribution and profit-sharing. In fact, there seemed to be little capital, except for certain agreements with a petroleum company (and these " hung at all times by the most tenuous thread ") and for the goodwill which had been built up. Lord Upjohn accepted the " robust way " in which the trial judge had, in the absence of evidence, taken the practical course of reducing the half share of profits which the respondents would have received had the partnership continued to a one-third share of the profits.

(*ii*) *Interest*. The alternative of a claim for interest has the advantage of simplicity accompanied, however, by the considerable disadvantage of a rate of interest bearing little relationship to current rates of inflation. The rate of interest will normally be simple, but in the case of partners clothed with the role of trustee who commit trust funds to the partnership business (and non-partner trustees who are implicated by reason of having notice of the breach of trust), the rate will be compound. [48]

The partner-trustee

It is not uncommon to find that a partner disposing of his partnership interest by will has appointed (or included) his fellow-partners as executors or trustees to his will in order that inexperienced persons are not called upon to administer that part of his estate comprised in the partnership property. If during the subsistence of the partnership, the testator dies and his executors or trustees carry on (or assist in carrying on) [49] the business without settlement of accounts, such persons, if also partners, fulfil dual roles. As partners, they are liable to account for profits to the deceased's estate; as executors or trustees, they owe duties towards the persons beneficially interested in the deceased's estate. It occasions no surprise that the duality in roles has occasioned no little subtlety in the cases.

If those seeking to assert their right to an account of profits proceed against executors as such for what is really a partnership liability, if any, and without bringing all the members of the firm before the court, they will not obtain full redress. A, who is in partnership with B and C, dies having appointed B his executor. B and C continue to employ A's capital in the business. B may be made liable to account for the profits received by him from the use of A's capital, but not for the whole profits received therefrom by the firm. Lord Cairns was unable in *Vyse* v. *Foster* [50] to find any case where one surviving partner, being an executor, had been held answerable for the whole of the profits which, in any case, had been received, not by the executor alone, but as one of a number of partners not all of whom were before the court and who were therefore not subject to any liability under a decree it might make. In *Stroud* v. *Gwyer*,[51] executors of the deceased partner allowed the latter's capital to remain in the firm beyond the permitted time. It was held that the continuing partners (one of whom had joined after the deceased partner's death) were not liable to the beneficiaries, inasmuch as the executors themselves were only liable to make good the amount of capital and interest. The moral is that those seeking to assert a claim to post-dissolution profits ought to make up their minds distinctly as to the capacity and duty of those whom they seek to hold accountable.

Option to purchase share given by partnership contract

It will be seen from subsection (2) that a partner who does not comply in all material respects with the terms of an option in the partnership contract to purchase the interest of a deceased or outgoing partner is liable to account in the same way as a continuing partner without such an option is liable. The dangers in non-compliance are exemplified by *Willett* v. *Blanford*.[52] In that case, A, B and C were partners under articles which provided that on A's death, B and C, or the survivor of them, might continue the business in partnership with A's representatives or nominees, taking at the same time an increased share in the profits; in that case, B and C, or the survivor of them, would be obliged to enter into new articles of partnership, to pay out in a specified manner the value of the part of A's interest taken over, and to give certain securities to A's representatives. B, and later A, died. C carried on the business without fulfilling the provisions of the articles as to entering into new articles, or paying out the value of the part of A's interest which he was entitled to acquire, or giving security. It was held that C was bound to account to A's estate for subsequent profits.

On the other hand, surviving partners who complied with articles providing for the ascertainment of the deceased partner's share and the payment of interest thereon but who, acting in good faith for the benefit of the persons interested, failed to comply with a requirement that the purchase price for the deceased partner's share be paid in instalments over two years were held not to be accountable for subsequent profits.[53]

Retiring or deceased partner's share to be a debt

" 43. Subject to any agreement between the partners, the

amount due from surviving or continuing partners to an outgoing partner or the representatives of a deceased partner in respect of the outgoing or deceased partner's share is a debt accruing at the date of the dissolution or death."

Statements to the effect that a surviving partner is a " trustee " in respect of a deceased or former partner's interest in the partnership assets were criticised as " metaphorical and inaccurate " in the last edition of Pollock. This criticism is in line with the decision and certain comments in *Knox* v. *Gye* [54] in which the House of Lords (Lord Hatherley L.C. dissenting) decided that the surviving partner is a debtor in respect of the deceased partner's interest in the partnership so that time under the Statutes of Limitation runs from the *punctum temporis* at which the partnership estate comes to be vested in such surviving partner. The limitation period does not commence to run in connection with a continuing partnership, including one in which there has been a discontinuance of the business without a winding up,[55] but will ordinarily commence when the partnership ceases and a cause of action accrues.[56] In *Betjemann* v. *Betjemann*,[57] in which two sons had carried on partnership after the death of their father, with whom they had been in partnership, it was held that after the death of one of the sons the surviving son could reopen the accounts prior to the date of the father's death on the grounds (a) that despite the dissolution of the partnership of the three by the father's death the partnership account had been carried on unbroken so that time did not commence to run at the father's death, or, alternatively, (b) that the concealed fraud of the father, who had drawn more than his entitlement, prevented time from running; in which connection it was no answer to say that due caution would have ensured the discovery of such fraud, partners being entitled to rely on each others' good faith.

In the Irish case of *Meagher* v. *Meagher*,[58] in which the date for the valuation of the deceased partner's interest was held to be the date of realisation and not the date of death (where a claim for post-dissolution profits is submitted), the court denied that section 43 meant that the valuation of the deceased partner's share must be made at the date of his death. The mode of ascertaining an outgoing or deceased partner's share will often depend on the partnership agreement.

Rules for distribution of assets on final settlement of accounts

On a dissolution, partners are free to make whatever dispositions of the partnership assets they wish. They may, for example, agree that continuing partners may take over the business and undertaking on agreed terms or that, in the event of a complete dissolution, the assets are to be distributed in a particular way. For example, in *Wood* v. *Scoles* [59] one clause in the articles provided for equal sharing in profits and losses whilst another clause provided for the distribution of capital, etc., to partners according to their " respective shares or interests therein." It goes without saying that whatever they may agree amongst themselves, the rights of creditors remain unaffected.

Subject to any special arrangements which may have been agreed, the broad procedure to be followed may be stated as follows:

(1) It may be necessary to " get in " the partnership assets, such as outstanding debts owed to the firm either by debtors or by the partners themselves, in order that one may start from what Kekewich J. in *Ross* v. *White*,[60] referred to as the " whole mass " of the assets. However, a partner's separate real estate, charged with payment of a partnership debt, passes to the partner's devisee free of the charge where the partnership assets are adequate to meet the claims of creditors.[61] We have already seen that the determination of what constitutes " partnership assets " is a question not free of difficulty (see p. 78 *et seq.*, above). Thus, a partner may not have brought in his agreed capital, or he may have drawn on capital. It may be that offices held by a partner in his individual capacity may nevertheless constitute part of the partnership assets, *e.g.* clerkships held by a solicitor,[62] an Army commission conferred upon a solicitor who responds to Kitchener's " Call " in 1914,[63] and a government mail contract,[64] examples which exemplify the sweeping aphorism of Lord Cairns L.C. in *Syers* v. *Syers* [65] that " A co-partnership in profits, as we all know, is a co-partnership in those assets by which the profits are made and produced." Sir G. J. Turner V.C. in *Smith* v. *Mules*, *supra*, seems to have accepted somewhat more cautiously that a distinction might in certain cases be drawn between offices and profits therefrom.

(2) The realisation by sale of such assets as can be sold. Subject to special agreement, every partner has the prima facie right to insist on a sale following a dissolution and the court will normally take this course.[66]

(3) The application of the proceeds of sale (including sums received on the valuation of assets incapable of sale) to the liquidation of the debts and liabilities of the firm, to the repayment of advances by partners, to costs of administration if the aid of the court has been enlisted, to repayments of capitals to partners and lastly to the partners according to their respective interests.

Section 44 follows the logical, although possibly distasteful, course of attributing responsibility for losses before dealing with the more agreeable question of distributing the assets:

" In settling accounts between the partners after a dissolution of partnership, the following rules shall, subject to any agreement, be observed:

(*a*) Losses, including losses and deficiencies of capital shall be paid first out of profits, next out of capital, and lastly, if necessary, by the partners individually in the proportions in which they were entitled to share profits:

(*b*) The assets of the firm including the sums, if any, contributed by the partners to make up losses or deficiencies of capital, shall be applied in the following manner and order:

1. In paying the debts and liabilities of the firm to persons who are not partners therein:

2. In paying to each partner rateably what is due from the firm to him for advances as distinguished from capital:

3. In paying to each partner rateably what is due from the firm to him in respect of capital:

4. The ultimate residue, if any, shall be divided among the partners in the proportions in which profits are divisible."

Losses

Subsection (*a*) allocates responsibility for a loss, a term which covers both (i) an excess of liabilities (excluding the claims of partners) over assets so that the partnership, viewed (as it is in bookkeeping) as a quasi-entity, is " insolvent," and (ii) the ability to meet debts and liabilities but an insufficiency of assets to repay the capital of the " proprietors." " In the absence of stipulation to the contrary," said Sir W. M. James V.-C. in *Nowell* v. *Nowell*,[67] " the

community of profit involves like community of loss," thus rejecting
the notion that loss of capital should be borne by the partner
providing it—the " heads, I win: tails you lose " argument. The
operation of this subsection may be made clear by means of examples.

Example

Partners A, B and C contribute £5,000, £3,000 and £1,000 respectively, A having made an advance of £1,000. On dissolution, the
assets realise £8,000 but the debts of the partnership amount to
£2,500.

(1) Creditors are paid off, leaving assets of £5,500;
(2) A's advance is paid off, leaving assets of £4,500;
(3) Assuming that there is no provision to the contrary in the
articles, profits and losses are shared equally (s. 24). The loss
on capital of £4,500 (£9,000 less net assets of £4,500) is borne
equally by A, B and C, *i.e.* each bears £1,500.

The result is that:

	Share of Net Assets
A brought in £5,000, less £1,500	£3,500
B brought in £3,000, less £1,500	£1,500
C brought in £1,000, less £1,500	(500)
	£4,500

NOTE.—If, in the example given, the partners shared profits in the
proportions in which they contributed capitals, the loss of £4,500 on
capital would be apportioned to A, B and C in the proportions 5:3:1.
The contributions towards the loss of £4,500 would therefore be:
A, 5/9 of £4,500, *i.e.* £2,500; B, 3/9 of £4,500, *i.e.* £1,500; C, 1/9 of
£4,500 *i.e.* £500.

	Share of Net Assets
A brought in £5,000, less share of loss @ £2,500	£2,500
B brought in £3,000, less share of loss @ £1,500	£1,500
C brought in £1,000, less share of loss @ £500	500
	£4,500

Garner v. Murray

In *Garner* v. *Murray* [68] (a case ranking high in accountancy folk-lore), the court was confronted with the problem of a partnership (providing for the unequal contribution of capital but the equal division of profits) in which (after payment of debts and advances to solvent partners) there was a deficiency of assets to which one of the partners was unable to contribute by reason of insolvency. Joyce J. could find nothing in the Act to oblige the solvent partners to make up the contribution of their insolvent co-partner.

Applying the facts in the example given above, except for the insolvency of C, the position is, as before, that the loss of capital is shared equally between the three partners. C's inability to contribute is ignored, so that the notional fund available for distribution consists of the net assets (£4,500), plus contributions of £1,500 from A and B (£3,000), that is to say £7,500. This fund is divided rateably between A and B, as follows:

A is entitled to 5/8 of £7,500, *viz.*   £4,687·50
B is entitled to 3/8 of £7,500, *viz.*   £2,812·50

                                                 £7,500·00

                                          Share of Assets

A receives £4,687·50, less share
    of loss £1,500   £3,187·50
B receives £2,812·50, less share
    of loss £1,500   £1,312·50
It will be seen that the losses suffered by A and B are:
A—£5,000, less sum received £3,187·50   £1,812·50
B—£3,000, less sum received £1,312·50   £1,687·50

Order of application of assets

Subsection (*b*) "marshals the assets" in a particular order to meet the claims of debts and liabilities, advances by partners, capital contributions by partners and lastly the claim of partners to any surplus remaining assets. As in the case of companies (confirmed by the much-criticised case of *Saloman* v. *Saloman and Co.* [69]) creditors take priority over members in the matter of repayment; this requires no further comment. The rule that advances rank before capital confirms the effect of decisions before the Act. [70] An advance differs from capital in that it is brought in *ultra* the stipulated amount of capital as a form of loan which is " not intended to be wholly risked in the business." [71] Next comes capital which, although treated as a " liability " in the balance sheet, is not a " debt " in the legal sense until such time as the amount is settled. In *Green* v. *Hertzog*,[72] an action during the subsistence of the partnership for money lent to the partnership as capital was held to be misconceived, the only claim being that which arises upon the taking of accounts under section 44 (*b*). Lastly, any remaining assets go to the partners in profit-sharing proportions.

Costs

The Act does not make provision for the question of costs when, as not infrequently happens, the aid of the court has been enlisted. Such costs are payable out of the assets, ranking after the claims of creditors and partners for their advances, but before the claims of the latter in respect of capital.[73] In order to ascertain the amount of the assets, it may be necessary that a partner restore amounts of capital withdrawn.[74] If the assets are insufficient to meet the costs, the deficiency must be made up by the partners in the proportions in which they share profits,[75] unless one or more of the partners has been guilty of negligence or misconduct, in which case he may be ordered to bear more than his *pro rata* share.[76]

Remaining provisions of the Act
Definitions of " court " and " business "

" 45. In this Act, unless the contrary intention appears, the expression ' Court ' includes every Court and judge having jurisdiction in the case. The expression ' business ' includes every trade, occupation, or profession."

Saving for rules of equity and common law

" 46. The rules of equity and of common law applicable to partnership shall continue in force except so far as they are inconsistent with the express provisions of this Act."

Provision as to bankruptcy in Scotland

" 47. (1) In the application of this Act to Scotland the bankruptcy of a firm or of an individual shall mean sequestration under the Bankruptcy (Scotland) Acts, and also in the case of an individual the issue against him of a decree of cessio bonorum.

(2) Nothing in this Act shall alter the rules of the law of Scotland relating to the bankruptcy of a firm or of the individual partners thereof."

Section 48 of the Partnership Act 1890 deals with repeals in the Schedule, sections 49 and 50 with the coming into force of the Act, and the short title.

1 *Moss* v. *Elphick* [1910] 1 K.B. 846 and commentary on s. 27, *supra*.
2 (1858) 4 K. & J. 656.
3 *Crawshay* v. *Maule* (1818) 1 Swanst. 495 at p. 508.
4 *Titmus* v. *Rose and Watts* [1940] 1 All E.R. 599.
5 *McLeod* v. *Dowling* (1927) 43 T.L.R. 655.
6 *Mellersh* v. *Keen* (1859) 27 Beav. 236.
7 *Griffiths* v. *Bracewell* (1865) 35 Beav. 43 at p. 46.
8 *Warder* v. *Stilwell* (1856) 26 L.J.Ch. 373.
9 (1927) 43 T.L.R. 655.
10 *Whitmore* v. *Mason* (1861) 2 J. & M. 204.
11 *Ex p. Smith* (1800) 5 Ves. 295 at p. 297.
12 *Craven* v. *Edmondson* (1830) 6 Bing. 734; see Bankruptcy Act 1914, s. 37; also ss. 45 and 46 for " protected " transactions.
13 *Brown, Janson and Co.* v. *Hutchinson* (*No.* 2) [1895] 2 Q.B. 126.
14 *Griswold* v. *Waddington* (1818) (Supreme Court, N. York) 15 Johns 57, 16 *ibid.* 438. *Esposito* v. *Bowden* (1857) 7 E. & B. 763. S. 45, *infra*, shows that the enemy alien is not rightless for all time.
15 Lindley, pp. 155, 575.
16 See the restrictions on partnership numbers, p. 22 *supra*.
17 [1969] 1 Ch. 545.
18 *Goodman* v. *Whitcomb* (1820) 1 Jac. & W. 589 at p. 592.
19 Mental Health Act 1959, s. 100.
20 County Courts Act 1959, s. 52 (1) (*f*), as amended.
21 *Jones* v. *Noy* (1833) 2 M. & K. 125.
22 *J.* v. *S.* [1894] 3 Ch. 72.
23 *Besch* v. *Frolich* (1842) 1 Ch. 172.
24 *Lyon* v. *Tweddell* (1881) 17 Ch.D. 529 at p. 531.
25 Lindley, p. 586.
26 *Whitwell* v. *Arthur* (1865) 35 Beav. 140.
27 *Essell* v. *Hayward* (1860) 30 Beav. 158.
28 (1868) 16 W.R. 654.
29 *Clifford* v. *Timms* [1908] A.C. 12.
30 (1830) 3 Sim. 8 at p. 11.
31 *Cheesman* v. *Price* (1865) 35 Beav. 142.
32 *Anderson* v. *Anderson* (1857) 25 Beav. 190.
33 *Jennings* v. *Baddeley* (1856) 3 K. & J. 78; *Handyside* v. *Campbell* (1901) 17 T.L.R. 623.
34 [1966] 1 W.L.R. 514 at p. 521.
35 [1916] 2 Ch. 426 (C.A.): also held that the arbitration clause could hardly be expected to cope with daily differences.
36 See *Baxter* v. *West* (1860) Drew. & Sm. 173: *Watney* v. *Wells* (1861) 40 Beav. 56.
37 As in *Harrison* v. *Tennant* (1856) 21 Beav. 482, in which a dissolution was granted to solicitors who, by sublimating their feelings, had acted as gentlemen.

[38] [1965] 1 W.L.R. 1051 at p. 1056.

[39] [1973] A.C. 360.

[40] [1970] 1 W.L.R. 592 at p. 597.

[41] (1889) 61 L.T. 629.

[42] [1959] 1 W.L.R. 551 (s. 35 (*f*) refers expressly to " the opinion of the court ").

[43] (1880) 14 Ch.D. 471.

[44] [1974] 1 W.L.R. 719.

[45] [1971] Ch. 758.

[46] *Adam* v. *Newbigging* (1888) 13 App.Cas. 308 (H.L.).

[47] Now Belfast for N. Ireland: S.R. & O. 1923.

[48] See *Court* v. *Berlin*, p. 62, *supra*.

[49] *Carter* v. *Whalley* (1830) 1 B. & Ad. 11.

[50] [1949] 2 K.B. 397.

[51] *Bradbury* v. *Dickens* (1859) 27 Beav. 53.

[52] See *Heath* v. *Sansom* (1832) 4 B. & Ad. 172.

[53] *Griffiths* v. *Bracewell* (1865) 35 Beav. 43 at p. 46: *Crawshay* v. *Maule* (1818) 1 Swanst. 495 at p. 508.

[54] *Re Bourne* [1906] 1 Ch. 113 : 2 Ch. 427 at pp. 430–431.

[55] *Smith* v. *Winter* (1838) 4 M. & W. 454.

[56] *Fraser* v. *Kershaw* (1856) 2 K. & J. 496. *Fox* v. *Hanbury* (1776) Cowp. 445 at p. 448.

[57] *Backhouse* v. *Charlton* (1878) 8 Ch.D. 444.

[58] *Lewis* v. *Reilly* (1841) 1 Q.B. 349: this decision is doubted by Lindley, p. 249.

[59] *King* v. *Smith* (1829) 4 C. & P. 108.

[60] *Butchart* v. *Dresser* (1853) 4 De G.M. & G. 542.

[61] *Re Hill* [1921] 2 K.B. 831.

[62] *Goldfarb* v. *Bartlett* [1920] 1 K.B. 639.

[63] (1808) 10 East 418.

[64] (1823) 1 L.J. (o.s.) K.B. 143.

[65] *Re Hill* [1921] 2 K.B. 831.

[66] For assets falling in after dissolution see *Gopala Chetty* v. *Vijayaraghava-chariar* [1922] A.C. 488 at p. 495.

[67] *Croft* v. *Pike* (1733) 3 P.Wms. 180.

[68] *Op. cit.* p. 375.

[69] [1906] 2 Ch. 427 at p. 434. See 12 M.L.R. 432.

[70] *Payne* v. *Hornby* (1858) 25 Beav. 280. See *Nerot* v. *Burnand* (1827) 4 Russ. 247.

[71] (1845) 9 Beav. 239 at p. 246.

[72] See *Valletort Sanitary Steam Laundry* [1903] 2 Ch. 654, referred to in *Re Bourne*.

[73] [1906] 2 Ch. 427, following *Re Langmead's Trusts* (1855) 20 Beav. 20.

[74] (1824) 1 S. & S. 600.

[75] *West* v. *Skip* (1749) 1 Ves.Sen. 239; *Skip* v. *Harwood* (1747) 2 Swanst. 586.

[76] *Inland Revenue Commissioners* v. *Muller and Co.'s Margarine Ltd.* [1901] A.C. 217 at pp. 223–224, *per* Lord Macnaghten.

[77] *Cruttwell* v. *Lye* (1810) 17 Ves. 335 at p. 346.

[78] [1934] 2 K.B. 35 at p. 42.

[79] *Ibid.* at p. 50.

[80] *Austen* v. *Boys* (1858) 2 De G. & J. 626 at p. 635; *Arundell* v. *Bell* (1883) 31 W.R. 477. But *Burchell* v. *Wilde* [1900] 1 Ch. 551 indicates that a solicitor's business may have goodwill of some value.

[81] *Levy* v. *Walker* (1879) 10 Ch.D. 436 at p. 466.

82 *Churton* v. *Douglas* (1859) Johns. 174, a leading case.
83 *Boorne* v. *Wicker* [1927] 1 Ch. 667.
84 [1896] A.C. 7 at p. 20.
85 *Ibid.* at p. 25.
86 *Curl Bros.* v. *Webster* [1904] 1 Ch. 685.
87 *Levy* v. *Walker* (1879) 10 Ch.D. 436; *Re David and Matthews* [1899] 1 Ch. 378.
88 *Thynne* v. *Shove* (1890) 45 Ch.D. 577 at p. 582.
89 *Townsend* v. *Jarman* [1900] 2 Ch. 698.
90 *Jennings* v. *Jennings* [1898] 1 Ch. 378.
91 *Smith* v. *Everett* (1859) 27 Beav. 446.
92 *Menendez* v. *Holt* (1888) 128 U.S. 514 at p. 522.
93 [1900] 1 Ch. 551.
94 *Cf. Sobell* v. *Boston* [1975] 1 W.L.R. 1587.
95 *Re David and Matthews* [1899] 1 Ch. 378.
96 (1872) 20 W.R. 508.
97 [1910] A.C. 465.
98 (1857) 24 Beav. 598.
99 (1823) Jac. 607 at pp. 620–621.
1 *Re David and Matthews* [1899] 1 Ch. 378 at p. 382.
2 [1898] 1 Ch. 378 at p. 384.
3 (1878) 10 Ch.D. 626.
4 *Hunter* v. *Dowling* (1895) 2 Ch. 223; *Chapman* v. *Hayman* (1885) 1 T.L.R. 397; *Scott* v. *Scott* (1903) 89 L.T. 582.
5 See *Taylor* v. *Neate* (1888) 39 Ch.D. 538.
6 *Ronbar Enterprises Ltd.* v. *Green* [1954] 1 W.L.R. 815 at pp. 820–821. *Cf. Jenkins* v. *Reid* [1948] 1 All E.R. 471, in relation to covenants taken from the spouse of the seller (or from employees of the old business).
7 [1952] Ch. 236.
8 [1965] 1 W.L.R. 1019.
9 [1969] 1 W.L.R. 1293.
10 [1972] 1 W.L.R. 8.
11 G. K. Morse in 35 M.L.R. 315.
12 *Re Cosh's Contract* (1896) 66 L.J.Ch. 28 at p. 30, *per* Russell C.J.
13 (1868) L.R. 3 Ch. 369.
14 *Lyon* v. *Tweddell* (1881) 17 Ch.D. 529, *per* Jessel M.R.
15 *Whincup* v. *Hughes* (1871) L.R. 6 C.P. 78.
16 (1818) 1 Swanst. 85.
17 (1868) L.R. 3 Ch. 369 at p. 372.
18 (1852–54) 2 Sm. & G. 479.
19 *Ibid.* at p. 486.
20 *Bury* v. *Allen* (1844–45) 1 Coll. 589. The same formula was applied in *Astle* v. *Wright* (1856) 23 Beav. 77: *Pease* v. *Hewitt* (1862) 31 Beav. 22: *Wilson* v. *Johnstone* (1873) L.R. 16 Eq. 606.
21 *Per* Sir John Wickens in *Wilson* v. *Johnstone* (1873) L.R. 6 Eq. 606 at p. 609.
22 *Bullock* v. *Crockett* (1862) 3 Giff. 507.
23 (1879) 12 Ch.D. 863.
24 As in *Astle* and *Bury*, n. 35, *supra*: *cf. Airey* v. *Borham* (1861) 29 Beav. 630.
25 (1817) 4 Pri. 161.
26 *Wilson* v. *Johnstone*, n. 36, *supra*, at p. 611.
27 (1851) 30 L.J.Ch. 857.
28 *Edmonds* v. *Robinson* (1885) 29 Ch. 170.
29 *Belfield* v. *Bourne* [1894] 1 Ch. 521.

[28] *Edmonds* v. *Robinson* (1885) 29 Ch. 170.

[29] *Belfield* v. *Bourne* [1894] 1 Ch. 521.

[30] *Seddon* v. *N.E. Salt Co.* [1905] 2 K.B. 86 (C.A.).

[31] *Law* v. *Law* [1905] 1 Ch. 140, discussed p. 106, fn. 25, *supra.*

[32] (1888) 13 App.Cas. 308.

[33] (1888) 13 App.Cas. 308 at p. 324.

[34] *Sub nom. Newbigging* v. *Adam* (1886) 34 Ch.D. 582 at p. 594.

[35] Higgins, *Law of Partnership* (*Australia and N. Zealand*), p. 214, citing *Powell* v. *Powell* (1932) 32 S.R. (N.S.W.) 407, in which s. 42 is treated as a " penalty " imposed on a wrongdoer.

[36] *Wedderburn* v. *Wedderburn* (1855–56) 22 Beav. 84 at p. 100.

[37] [1927] 1 Ch. 157 at p. 163.

[38] (1855–56) 22 Beav. 84.

[39] (1842) 1 Hare 253 at p. 272.

[40] *Wood* v. *Scoles* (1866) 1 Ch.App. 369.

[41] *Dinham* v. *Bradford* (1869) 5 Ch.App. 519 at p. 524.

[42] *Willett* v. *Blandford* (1842) 1 Hare 253.

[43] [1961] I.R. 96: distinguishing *Syers* v. *Syers* (1876) 1 App.Cas. 174.

[44] [1911] 1 Ch. 92.

[45] (1880) 13 Ch.D. 839 at p. 843, *cf. Crawshay* v. *Collins* (1826) 2 Russ. 325.

[46] *Op. cit.* p. 605.

[47] [1967] 1 A.C. 233.

[48] *Jones* v. *Foxall* (1852) 15 Beav. 388.

[49] As in *Flocton* v. *Bunning* (1868) L.R. 8 Ch. 323.

[50] (1874) L.R. 7 H.L. 318.

[51] (1860) 28 Beav. 130.

[52] (1842) 1 Hare 253.

[53] *Vyse* v. *Foster* (1874) L.R. 7 H.L. 318.

[54] (1871–72) L.R. 5 H.L. 656.

[55] *Miller* v. *Miller* (1869) L.R. 8 Eq. 499.

[56] *Barton* v. *North Staffordshire Railway Co.* (1887) 38 Ch.D. 458.

[57] [1895] 2 Ch. 474.

[58] [1961] I.R. 96.

[59] (1866) 1 Ch.App. 369.

[60] [1894] 3 Ch. 326 at p. 333.

[61] *Re Ritson* [1899] 1 Ch. 128.

[62] *Smith* v. *Mules* (1852) 9 Ha. 556.

[63] *Carlyon-Britton* v. *Lumb* (1922) 38 T.L.R. 298.

[64] *Ambler* v. *Bolton* (1871) L.R. 14 Eq. 427.

[65] (1876) 1 App.Cas. 174 at p. 181.

[66] *Cook* v. *Collingridge* (1823) Jac. 607, but for an interesting and justifiable example to the contrary, see *Syers* v. *Syers* (1876) 1 App.Cas. 174.

[67] (1869) L.R. 7 Eq. 538 at p. 541.

[68] [1904] 1 Ch. 57.

[69] [1897] A.C. 22.

[70] *Wood* v. *Scoles* (1886) 1 Ch.App. 369.

[71] See Lindley, p. 347: *Barfield* v. *Loughborough* (1872) L.R. 8 Ch. 1.

[72] [1954] 1 W.L.R. 1309.

[73] *Potter* v. *Jackson* (1880) 13 Ch.D. 845.

[74] *Ross* v. *White* [1894] 3 Ch. 326.

[75] *Austin* v. *Jackson* (1879) 11 Ch.D. 942n.

[76] *Hamer* v. *Giles* (1879) 11 Ch.D. 942.

CHAPTER SIX

PROCEDURE IN ACTIONS BY AND AGAINST PARTNERS

BECAUSE they are not covered by the Partnership Act 1890, it may be convenient to give some account of the Rules of Court governing the procedure to be followed in actions by and against partners, although such an account cannot afford more than a general outline in a work of this kind.

In the rules concerning actions (as well as those concerning proof in insolvent estates) it is necessary to bear in mind that partnership debts are normally joint, but may be joint and several if there is an express contract to this effect or in relation to the estate of a deceased partner. For wrongs other than breach of contract, namely torts, the misapplication of money or property received for or in the custody of the firm, and breaches of trust, liability is joint and several.

If liability is joint, all the partners should be sued. If they are not so sued, the defendant may have the action stayed until joinder.[1] To this rule there are exceptions,[2] of which the most important for our purposes is that objection cannot be taken to the non-joinder of an undisclosed sleeping partner.[3] In practice, however, the action on a joint obligation should always be brought against all the partners, for the very good reason that the plaintiff may find that his rights against those not sued are barred by the rule in *Kendall* v. *Hamilton*.[4] To obviate the risk that there may be undisclosed partners, the firm should always be sued in the firm-name under the appropriate Rules of Court.[5] Order 81 of the Rules of the Supreme Court 1965 is the current Order. The terms of Rule 1 are as follows:

" Actions by and against firms within jurisdiction:

1. Subject to the provisions of any enactment, any two or more persons claiming to be entitled, or alleged to be liable, as partners in respect of a cause of action and carrying on business within the jurisdiction may sue, or be sued in the name of the firm (if any) of which they were partners at the time when the cause of action accrued."

Persons carrying on business together may thereby sue or be sued in their firm-name, without the necessity of setting out the names of the individual partners. However, foreign firms cannot sue or be sued under this rule unless they carry on business within the jurisdiction, which they may do even though the partners reside outside the jurisdiction.[6] An action against the firm in the firm-name is not defective by reason of the disability of one of the partners, but judgment against a firm having a member who is a minor[7] may only issue against the firm other than the minor.[8] An action may be brought against a firm for a debt incurred on behalf of the firm during the partnership.[9]

Rule 2 of Order 81 enables a defendant being sued by a plaintiff firm to serve notice upon that firm to disclose the names and addresses of all the partners *at the time when the cause of action accrued.* This Rule applies whether or not the firm is out of the jurisdiction. If the notice is not complied with a court order may be obtained compelling disclosure or staying the action. When the names and addresses of the partners have been declared the proceedings continue in the firm-name " but with the same consequences as would have ensued if the persons whose names have been so declared had been named as plaintiffs in the writ." [10] This Rule similarly enables a plaintiff suing a defendant firm to serve notice on that firm to disclose the names and addresses of all partners at the time when the cause of action accrued. In default, an order may be obtained compelling disclosure. There is, therefore, now no excuse for a plaintiff who finds himself caught by the rule in *Kendall* v. *Hamilton.*

Rule 3 of Order 81 deals with the service of the writ. It applies only where the writ has been issued against the firm in their firm-name under Rule 1. Paragraph 1 provides that (subject to one exception) the writ may be served:

" (*a*) on any one or more of the partners, or

(*b*) at the principal place of business of the partnership within the jurisdiction, on any person having at the time of service the control or management of the partnership business there. . . ." [11]

Writs served in accordance with this rule are deemed to have been served on the firm, whether or not any partner is out of the jurisdiction.

We have already seen that foreign firms cannot be sued under Rule 1. Such firms (unless they carry on business within the jurisdiction) may only be sued by naming each partner in the writ.[12] If there is good reason for effecting service on a partner in a firm sued under Rule 1 who is out of the jurisdiction, he must be sued personally as well as under the firm's name (or alternatively all persons may be sued personally with a suffix indicating their trade name).[13] The whole rule has been characterised as " illogical " but as an example, in English law, of the sacrifice of principle to expediency.[14]

The second paragraph of Rule 3 gives the exception to the above rule and reads as follows:

" (2) Where a partnership has, to the knowledge of the plaintiff, been dissolved before an action against the firm is begun, the writ by which the action is begun must be served on every person within the jurisdiction sought to be made liable in the action " [15]

Thus, if the plaintiff has knowledge of the dissolution, an out-going partner may only be made liable for the debt, even if he was a partner when the debt was contracted, if the plaintiff serves a writ upon him.

The final paragraph of Rule 3 states that everyone upon whom a writ is served under paragraph 1 must at the same time be given a written notice stating whether he is sued as a partner or as a person having the control or management of the partnership business or as both. In fact, it is not necessary to give notice if he is served as a partner, because the Rule goes on to provide that where notice is not given he is deemed to be served as a partner.

The opening paragraph of Rule 4 reads as follows:

" Entry of appearance in an action against firm
4.—(1) Where persons are sued as partners in the name of their firm, appearance may not be entered in the name of the firm but only by the partners thereof in their own names, but the action shall nevertheless continue in the name of the firm."

Even if one of the partners sued in the firm-name dies after writ and appearance, the survivor must not put in a purely personal defence. He must defend in the name and on behalf of the firm.[16] In an action against the firm, the appearance of one of several partners is sufficient to ground proceedings under Order 14, Rule 1,[17] and service under Order 81, Rule 3, on one of two foreigners trading in partnership in England will be good.[18] A solicitor employed by the managing partner of a firm to defend an action brought against the firm has authority to enter an appearance in the names of each of the partners individually.[19]

The Rule goes on to state that if the writ was served on a person as a partner who denies that he was a partner, or liable as such at any material time, then that person may enter an appearance in the action and state that he does so as a person served as a partner in the defendant firm but who denies that he was a partner at any material time. Unless and until such an appearance is set aside it is treated as an appearance for the defendant firm. The plaintiff may apply to the court to set the appearance aside on the ground that the defendant was a partner, or liable as such at a material time, or he may leave that question to be determined later. The defendant may apply to the court to set aside the service of the writ on him on the ground that he was not a partner or liable as such at a material time. Alternatively, he may serve a defence on the plaintiff denying either his liability as a partner or the liability of the defendant firm, or both. The court itself may at any stage of the proceedings order that any question as to the liability of the defendant or the defendant firm be tried in such manner and at such times as the court directs. Where the writ was served on a person as a person having the control or management of the partnership business then that person may only enter an appearance in the action if he is a member of the firm sued.

The fifth Rule of Order 81 deals with enforcement of the judgment or order against the firm. It provides that, subject to certain exceptions, execution to enforce the order may issue against any of the firm's property within the jurisdiction and against any person who entered an appearance as a partner, or any person who admitted in his pleading or was adjudged to be a partner, or any person served as a partner who failed to enter an appearance in the action but only if there has been no dissolution or none to the knowledge of the plaintiff.[20] If the leave of the court is obtained judgment may be issued against the private property of any other person who is liable to satisfy the judgment or order as a member of the firm. The application for leave must be made by a summons served personally on that person. If he disputes his liability the court may order that the liability be tried and determined; if he does not dispute his liability the court may give leave to issue execution against him. The form of issue may be " whether the said . . . was, or had held himself out to be, a partner." [21]

Execution may not issue against a member of a firm who was out of the jurisdiction when the writ was issued unless he made an appearance as a partner, or was served with the writ as a partner either within the jurisdiction, or outside the jurisdiction with leave of the court given under Order 11. Otherwise, except in so far as the judgment is issued against the personal property of the firm, any judgment made against a firm shall not affect a member who was out of the jurisdiction when the writ was issued. Where judgment has been obtained against the firm, a bankruptcy notice cannot be issued against an individual member of it, unless execution can issue against him under this Rule.[22]

Rule 6 imposes a general restrictilon on Rule 5. It is concerned with the enforcement of a judgment or order in an action between partners. It provides that a judgment may issue only with leave of the court in:

" (a) an action by or against a firm in the name of the firm against or by a member of the firm; or

(b) an action by a firm in the name of the firm against a firm in the name of the firm where those firms have one or more members in common." [23]

When hearing an application under this Rule the Court may give such directions as may be just.

At one time it was doubtful whether the firm-name could be used in actions between a firm and any of its own members, or between firms having a member in common. R.S.C., Ord. 48A, r. 10 (now Ord. 81, r. 6) removed that doubt, although the leave of the court is required to levy execution. The rule does not authorise an action in the firm-name if the effect would be in substance, according to settled partnership law, to make a partner both plaintiff and defendant.[24]

Rule 7 provides that an order may be made, under Order 49, rule 1, in relation to debts due or accruing due from a firm carrying on business within the jurisdiction notwithstanding that one or more members of the firm is not resident within the jurisdiction. However, the order must be served on a member of the firm within the jurisdiction or on a person having the control or management of the partnership business. If the order requires the firm to appear before the court, an appearance by a member of the firm constitutes a sufficient compliance.

Rule 8 simply states that Rules 2 to 7 shall apply in relation to actions begun by originating summons as they apply in relation to actions begun by writ.

Rule 9 deals with the application of all the above rules to a person carrying on business in another name. It provides that any person who carries on business within the jurisdiction in a name or style other than his own may be sued in that name or style as if it were the name of a firm. Rules 2 to 8 apply as if he were a partner and the name in which he carries on business were the name of his firm. This Rule does not apply to a foreigner resident out of the jurisdiction.[25]

A domiciled Scot resident in Scotland is a foreigner for this purpose and must be sued in this country under Order 11.[26]

Rule 10 deals with applications for charging orders on a partner's interest in the partnership property, on which see section 23 of the Partnership Act discussed above.

[1] See third party procedure under R.S.C., Ord. 16.

[2] For details of these and generally, see Glanville L. Williams, *Joint Obligations*, Chap. 2.

[3] *De Mautort* v. *Saunders* (1830) 1 B. & Ad. 399.

[4] (1879) 4 App.Cas. 504: see p. 43, *supra*.

[5] For county courts, see County Court Rules 1936 (S.R. & O. 1936, No. 626).

[6] *Worcester City Banking Co.* v. *Firbank and Co.* [1894] 1 Q.B. 784. See r. 3 (1) for service of writ on person having control or management of the firm.

[7] See Family Law Reform Act 1969.

[8] *Lovell* v. *Beauchamp* [1894] A.C. 607.

[9] *Re Wenham* [1900] 2 Q.B. 698.

[10] r. 2 (2).

[11] r. 3 (1).

[12] See Ord. 11 on service of writ out of jurisdiction.

[13] *West of England Steamship Owners Protection and Indemnity Association* v. *John Holman and Sons* [1957] 1 W.L.R. 1164.

[14] *Ibid.*

[15] *Wigram* v. *Cox, Sons, Buckley and Co.* [1894] 1 Q.B. 793.

[16] *Ellis* v. *Wadeson* [1899] 1 Q.B. 714.

[17] *Lysaght* v. *Clark* [1891] 1 Q.B. 552 at p. 556.

[18] *Ibid.*

[19] *Tomlinson* v. *Bradsmith* [1896] 1 Q.B. 386.

[20] *Per* Cave J. in *Wigram* v. *Cox and Co.* [1894] 1 Q.B. 793 at p. 795.

[21] See *Davis* v. *Hyman and Co.* [1903] 1 K.B. 854 (C.A.).

[22] *Re Ide* (1886) 17 Q.B.D. 775.

[23] r. 6 (1).

[24] *Meyer and Co.* v. *Faber* [1923] 2 Ch. 421. For county courts, see County Court Rules 1936, Ord. 25.

[25] *De Bernales* v. *New York Herald* [1893] 2 Q.B. 97n; *cf. St. Gobain* v. *Hoyermann's Agency* [1893] 2 Q.B. 96 (C.A.).

[26] *MacIver* v. *Burns* [1895] 2 Ch. 630.

CHAPTER SEVEN

BANKRUPTCY AND ADMINISTRATION OF PARTNERSHIP ESTATES

I. PROCEDURE IN BANKRUPTCY AGAINST PARTNERS

Adjudication and process in bankruptcy

In bankruptcy two separate cases have to be considered. One partner may be made bankrupt in respect of his separate debts, his co-partners remaining fully solvent. In such a case the partnership creditors are legally entitled to prove in his bankruptcy, but normally will not have to do so, since the solvent partners will pay them off and then themselves prove for a contribution. The only effect on the partnership is that it is dissolved in accordance with section 33, *supra*. Alternatively, bankruptcy proceedings may be taken in respect of a firm debt, and it is principally this type of case which is dealt with in what follows. Normally all the partners will then be made bankrupt and section 119 of the Bankruptcy Act 1914 provides that bankruptcy proceedings up to actual adjudication may be taken against the firm in the firm-name. But an order of adjudication cannot be made against the firm in the firm-name. Rule 288 of the Bankruptcy Rules 1952 states that it must be made against the partners individually. Their personal liability to such proceedings cannot be enlarged by previous action against the firm. If one of the partners is a minor, a receiving order cannot be made against the firm in respect of a debt for which that minor would not be liable; but it may be made against the firm " other than " the minor.[1] The same rule would seem to hold as to judgments against a firm. But if the obligation is one for which the minor is liable (*e.g.* in respect of a tort or taxation) judgment may be recovered against the whole firm, including the minor, and all of them may be adjudicated bankrupt.[2]

Procedure

The following provisions, dealing with procedure, are found in sections 110 to 119 of the Bankruptcy Act 1914.

Where two or more petitions are presented against the same debtor or joint debtors the court may consolidate all or any of the proceedings as it thinks fit.[3] A creditor who is entitled to present a bankruptcy petition against all the partners may present it against any one or more. Indeed, if there are more respondents than one, the court may dismiss the petition as to some only of them, without affecting the position of the remainder. If a receiving order has been made on a bankruptcy petition by or against one member of a partnership, any other bankruptcy petition by or against a member of the same partnership must be filed in or transferred to the same court. Furthermore, the same trustee will be appointed in respect of all the partners and the court may give directions for consolidating the proceedings. There is jurisdiction to consolidate proceedings under separate receiving orders even if they are made after a dissolution.[4] Where a trustee of the joint estate is appointed, the separate estates also vest in him at once.[5] Rule 13 of Schedule 1 to the Bankruptcy Act 1914 provides that if a receiving order is made against one partner any creditor to whom that partner is indebted jointly with any of the other partners may prove in a separate bankruptcy for the purpose of voting at a creditors' meeting.[6]

If a creditor is indebted jointly to a bankrupt partner and any other partners of the firm, then section 63 of the Bankruptcy Act 1914 provides that he cannot receive a dividend out of the separate property of the bankrupt until all separate creditors have received the full amount of their respective debts. It goes on to state that if joint and separate properties are being administered, the dividends on both are to be declared together and the expenses of and incident to such dividends are to be fairly apportioned between the joint and separate properties. However, the Board of Trade may direct otherwise on the application of any person interested.[7] If a member of a partnership is adjudged bankrupt the trustee may, with court authorisation, commence and prosecute any action in the names of the trustee and of the bankrupt's partner. A release by the solvent partner of the debt or demand to which the action relates is void. However, he may show cause against the application for authority whereupon the court may direct that he shall receive his proper share of the proceeds of the action. The partners may take proceedings, or be proceeded against in the firm-name, but the court may, on application by any person interested, order the names of the partners to be disclosed. This procedure is applicable after dissolution, if founded on a judgment in an action for a partnership debt incurred before dissolution.[8]

II. ADMINISTRATION OF PARTNERSHIP ESTATES
General rule of administration as to joint and separate estate

(1) In the administration by the High Court of Justice of the estate of deceased partners and of bankrupt and insolvent partners, the following rules are observed, subject to certain exceptions, discussed below:

(a) The partnership property is applied as *joint estate* in payment of the debts of the firm, and the separate property of each partner is applied as *separate estate* in payment of his separate debts.

(b) After such payment the surplus, if any, of the joint estate is applied in payment of the separate debts of the partners, or the surplus, if any, of the separate estate is applied in payment of the debts of the firm.

This rule, established since 1770, has been sanctified by statute, currently section 33 (*b*) of the Bankruptcy Act 1914. In fact, because of section 34 of and paragraph 2 of Schedule 1 to the Administration of Estates Act 1925, the rule is also applicable to the administration of the estates of deceased persons.

Because a partnership is not a legal entity separate and distinct from those who compose it, there is no point in segregating joint estate and separate estate on the one hand and joint creditors and separate creditors on the other where the partners are solvent; all will be paid. Thus, in *Ridgway* v. *Clare*,[9] A, who had been in partnership with B, died and his estate was administered by the court, both A's estate and B being solvent. It was held that no distinction need be made between A's joint and separate creditors inasmuch as all might come in *pari passu* and claim their debts on his estate, although, of course, payments thus made to creditors of the firm must then be allowed by B in account with A's estate as payment made on behalf of the firm, and A's estate would accordingly be credited when it came to ascertaining his share of the partnership property. If, in the example just given, it were shown that A's estate was insolvent, and that the creditors had not unnaturally gone against the solvent partner for their debts, B would then rank as a creditor of A's separate estate for the amount of the partnership debts paid by him beyond the proportion which he ought to have paid under the partnership contract. If, to utilise the example further, A's estate and B are both insolvent, different considerations obtain for the simple reason that where there is an insufficiency of assets it becomes a matter of importance to determine how the rights of creditors are to be regulated.

Joint estate

Unlike the Indian Partnership Act, which refers to " the property of the firm," the present subsection uses the rather more obscure expression " joint estate." We have already seen that partners may own property jointly without such property ranking as partnership property (*supra*, pp. 12 and 78). Nevertheless, it is safe to assume that such property would for present purposes be available only for separate debts and not partnership debts, *i.e.* " joint estate " can be taken as " joint *partnership* estate." Property, once stamped as partnership property or separate property does not necessarily retain that stamp immutably; partners may agree that what has been joint estate shall henceforth belong to one or more of the partners whilst, conversely, separate property may be brought into the partnership pool. If completed in good faith such dispositions cannot be overturned at the suit of creditors who claim a lien on the property affected.[10]

The same effect may result from the partnership articles as in *Re Simpson*[11]—" a peculiar case " according to Pollock, where A, B, C and D had been partners for a term under articles which provided that the death of any one of them should not dissolve the partnership, but that the survivors or survivor should carry on the business and the share of the deceased partner should be ascertained and paid out on terms set out therein. A and B died during the term, and afterwards C and D became liquidating debtors. It was held that the whole interest in the assets passed immediately on the death of one partner to the survivors so that the creditors of A, B, C and D, had no right to have the property of that firm, so far as still found existing in the hands of C and D, applied in payment of their debts in preference to the creditors of the new firm of C and D. But the joint assets were held not to have been converted in *Ex p. Morley*,[12] where a provision in the articles that on the death of one of the partners the other's share of profits should belong to the deceased's representative on agreed compensation terms was held not to work a conversion of partnership property into the separate property of A, with the consequence that the partnership property still found in the hands of A's representative at the time of a subsequent liquidation was held to be applicable in the first place to the creditors of the firm.

It may also be noted here that, by section 38 of the Bankruptcy

Act 1914, goods not belonging to the partnership may nevertheless go to swell the assets of the insolvent partners in the event of bankruptcy, if such goods are at the commencement of the bankruptcy in the possession, order or disposition of the bankrupt in his trade or business by the consent and permission of the true owner, under such circumstances that he is the reputed owner thereof. In *Ex p. Hare* [13] it was held (and cases of this must be not uncommon) that a partner who had permitted his own furniture to be used in the partnership business could not reclaim the furniture from the assets available for creditors. However, this reputed ownership section does not operate if the goods are in the joint possession of partners, one or some only of whom are adjudicated bankrupt. [14] Furthermore, a new section 38A, added by the Consumer Credit Act 1974, [15] will have the consequence, when it is brought into force, that goods subject to certain credit agreements, including hire-purchase agreements, are not treated as the property of the bankrupt until the default notice has expired or been complied with. Those whose goods are made available for creditors under the reputed ownership section can, of course, prove for their value in the bankruptcy. [16]

Section 33 (*b*) has not abrogated the power of the court to consolidate joint and separate estates if they are " inextricably blended " [17] nor does it prevent the joint and separate creditors from agreeing that the two funds shall be treated as one.

Rationale of the rule

Although the rule has been characterised as a sort of rough code of justice, it is clear that it has been chosen empirically on the ground of administrative convenience. In *Read* v. *Bailey*, [18] Lord Blackburn would not commit himself to any endorsement of the rightness of the rule. Indeed the rule itself has been criticised for producing results which are at variance with the doctrine of equality. Partners may as such incur huge liabilities yet own little partnership property, whilst at the same time they may own considerable personal estate, with the possible result that their separate creditors are paid in full whereas their joint creditors receive hardly anything. Turner L.J. justified the rule on the grounds of convenience, but he thought it unfair if joint creditors were let in on both funds. [19]

Exceptional rights of proof in certain cases—when creditors of firm may prove against separate estate

(2) (a) A creditor of the firm may nevertheless (it seems)

prove his debts in the first instance against the separate estate of
a partner *pari passu* with the separate creditors if there is no
joint estate.

The old authorities permitted joint creditors to prove in the first
instance against a partner's separate estate if there was no joint
estate, an exception which might produce capricious results in that
the existence of *some* joint estate, however small in value (such as
office furniture worth a few shillings) sufficed to exclude the exception. Be that as it may, arguments based upon the tacit abrogation
of the exception by section 40 of the Bankruptcy Act 1883 (re-enacted
in s. 33 of the 1914 Act), which makes no mention of it, were dismissed for the reason that such a long-established exception could
not be treated as altered by a mere negative implication. Accordingly,
the exception continues in force.[20]

The exception applies mainly to the bankrupt firm without property but also applies to the case of a firm in which the only solvent
partner is abroad, or in which the only solvent estate is that of a
deceased partner.

(b) Where the liability is joint and several, then:

> (i) If it arises out of contract, the creditor may prove
> against the joint and separate estates;
>
> (ii) If it does not arise out of contract, but is nevertheless
> a provable debt, the creditor must elect whether he will
> proceed as a creditor of the firm or as a separate creditor
> of the partners.

(i) This part of the exception is based upon rule 19 of Schedule 2
to the Bankruptcy Act 1914, which reads as follows:

> " If a debtor was, at the date of the receiving order, liable in
> respect of distinct contracts as a member of two or more distinct
> firms, or as a sole contractor, and also as member of a firm, the
> circumstances that the firms are in whole or in part composed of
> the same individuals, or that the sole contractor is also one of
> the joint contractors, shall not prevent proof in respect of the
> contracts, against the properties respectively liable on the con-
> tracts."

The separate contracts may be contained in the same instrument
as in *Ex p. Honey* where a single promissory note had been signed,
inter alia, by firm A and Co. (comprising A and B) and by A and B
separately. Sir G. Mellish L.J. considered that " a joint and several
promissory note, though it is one instrument, contains both a joint

contract and distinct separate contracts by the several makers." [21]
Nor need it appear overtly from the contract that partners are
signing as such in respect of a debt due from the firm when they
covenant jointly and severally to pay the debt; external evidence may
be led to show that the joint contract of A and B is in fact the
contract of their firm, the joint estate of which is, in addition to the
separate estates of A and B, available in connection with the debt
thus arising.[22] If an express trustee joins with other members of his
firm in misapplying the trust funds, such as those handed to the
firm for investment, double proof under rule 19 of Schedule 2
(*supra*) is possible because two liabilities have arisen, *viz.* (a) the
joint liability of the firm in respect of its contract to invest the funds
or, failing investment, to restore them, and (b) the distinct liability
of the trustee for the breach of trust committed by him. In *Re
Parkers*, where the above facts occurred, Cave J. pointed out that
" The liability of a trustee in respect of a breach of trust was always
provable in bankruptcy, . . . as a liability arising from a contract to
perform his trust and not from mere tort." [23]

(ii) The second part of the exception is limited in its application.
Although, by section 30 (1) of the Bankruptcy Act 1914, demands in
the nature of unliquidated damages arising otherwise than by reason
of a contract, promise, or breach of trust are not provable in bankruptcy, the courts have given a liberal interpretation to rule 19 of
Schedule 2, as is shown by their acceptance of claims arising by reason
of fraud or breach of trust, subject to the requirement that persons
submitting a proof for these reasons must elect between proceeding
against the joint or the separate estates. Thus, a person induced to
accept bills of exchange by the fraud of partners who have gone
bankrupt may prove at his election against the joint estate or the
separate estate of the partner; such proof is not for fraud or tort but
rather for " an equitable debt or liability in the nature of a debt."
In the case furnishing the facts just given,[24] James L.J. adverted to
the " slight inaccuracy " involved in the statement that fraud and
breach of trust give rise to joint and several liability where the joint
liability arises because the fraud (*and the same applies to the breach
of trust*) is connected with a partnership, illustrating his point with
the example of a partnership of A, B, C and D, in which A and B
perpetrate a fraud on a customer in a partnership matter; in such a
case A and B would be severally liable and the joint estate would be
liable to make restitution, but the separate estates of C and D would

be free of liability.[25] This point cannot be taken as settled since it was expressly left open by the Court of Appeal in the later case of *Ex p. Salting* [26] (which makes no reference to *Re Adamson*). Like fraud, a breach of trust, subject to the qualification just mentioned, gives rise to a joint and several liability between which the *cestui que trust* must make his choice. In *Re Kent County Gas Light and Coke Co.*[27] it was held that a company liquidator who had proved for damages against one of two partners in a firm which had, in breach of a promoter's fiduciary duty, sold property to the company at a large secret profit, could not proceed against the firm on the ground that only one breach of contract had been shown, namely, the making of the secret profit, so that rule 18 of Schedule 2 to the Bankruptcy Act 1883 (now rule 19 of Schedule 2 to the 1914 Act) was inapplicable.

It will be recalled that quite apart from the case of bankruptcy a partnership creditor is entitled to a remedy against the estate of a deceased partner concurrently with his right of action against any surviving partner, but subject to the prior claims of the deceased partner's separate creditors; and that it is immaterial in what order these remedies are pursued if the substantial conditions of not competing with separate creditor, and of the surviving partner being before the court, are satisfied in the proceedings against the deceased partner's estate.

Rule against proof by partners in competition with creditors

> (3) Where the joint estate of a firm or the separate estate of any partner is being administered, no partner in the firm may prove in competition with the creditors of the firm either against the joint estate of the firm or against the separate estate of any other partner until all the debts of the firm have been paid.[28]

The basis of this rule is put by Lord Eldon in *Ex p. Sillitoe* [29] as follows: " A partner in a firm against which a commission of bankruptcy issues shall not prove in competition with the creditors and shall not take part of the fund to the prejudice of those who are not only creditors of the partnership but of himself." The rule applies to the personal representative of a deceased partner who, at his death, was a co-debtor for the debts of the firm and a creditor for his share of assets therein. It is otherwise if partnership debts have been paid during the deceased partner's lifetime, unless his share of capital was to remain in the business, in which event his estate " would stand in the position of a partner and be liable for debts." The rule encompasses a person who, not being in fact a partner, has by " holding out " become liable as a partner to the creditors of the firm, but does not cover someone who has become liable in this way to some only of the creditors.

The rule loses its *raison d'être* if no case of competition with joint creditors arises, as where a solvent partner has paid off all the joint creditors, in which event he becomes entitled to prove in respect of his claim for contribution *pari passu* with his co-partner's separate creditors.[30] Again, if on a dissolution of partnership between A and B, B transfers his interest in the partnership to A in return for a bond of £10,000 with interest, and A subsequently becomes bankrupt, B's trustees (to whom he has assigned his separate property for the benefit of the creditors of the firm) cannot prove the bond debt against A's estate until either all the debts of the firm have been paid, or until such time as all the creditors of the firm have accepted the assignment of B's property in settlement of their debts and as a release of the joint liability of A and B.[31]

If the separate estate of the co-partner is insolvent, so that the joint creditors cannot resort to it under rule 1, above, a partner may prove against such co-partner's estate. *Ex p. Topping* [32] was a case in which A and B had been partners in a partnership which had become bankrupt after A had become indebted to B upon a contract independent of the partnership. It was held that B might prove his debt in A's separate estate for the reason that in so doing he did not come into competition with the creditors of the firm in view of the known fact that there was no surplus on A's estate after the satisfaction of his separate creditors, whether or not B's debt was taken into account. It is no objection to such proof to say that the dividend received by B will go to swell the surplus available to pay the joint debts of the partnership; the fact is that by the time the dividend has reached the joint creditors it has ceased to be the separate estate of the partner from whose estate it is paid.

There is a line of cases, of which *Ex p. Grazebrook* [33] is not untypical, in which a partner has been allowed to prove in respect of a *separate* debt. There B took over the business of a firm by agreement with his co-partner, A (who had been a dormant partner) and an account stated was agreed between the two showing a balance due to A. B was thenceforth treated as sole debtor by the firm's creditors. A signed judgment for his debt in an undefended action against B. It was held that A might prove in B's bankruptcy because the partnership debts had been converted into the separate debts of B, whose debt on the account stated was a purely separate debt.

It is, perhaps, opportune to recall at this stage the rule in *Garner* v. *Murray* (p. 156, *supra*) under which the contribution to loss of capital which an insolvent partner should make is ignored in ascribing responsibility for loss and in distributing the assets under section 44 of the 1890 Act. Nevertheless, the fact remains that the solvent partners have borne more than their share of the loss and this entitles them, in the event of the bankruptcy of the insolvent partner, to prove for the extra loss in the latter's estate.

Exceptions in special circumstances

Partners may nevertheless prove against the joint estate of the firm, or the separate estate of a partner, as the case may be, for debts which have arisen under any of the following states of fact:

(a)   where two firms having one or more members in common, or a firm and one of its members, have carried on business in separate and distinct trades and dealt with one another therein, and one firm or trader has become a creditor of the other in the ordinary way of such dealing.

In the words of the ubiquitous Lord Eldon: " Another relaxation of the rule was therefore admitted, that where there is a demand arising from a dealing by the partnership in a distinct trade, proof might be admitted; but then the question, what is a dealing in a distinct trade, is always to be looked at with great care." In *Ex p. Sillitoe*,[34] from which this dictum is taken, two of the partners in a banking firm indorsed bills remitted to them in the name of an ironmongers' firm of which they were the members, thus enabling the bills to be discounted on the credit of the indorsements. It was held that the two partners could not, on the bankruptcy of the banking firm, prove against its assets in respect of these transactions which had not been conducted in the course of a separate trade but which were only " for the convenience of the general partnership." [35] Nor would it have made any difference if the ironmongers' firm had been, instead, another firm of bankers. The two requirements, *viz.* (i) separate firms, and (ii) dealings in the ordinary course of business, were both fulfilled in *Ex p. Castell*,[36] in which a banking partnership at York (consisting of A, B, C, D and E) which had become bankrupt was allowed to prove in the bankruptcy of another banking firm in Wakefield (consisting of A, B, C and D, and, therefore, necessarily bankrupt). Doubts whether or not the smaller firm whose membership is contained in the large firm can prove in the latter's bankruptcy were resolved by *Ex p. Cook* [37] which held that it can.

> (b) where the separate property of a partner has been fraudulently converted to the use of the firm, or property of the firm has been fraudulently converted to the use of any partner, without the consent or subsequent ratification of the partner or partners not concerned in such conversion.

After a period of some doubt, it is clear that an exceptional right of proof exists in those cases where there has been fraudulent conversion of partnership property to the use of one or more partners [38] (and vice versa), although it must be added that the limits of the right of proof under this head cannot be stated with complete exactitude. Fortunately the lucid judgment of Jessel M.R. in *Lacey* v. *Hill*,[39] affirmed in the House of Lords *sub nom. Read* v. *Bailey*,[40] has done much to clear the air. Using this case as our lodestone, the following main points emerge.

Fraud

In *Lacey*, K, a country gentleman, had entered into a banking partnership in which H was the managing partner. Despite articles of partnership which forbade overdrawings by partners, H withdrew very large sums from the funds of the bank with which he gambled on the Stock Exchange, using fictitious credits and forged acceptances to conceal his malversation, of which K was unaware. The unhappy sequel was that H, to use Jessel M.R.'s phrase, " withdrew himself from earthly justice " by the expedient of committing suicide leaving the bank insolvent. K was adjudicated bankrupt. Holding that K could prove in H's estate for the partnership moneys which had been misappropriated, the Master of the Rolls allowed the proof because of H's conduct which he could only describe as "simple stealing " adding, however, that it would not always be necessary to put the case so high.[41] It suffices if the conversion was for private purposes and done without the knowledge, consent, privity or subsequent approbation of the other partners. The cases which have caused difficulty, such as *Ex p. Harris*,[42] can perhaps be explained on the footing that in those cases what took place was an abuse of authority rather than a fraud. In the last-named case, which concerned a bankrupt partnership, it was held that the trustees of the joint estate could not prove in the estate of the active partner who had, in breach of the articles of partnership, overdrawn partnership moneys for his own use. The partnership fund had been confided to the active partner into whose private account the moneys were paid. Lord Blackburn dealt with the case in *Read* v. *Bailey*,[43] saying: " I recollect that in that case the dormant partner had, by deed, given the acting partner who carried on the business the amplest authority to invest the money in any way he pleased, and he pleased to invest it by lending to himself, to pay his private debts. That was a very wrong thing indeed; it was, as Lord Eldon afterwards expressed it, an abuse of his authority—a most improper use of his authority— but he did act upon the authority." Lord Cairns L.C. in the same case, drew a distinction between fraud and some mere excess in degree in connection with some act authorised in kind, giving the example of an overdraft entered into the books without concealment.[44]

Consent or ratification

In addition to express consent or ratification of a partner's " fraud," it would seem that consent or ratification may be implied from conduct. Nevertheless, despite certain dicta [45] indicating an application of the doctrine of constructive notice in the present context, it seems to be reasonably clear that *Lacey* has administered the quietus to this notion; a real consent or acquiesence is needed and not merely the existence of facts unknown to the other partner. It is necessary to make out knowledge on the part of the non-fraudulent partner and then to show that he stood by and allowed the fraudulent state of affairs to continue without remonstrance. Even if the firm's clerks in *Lacey* had some inkling of what was going on, the court would not affix their suspicions upon the inactive partner; a clerk or employee may be the agent of the firm to receive information from a person outside the partnership; he is indubitably not an agent for the purposes of constructive notice *quoad* the partners *inter se*.

No estoppel by negligence

Neither can the result aimed at by the theory of constructive notice be obtained by putting it on the ground of estoppel by negligence, any more than the pickpocket can complain that the person whose pocket he has just picked ought to have kept it buttoned up. It is true, as we have already seen, that Lord Cairns L.C. considered that an excessive overdrawing entered openly in the books would be a different thing, but this would only go to prove that the conduct of the partner overdrawing his account was not fraudulent; it would not go to support the application of the doctrine of constructive notice in relation to the fraud under discussion.

Enlargement of separate fund available to creditors need not be shown

The argument that it must be shown that the separate estate (*i.e.* the fund available for separate creditors) has been enriched by the sums misappropriated found no favour with the court. The exception allowing proof applies indifferently to cases in which the separate estate has been enlarged by the fraud and to cases in which no such result has ensued as where the money has been dissipated. It may be mentioned here that the court rejected the argument that a partner drawing out partnership funds for his own use might be deemed to draw on his own capital in the partnership. Partnership capital is joint capital during the subsistence of the partnership and neither partner can point to " mine " and " thine," [46] for which reason *Clayton's* case was inapplicable.

Tracing

Finally, it should be observed that the ambit of the exception concerning fraud is restricted by the device of " tracing." In *Lacey*, the decision was rested on the misapplication of partnership property in some way rendering such property untraceable. The doctrine of proof presumes that the property cannot be identified and taken back and hence can only be the subject of proof. In the light of the clarification of the rules relating to tracing in decisions such as *Re Diplock* [47] (discussed in connection with s. 13, p. 58, fn. 14, *supra*), a claim *in rem* for the recovery of misappropriated partnership property will often be the proper remedy.

Rights of joint creditors holding separate security, or conversely

(4) Any creditor of a firm holding a security for his debt upon separate property of any partner may prove against the joint estate of the firm, and any separate creditor of a partner holding a security for his debt upon the property of the firm may prove against that partner's separate estate, without giving up his security: provided that the creditor shall in no case receive in the whole more than the full amount of his debt.

In bankruptcy law, a secured creditor may do one of several things. (a) He may rest content with his security. (b) He may realise his security and, if necessary, prove for any balance. (c) He may make a philanthropic gesture by surrendering his security for the benefit of the bankrupt's creditors and join them in proving for a dividend. (d) He may prove for the debt, less the sum at which he values his security. What he *cannot* do is keep his security to himself and put in a proof for his whole debt.

To the general position outlined above there is one clearly established exception and that concerns the creditor who holds a security over the property of a third person. It is in this connection that the distinction between " joint estate " and " separate estate " becomes one of more than purely formal importance, for it has been decided that a joint creditor holding a security over the joint estate may prove in the separate estate without giving up his security, provided of course that in either case he receives no more than a hundred pence in the pound.[48] In such a situation it cannot be a matter of complaint that a creditor should secure himself *aliunde* and yet come in to share *pari passu* with other creditors.[49] The distinctions between joint and separate estates may not always be easy. One example of the " blurring " of estates occurred in *Ex p. Turney*.[50] There, A was in partnership with his son B, both executing a joint and several bond in favour of C, a creditor of the partnership, to whom A also gave an equitable mortgage over his separate property. The partnership was later dissolved, following which A died intestate and B became bankrupt. Holding that C might prove his debt in B's bankruptcy without surrendering his security, the court realised that the mortgaged estate descended to the son, B, but also took into account the circumstance that such descent would only occur subject to the father's debts, and since these exceeded his assets, quite apart from the mortgage debt, the son could have no beneficial interest in the mortgaged estate, for which reason it was untrue to say that C's security lay over B's estate.

Another example is provided by *Ex p. Manchester and County Bank*,[51] where it was held that an incorporated bank could not prove against the joint estate of partners A and B in respect of a joint debt, whilst treating as quite separate shares in the bank held by A, over which the bank had a lien. In fact A's shares in the bank were partnership property, although this was unknown to the bank. The result was that the bank could not say that it was a case of a joint debt and a security on the separate estate of one partner; it was a case of a joint debt and, *de facto*, a joint security against the same persons.

However, a creditor holding a security which he can apply to one or other of two debts can exercise that right in any way he thinks fit, as for example where a bank having the accounts of a firm and one of the partners therein, takes a security from the latter to secure any balance which may become due not only from him but also from his firm.

Effect of separate discharge of partner

(5) Where the discharge of any member of a partnership firm is granted to him in his separate bankruptcy, he is thereby released from the debts of the firm as well as from his separate debts.

---

[1] *Lovell* v. *Beauchamp* [1894] A.C. 607.
[2] *Re a Debtor (No. 564 of* 1949) [1950] Ch. 282 (C.A.).
[3] See *Ex p. Mackenzie* (1875) L.R. 20 Eq. 758.
[4] *Re Abbot* [1894] 1 Q.B. 442.
[5] *Ex p. Philps* (1874) L.R. 19 Eq. 256.
[6] As to the distribution of the estates see further, p. 164 *et seq., infra*
[7] See *Ex p. Dickin* (1875) L.R. 20 Eq. 767.
[8] *Re Wenham* [1900] 2 Q.B. 698 (C.A.). See on Ord. 81, r. 1, *supra*.
[9] (1854) 19 Beav. 111.
[10] *Ex p. Ruffin* (1801) 6 Ves. 119.
[11] (1874) L.R. 9 Ch. 572.
[12] (1873) L.R. 8 Ch. 1026.
[13] (1835) 1 Deac. 16.
[14] *Ex p. Dorman* (1872) L.R. 8 Ch.D. 51.
[15] s. 192 (3) (*a*) and Sched. 4, para. 6.
[16] *Re Button* [1907] 2 K.B. 180.
[17] *Ex p. Trotman* (1893) 68 L.T. 588.
[18] (1877) 3 App.Cas. 94 at p. 102.
[19] *Lodge* v. *Pritchard* (1863) 1 De G.J. & S. 610, at pp. 613–614.
[20] *Re Budgett, Cooper* v. *Adams* [1894] 2 Ch. 555.
[21] (1871) L.R. 7 Ch. 178 at p. 183.
[22] *Ex p. Stone* (1873) L.R. 8 Ch. 914.
[23] (1887) 19 Q.B.D. 84 at p. 87.
[24] *Ex p. Adamson* (1878) 8 Ch.D. 807 at p. 820.
[25] *Ibid.*
[26] (1883) 25 Ch.D. 148.
[27] [1913] 1 Ch. 92.
[28] For the postponement of lender to the partnership and seller of goodwill see s. 3 of 1890 Act (preserved by Bankruptcy Act 1914, s. 33 (9); also Bankruptcy Act 1914, s. 36 (postponement of husband's and wife's claim) and the rule in *Re Meade* [1951] Ch. 774 concerning postponement of creditors, sometimes termed " quasi-partners," who provide capital for a business in which they have a direct interest and which is carried on for their joint benefit.
[29] (1824) 1 Gl. & J. 382.

[30] See *Ex p. Yonge* (1814) 3 V. & B. 31; 2 Rose 40.

[31] *Ex p. Collinge* (1863) 4 De G.J. & Sm. 533.

[32] (1865) 4 De G.J. & Sm. 551.

[33] (1832) 2 D. & Ch. 186; *Ex p. Atkins* (1820) Buck 479.

[34] (1824) 1 Gl. & J. 382.

[35] *Ibid.*

[36] (1826) 2 Gl. & J. 124.

[37] (1831) Mont. 228.

[38] *Ex p. Yonge* (1814) 3 V. & B. 31; 2 Rose 40.

[39] (1876) 4 Ch.D. 537.

[40] (1877) 3 App.Cas. 94.

[41] (1876) 4 Ch.D. 537 at p. 543.

[42] (1813) 2 V. & B. 210.

[43] (1877) 3 App.Cas. 94 at p. 103.

[44] *Ibid.* at pp. 98–99.

[45] Lord Eldon in *Ex p. Yonge* (1814) 3 V. & B. 31 at p. 36: Knight Bruce V.-C. in *Ex p. Hinds* (1849) 3 De G. & Sm. 613 at pp. 616–617.

[46] See n. 39 at p. 546.

[47] [1948] Ch. 465 (C.A.) affirmed *sub. nom. Ministry of Health* v. *Simpson* [1951] A.C. 251.

[48] *Re Plummer* (1841) 1 Ph. 56 at p. 59, *per* Lord Chancellor Lyndhurst.

[49] *Rolfe* v. *Flower, Salting and Co.* (1865) L.R. 1 P.C. 27.

[50] (1844) 3 M. & D. 576.

[51] (1876) 3 Ch.D. 481.

CHAPTER EIGHT

TAXATION OF PARTNERSHIPS

SINCE 1860, when Nathaniel Lindley (later Lord Lindley) produced his work on the Law of Partnership, taxation of income and, more recently, taxation of capital, have increasingly demanded attention in the treatment of business associations. The State is no longer satisfied with a small share of the income and capital of its citizens and pre-empts a proportion of both which would have surprised Lord Lindley.

In this Chapter, the following topics are discussed:

I. Partnership versus Company—the tax aspects

II. Taxation of Partnership Profits

III. Capital Gains Tax

IV. Capital Transfer Tax

I. PARTNERSHIP VERSUS COMPANY—THE TAX ASPECTS

Income tax versus corporation tax

For those with freedom of choice one of the most important considerations influencing the choice of a legal vehicle for business is the burden of taxation as between the partnership and the company. Although the taxation of partnership profits is discussed in some detail below, it may be useful to set out here some of the main attributes of the personal income régime to which partnerships are subject in contrast to the régime of corporation tax which affects companies, a contrast on which the worked examples at the end of this section may provide some guidance.

The easiest, but by no means safest, comparison is that between the rate of income tax and the rate of corporation tax. Because the respective rates of these taxes are subject to alteration, it is impossible to make a once-and-for-all judgment as to the relationship between the two. In 1976, income tax was charged at the basic rate of 35 per cent. on taxable income of £5,000 or less, a rate of tax which increases in progressive bands until it reaches 83 per cent. on taxable incomes over £20,000 (the higher rates of income tax replacing the old surtax rates and the rates for unearned income). An additional rate of tax is levied on investment income exceeding a certain figure, *viz.* 10 per cent. on investment income over £1,000, and 15 per cent. on such income over £2,000, which would bring the highest marginal rate of income tax to 98 per cent. Clearly the investment income surcharge will not be popular with the " sleeping partner " who receives a share of profits, or with the retired partner who receives a share of profits, unless by means of a properly-drawn consultancy agreement he can demonstrate services in consideration for his share of profits or salary.

Companies, for their part, are regulated by a separate system of corporation tax introduced in 1965. A company's profits, whether distributed or not, are subject to corporation tax at rates which have increased since 1965 (the rate for 1976 was 52 per cent.). Prior to the changes wrought by the Finance Act 1972, the Revenue had in effect " two bites at the apple," namely, corporation tax on the company's profits and income tax at the standard rate deducted from distributions and accounted for to the Revenue, a system which was said to encourage profit-retention policies on the part of companies.

A new system of " imputation " was introduced by the Finance Act 1972, avowedly upon a " neutral " principle with regard to company profits irrespective of whether or not those profits are distributed. Under this new system, a company is charged corporation tax on its profits (as before), but instead of deducting income tax on a distribution of profits, it is required to make an advance payment of corporation tax (ACT) at a certain rate (35/65ths of the value of the distribution for the financial year). ACT payments in respect of dividends and other qualifying distributions go to reduce the amount of corporation tax payable for the financial year in question and, furthermore, also go to satisfy the basic rate income tax liability of the person receiving the qualifying distribution. In other words, ACT is " imputed " to the shareholder to the extent of his basic rate tax liability, if any.

Small companies pay corporation tax at a lower rate (42 per cent. since 1973). A small company is defined as a company with taxable profits (including chargeable capital gains) not exceeding a certain maximum amount over an accounting period (the maximum for 1976 was £30,000) with tapering arrangements up to a further amount (£50,000 in 1976) beyond which the full rate of corporation tax is payable. It will be seen that the " small companies' rate " affords a substantial tax concession to small companies, particularly in view of a definition which defines the small company not by reference to its profits but its *taxable* profits.

The so-called " neutrality " of the law as between distributed and retained profits is abandoned when one comes to the " close " company, a company with a complex definition and subject to complex tax regulation. Broadly speaking a " close company " is a company resident in the United Kingdom and under the control (a term of wide import) of five or fewer " participators " or of participators (irrespective of number) who are directors. In practice, the close company is usually a private company of the family type. We have seen that distributions of profits, whilst they will involve a tax credit at the basic rate by virtue of the imputation system, will not confer tax credits in respect of higher rate income tax and, because the distribution does not rank as earned income in the hands of the recipient, will attract the investment income surcharge. Those who control a company might therefore be tempted to minimise income tax liability by ploughing back profits rather than distributing them as dividends and, wherever possible, striving to receive income from the company as earned income rather than investment income. The tax treatment of the " close company " places obstacles in the way of those who control such a company and who might be tempted to succumb to that temptation.

To deal with a situation in which income tax liability might be minimised by the retention of profits in the company, the " relevant income " of the company for any accounting period may be apportioned by the Revenue amongst the participators who are then treated as having received the apportioned income and thereby liable to higher rate income tax and investment income surcharge where applicable. The discretion given to the Revenue is not uncontrolled. Apart from the definition of the " close company," the following points may be noted.

First, it is only the " relevant income " of the company which may be apportioned, and this is defined in relation to a trading company as " so much of its distributable income . . . as can be distributed without prejudice to the requirements of the company's business " (see Finance Act 1972, Sched. 16, para. 8, as amended, with respect to non-trading companies having estate or trading income, and other companies). Justification for retaining income extends not only to income retained for current requirements of the company's business, but also for such other requirements as may be necessary or advisable for the maintenance and development of that business.

Secondly, subject to certain exceptions, the relevant income must not be taken to exceed the company's distributable investment income for the accounting period plus 50 per cent. of the estate or trading income for that period. This means that a company may retain 50 per cent. of its trading income without apportionment and may retain more than 50 per cent. where this can be justified by the requirements of the business as described above. Trading companies with small estate or trading incomes over an accounting period are given the further advantage that their relevant income is treated as nil, or reduced, according to their amount (nil, if less than £5,000, with tapering provisions between £5,000 and £15,000, as the position stood in 1976).

Certain other factors need to be taken into account in evaluating the tax position of the partnership and the company.

It is broadly true to say that the personal nature of the income tax system enables it to reflect the composition of the partnership and the tax attributes of its members. The tax liability of a partner will depend upon the number of partners and will take account of personal allowances and reliefs to which he may be entitled (with the possibility that it may be possible to introduce a wife as partner who, if she takes an active part in the business, may elect for separate taxation of her earned income). Thus, the total tax liability of a partnership rests on " personal " factors in contrast to the " impersonal " nature of company taxation. Corporation tax is payable on the profits of a company as a legal entity without regard to the number of corporators or their personal tax positions. On the other hand, distributions raise questions which are personal to the recipients, e.g. some recipients may be able to reclaim the basic rate of tax imputed to the distribution whilst others may be liable to higher rate income tax and investment income surcharge.

Although it is broadly true to say that income is computed for corporation tax purposes in accordance with income tax principles, there are certain significant differences only some of which can receive attention here. In the case of a company, expenses wholly and exclusively incurred in running the company are deducted from profits for the purposes of corporation tax, e.g. the remuneration of directors (who will, of course, be taxed on that remuneration). Unlike the director with a service contract, the partner is not entitled to a redundancy payment, or a " golden handshake " which is tax-free up to the £5,000 limit, if his services are no longer required. A person may be a partner notwithstanding that he is remunerated entirely by salary (see the *Stekel* v. *Ellice* type of case and in such a case salary is not deductible from profits for tax purposes but is treated as a partner's share of profits taxable under Schedule D, Cases (I) or (II). Salaries or wages paid to employees of the partnership are however deducted from profits for tax purposes and this includes payments from profits. Whereas interest on loans is deductible as an expense from company profits, partners themselves are not entitled to interest on capital unless there is agreement to that end and, in that event, the interest is not deductible from profits for the purposes of tax but is credited to the partner as profits. A partner who lets premises for use by the firm receives the rent as unearned income according to the Revenue, from which it follows that he may be liable to investment income surcharge according to the amount of such income. Clearly, the partner in such a situation would be well advised to take a low rent in exchange for a larger share of profits or a salary. For the different treatment of plant and machinery, see the specialist works on taxation.

As will be seen, a partnership is normally assessed to income tax on a preceding year basis (see *infra*), which can be advantageous if the graph of profits shows an upward trend, particularly where there is an advantageous allocation of profits amongst the partners in the year of assessment (see p. 202), although this advantage turns into a disadvantage if the graph shows a downward trend. Corporation tax is charged on the profits of a company for a financial year whereas the assessment to corporation tax is made by reference to an accounting period (not exceeding one year) with power to apportion where the latter period straddles two financial years. The rate of corporation tax is fixed in arrears and once assessed for an accounting period is generally payable within nine months from the end of that period (or if assessed later, one month from the date of assessment). A company resident in the United Kingdom is liable to pay ACT on qualifying distributions. Subject to certain exceptions, this ACT can be set-off against the corporation tax charged for the same accounting period. It will however be seen that distributions mean that the company cannot wait until the end of the accounting period and then pay corporation tax at the end of that period.

It is impossible to generalise with any degree of exactitude on the respective merits of the partnership and the company so far as the taxation of profits is concerned since these can only be ascertained in the circumstances of particular cases. It is for this reason that the following examples are proffered in the hope that a meaningful comparison can be made at certain levels of profit against the background of certain assumptions. Bearing in mind that those assumptions include the pessimistic assumption that only the minimum retention of profits under close company legislation is permitted it will be seen that even so, the company has the advantage at all levels of profit, except Example C, in which the partnership only manages to " break even " with the company.

COMPARISON OF TOTAL TAX PAYABLE UNDER PARTNERSHIP OR COMPANY

Assumptions

1. Two individuals are involved either as partners or directors of a company on an equal sharing basis. Both are married with two children over 11 but under 16 years.

2. Neither has any other income.

3. The requirements of the company's business do not justify any retention of profits above the maximum allowed by the close company legislation.

4. Rates of tax are as specified in the Finance Act 1976.

5. Any losses will be made up in future profits.

PARTNERSHIP

	£	Tax £
A *Loss or Profits Nil*		
Personal allowances wasted totalling £3,510		nil
B *Profits below £3,510*		
Some waste of personal allowances		nil
C *Profits £14,510*		
Profits	14,510	
Allowances	3,510	
Taxable	11,000	
10,000 @ 35%		3,500
1,000 @ 40%		400
		3,900
Marginal Rate		40%
D *Profits £23,130*		
Profits	23,130	
Allowances	3,510	
	19,620	
first 11,000 as in C		3,900
2,000 @ 45%		900
2,000 @ 50%		1,000
2,000 @ 55%		1,100
2,620 @ 60%		1,572
		8,472
Marginal Rate		60%

COMPANY

	£	*Tax* £
A *Loss or Profits Nil*		
Directors' Salaries £1,755 each		
Loss created for company of £3,510 to carry forward against future profits and save Corporation Tax at 42% amounting to		(1,474)
B *Profits below £3,510*		
Directors' salaries as above		
Some loss which is extent of deficiency of profits below £3,510		
C *Profits £14,510*		
Directors' salaries £7,255 each	14,510	
Company profits	nil	
Personal tax as partnership		
		3,900
Marginal Rate	40%	
D *Profits £23,130*		
Directors' salaries as in C	14,510	
Tax thereon		3,900
Company's profits	8,620	
Corporation Tax @ 42%	3,620	3,620
	5,000	
Abatement $\dfrac{15,000-5,000}{2}$	5,000	
Distributable	nil	
		7,520
Marginal Rate	42%	

E *Profits* £26,000

Tax as in D		8,472
Further 380 @ 60%	228	
2,490 @ 65%	1,618	1,846
		10,318

F *Profits* £45,000

On £26,000 as in E		10,318
Further 1,510 @ 65%	981	
6,000 @ 70%	4,200	
10,000 @ 75%	7,500	
1,490 @ 83%	1,237	13,918
		24,236

G Any additional profits will be charged at 83% leaving a maximum of 17% to partners

E *Profits £26,000*

Directors' salaries as in C	14,510	
Tax thereon		3,900
Company's profits	11,490	
Corporation Tax @ 42%	4,826	4,826
	6,664	
Abatement $\dfrac{15,000-6,664}{2}$	4,168	
	2,496	
Apportioned to members 50%	1,248	
Gross income to members	1,920	
Tax @ 45%	864	
Tax credit 35%	672	
		192
		8,918

F *Profits £45,000*

Directors' salaries £16,750 each	33,500	
Tax on £26,000 as in E		10,318
1,510 @ 65%	981	
5,990 @ 70%	4,193	
		5,174
Company's profits	11,500	
Corporation Tax @ 42%	4,830	4,830
	6,670	
Abatement $\dfrac{15,000-6,670}{2}$	4,165	
	2,405	
Apportioned to members 50%	1,203	
Gross income to members	1,850	
Tax 10 @ 70%	7	
1,840 @ 75%	1,380	
	1,387	
Tax credit @ 35%	647	
		740
		21,062

G At least 24% of profits can be retained (after tax) by the company plus a minimum of 2% by the members.

II. TAXATION OF PARTNERSHIP PROFITS

Two or more persons who carry on jointly a trade, profession or vocation constitute a partnership for the purposes of tax law. In the sense of a " calling," " vocation " would seem to add little to " trade or profession " and in its popular sense is wide enough to include contracts of service which are taxed under Schedule E, unlike partners, including the so-called " salaried partner," who are taxed under Schedule D.[1] In determining the existence of a partnership regard is had to the substance of the relationship which may lie behind a verbal smokescreen or even a clause in the agreement purporting to negative a partnership. Although the definition for tax purposes generally accords with that given in section 1 of the Partnership Act 1890, the tax definition has a slightly wider ambit. First, it would seem that persons who are not animated by the " profit motive " may carry on a trade, profession or vocation, as in cases of charitable or mutual trading. Profits derived from the carrying on of the business of a partnership which has been dissolved and arising from the performance of pre-dissolution contracts have been held to be trading receipts and as such assessable to tax, even though the purpose of fulfilling these contracts was to enable the business to be wound up under section 38 of the Partnership Act.[2] Secondly, the collectors of taxes are not too proud to soil their hands with the " wages of sin." They had no compunction in collecting tax assessed on the profits of an illegal partnership formed to run whisky into the United States of America during the so-called " Prohibition Era "[3] and it seems clear that any trading or professional activity (including that of the oldest profession in the world) will not escape their attention if carried on in an illegal manner. In cases outside tax law the courts refuse to recognise the existence of a partnership tainted with illegality and a lawful partnership is, as we have seen, dissolved when to carry it on would be illegal.

Thirdly, whilst a partnership is not for the purposes of ordinary partnership law a legal *persona* (Scotland excepted), tax law has oscillated between the qualified acceptance of the partnership as a separate entity for certain tax purposes and the orthodox view taken in partnership law. A leading case on the tax status of partnership is *Income Tax Commissioners* v. *Gibbs*,[4] in which the House of Lords cautiously conceded that a partnership consisting of A, B, C and D, could be succeeded as a " person " by a partnership consisting of A, B, C, D and E, although it was made clear that it was not the firm which carried on the business or was liable for tax. Lord Denning M.R., however, would have none of this qualified personification of partnerships which he considered to be incorrect in *Harrison* v. *Willis Bros.*,[5] stating: " The partnership firm is not an entity for taxing purposes or any other purposes. Its name is simply a convenient way of describing the persons who constitute the firm." In other words, the partnership name is used as mere machinery in order to designate the partners during the years in which profits are made, much as Order 81 of the Rules of the Supreme Court permits the use of the firm-name in actions by and against the firm. Even if Lord Denning's view proves to be the correct one, the profits of the firm require treatment quite separate from other income which a partner may derive from non-partnership sources.

Partnership return

Apart from any other returns of income which the partners as individuals may be obliged to make, a separate return of the profits or gains of a trading or professional partnership during a specified year of assessment is required by section 9 of the Taxes Management Act 1970. The obligation to make the return on behalf of himself and the other partners normally falls upon the " precedent partner," although the inspector may require a return from every partner, save such as are corporate partners. The " precedent partner " is the partner who, being resident in the United Kingdom, is first-named in the partnership agreement other than a dormant partner (in which case it means the first-named acting partner) or, if there is no agreement, the partner who is named singly or with precedence in the usual name of the firm.

Joint liability

A joint assessment is made in the partnership name and the income tax of the partnership is computed and stated jointly in one sum, being separate and distinct from any other tax chargeable on the partners as individuals. The nature of a partnership's tax liability was examined in *Stevens* v. *Britten*,[6] where a deed dissolving the partnership contained a clause whereby the continuing partner covenanted to pay and satisfy all debts and liabilities of the partnership and also to indemnify the retiring partner against such debts and liabilities. After paying half of the tax assessed on the trading profits in the last year of the partnership, the retiring partner claimed indemnity under the relevant clause and was upheld by the Court of Appeal which equated tax liability with that for debts and liabilities, *i.e.* it was a joint liability (not joint and several) which might be enforced *in toto* against any or all of the partners. Evershed M.R. recognised that the parties might lawfully have inserted some phrase such as " other than income tax " in the relevant clause, but felt unable to supply the *casus omissus*, if such it was. A further consequence of joint liability was brought out in *Harrison* v. *Willis Bros.* [7] There, two brothers, HW and WW, carried on a dairying partnership under the name of " W Bros." until 1950, when the partnership was dissolved, HW carrying on alone until his death in 1957. In 1962 additional assessments under Case I of Schedule D were made on the firm for the years 1941/42 to 1947/48, inclusive. Holding that the firm's tax liability was joint, the Court of Appeal applied the common law rule as to survivorship, with the consequence that the liability passed to WW on the death of HW, thereafter devolving on WW's personal representatives when he died. " It is an ordinary common law case of the survivor of two joint debtors," said Harman L.J. [8] In any event, the ordinary time-limit of six years for the assessment of tax had passed, and the exception to that time-limit in cases of fraud or wilful default was in any case inapplicable to assessments on personal representatives, who cannot be assessed on income or chargeable gains of the deceased after the end of the third year from the year of assessment in which the deceased has died. [9]

Partnership profits

The profits or gains arising or accruing from any partnership trade or profession are chargeable to tax under Cases I and II of Schedule D. [10] Profits or gains consist in the excess of receipts [11] over the expenses incurred in earning those receipts and are found by applying ordinary accounting principles, subject, however, to income tax legislation. The ascertainment of profits can frequently pose accountancy and legal problems, except in the simplest of cases where profits are found on a " cash basis " by offsetting expenses against receipts. Generally, profits are found on an " earnings basis " under which matters other than receipts and expenses may have to be taken into account, such as the value to be placed upon stock and trade debts at the beginning and end of the relevant accounting period. Even trading receipts may be difficult to identify, as in *Orchard Wine and Spirit Company* v. *Loynes*, [12] where the commission on whisky liqueur (manufactured by the assignee of the trade mark and formula of the liqueur) which was paid to the assignor pursuant to an agreement between the two was held to be a taxable trading receipt in the hands of the assignor. A solicitor-partner who receives costs in relation to his work as a trustee must bring those costs into the partnership account for taxation under Schedule D [13] and, conversely, a partner who permits the partnership to have the use and occupation of premises belonging to him at a fair and proper rent is entitled to have that rent deducted in the same way as though the rent had been paid to an independent person.[14]

Statutory income

" The income of the firm which has to be assessed is not . . . the actual income of the firm for the year of assessment, but what is called the statutory income," said Finlay J. in *Lewis* v. *I.R.C.*[15] paraphrasing the expression in income tax legislation that the profits are " estimated according to the provisions of the Income Tax Acts." Two important features of the " statutory income "—" a mere imaginary income " as Lord Hanworth M.R. termed it [16]—are, (a) the manner of its assessment, and (b) the manner of allocating the assessed liability of the partnership amongst the individual partners.

(1) *The manner of assessment*
   This may be illustrated by examples:

PRECEDING YEAR BASIS
   A trading or professional partnership charged with tax under Cases I or II of Schedule D (and there is little practical difference between the two cases) in respect of profits or gains is not assessed on the actual profits of the particular year of assessment concerned but on the profits during the basis period. In most instances this will be the accounting year ended in the previous year of assessment.[17]

   EXAMPLE 1. Profits in a continuing partnership are £15,000 and £6,000 for the calendar years ending December 31, 1975 and 1976, respectively.
   The assessments for the tax years 1976/77 and 1977/78 will be £15,000 and £6,000, respectively.

EXCEPTIONS TO PRECEDING YEAR BASIS
   The preceding year basis (occasionally a matter for envy on the part of " wage-slaves," the emoluments of whose offices or employments

are deducted at source under Schedule E) is not always utilised. Departures from the principle are as follows.

(a) *Commencement*.[18] A trading or professional partnership which has made profits from its commencement will be assessed from the date of such commencement to April 5 following thereon. If the partnership makes up its accounts on a tax-year basis, the first account up to April 5 will be the basis of the first assessment. If, as is more likely, the accounting period and the tax year differ, apportionment of the former is needed.

EXAMPLE 2. A partnership commences business on July 6, 1975, and makes statutable profits of £18,000 in its first year ending July 5, 1976. Its assessment for the tax year 1975/76 will be 9/12ths of £18,000, *i.e.* £13,500.

The second year of assessment will be based upon the statutable profits of the first 12 months; in Example 2 above, for 1976/77, this would be the profits of £18,000, subject to the option conferred by section 117 of the Income and Corporation Taxes Act 1970. In the third year of assessment and thereafter (but subject to the discontinuance provisions), the normal preceding year basis of assessment will be used; taking Example 2 again the 1977/78 assessment would be based on the year ended July 5, 1976, giving an assessment of £18,000. If the option is not used, it will be apparent that the first year's profits of £18,000 have been used three times for the purposes of assessment, *viz.* £13,500 thereof in the first, and £18,000 in each of the second and third years of assessment respectively.

The option, to which reference has been made, enables the partnership to elect to have the assessments for the second *and* third years (but *not* one without the other) charged upon the statutory profits of those two years. This option is available within the seven years of the end of the second year of assessment and must be given by notice in writing to the inspector of taxes. It may be withdrawn within six years of the end of the third year of assessment.

EXAMPLE 3. Suppose the business in Example 2 shows profits for the second and third accounting years of:

Year ended July 5, 1977	£16,800
Year ended July 5, 1978	£17,400

A claim under section 117 of the Income and Corporation Taxes Act 1970 would give:

1976/77

		£	£
3/12ths of £18,000		4,500	
9/12ths of £16,800		12,600	
		———	
			17,100

1977/78

		£	£
3/12ths of £16,800		4,200	
9/12ths of £17,400		13,050	
		———	
			17,250

instead of the two assessments of £18,000 previously calculated.
The assessments for the next two years of assessment would be:

	£
1978/79 based on profits to July 5, 1977	16,800
1979/80 based on profits to July 5, 1978	17,400

(b) *Discontinuance*.[19] If a partnership trade or profession is
permanently discontinued in a particular year of assessment, either
because the business is closed down or sold, or by reason of a change
in the membership of the partnership (unless, in this latter case,
certain partners continue after the change and both the former and
new partners agree to exercise the option to treat the business as
continuing),[20] the basis year for that year of assessment is the period
from the commencement of that year to the date of discontinuance.
Furthermore, with the exception of discontinuance caused by
nationalisation, the inspector may choose to revise the assessments
for the two preceding years of assessment if the aggregate of profits
in those years exceeds the aggregate of the amounts on which the
partnership has been charged for those two preceding years. This
facultative provision, which was introduced in order to prevent
persons from avoiding tax by choosing a suitable date for discontinuance, allows the Revenue to take into account the actual profits
of the penultimate and antepenultimate two years next preceding the
final year of assessment.

EXAMPLE 4. Partnership closes down on January 5, 1976. Revenue
does not exercise option.

		£
Profits: Years to July 5,	1972	14,400
	1973	13,800
	1974	13,200
	1975	12,600
Period to January 5,	1976	6,000

Assessments		£
1973/74 Year ended July 5, 1972		14,400
1974/75 Year ended July 5, 1973		13,800
1975/76 April 6, 1975 to January 1976		
$(3/12\text{ths} \times 12,600)+6,000$		9,150

The profits of the period from July 6 1973 to April 5 1975 escape assessment. This compensates for the treble assessment of some profits in the opening years, previously referred to.

EXAMPLE 5. Partnership closes down on January 5, 1976. Revenue exercises option.

		£
Profits: Years to July 5,	1972	12,000
	1973	12,600
	1974	13,200
	1975	13,800
Period to January 5,	1976	7,200

Assessments	£
1973/74 Originally year ended July 5, 1972	12,000
Amended to	
April 6, 1973 to July 5, 1973	3,150
July 6, 1973 to April 5, 1974	9,900
	13,050

	£
1974/75 Originally year ended July 5, 1973,	12,600
Amended to	
April 6, 1974 to July 5, 1974	3,300
July 6, 1974 to April 5, 1975	10,350
	13,650

1975/76 April 6, 1975 to July 5, 1975	3,450
July 6, 1975 to January 5, 1976	7,200
	10,650

In this example the profits from July 6, 1971 to April 5, 1973 escape assessment.

(c) *Change of partners.* For the purposes of the law of partnership the term " dissolution " covers both a complete dissolution of the firm in its ordinary sense, as where the partners retire and close down the business, and a dissolution in which the composition of the firm is changed, as where new partners are introduced into the firm or former partners retire, become bankrupt or die, and one or more of the original partners continues his membership of the firm. For tax purposes, the latter type of dissolution—sometimes inaccurately termed a " partial dissolution "—works a discontinuance of the old business and a commencement of the new business, *unless all the partners* (*i.e.* the old partners, including the personal representative of any deceased partner, *and* any new partners) elect by notice in writing, signed within two years after the date of change, to have the business treated as continuing notwithstanding the change.[21] If the option is used, the result is that a change of partners in which one or more of the partners continues does not disturb the preceding year basis of assessment. Income tax is assessed and charged separately on the former and new partners who exercise the option, subject to a just apportionment of the tax, on which there may be an appeal to the General or Special Commissioners.[22] Normally, it will be advantageous for a changed partnership to use the option where the business discloses a rising trend in profits. Even so, it is also clear that the exercise of the option may well prejudice the position of one or more of the partners who may, if there is no provision covering the matter in the articles of partnership, " stymie " the election for a continuance unless they receive an indemnity against the extra tax liability which they may incur.

Since 1960, there has been provision for assessing certain receipts made after the permanent discontinuance of the partnership trade or profession, but arising out of such trade or profession before its discontinuance. In so far as such receipts have not been brought into account in computing pre-cessation profits, they will, under sections 143 to 147 of the Income and Corporation Taxes Act 1970, be charged under Case VI of Schedule D. The references in those sections to permanent discontinuance include a change in the partnership ranking as a permanent discontinuance under section 154 of that Act, unless the partners take up their option to treat the partnership as continuing.

(2) *Division amongst partners*

However much one may refer to the partnership as a separate entity for certain tax purposes, the inescapable fact remains that a partnership is merely so many persons who bear the incidence of the tax. The income of a partner is " deemed " to be the share to which he is entitled during the year to which the claim relates in the partnership profits.[23] However anomalous it may appear, the result will be that A and B sharing profits equally in the basis period, and joined by C in the year of assessment (the three sharing equally), do not have an equal half share of the assessment but an equal third share of the assessment (C included), for the reason that what is taken into account is the division of profits *in the year of assessment*. The same result will follow if, in the latter year, A and B agree to vary their profit-sharing ratios.

Quite apart from the sharing of profits, the partners may have agreed on certain payments which are to be made to one or more of the partners, *e.g.* the payment of a salary, interest on capital or commission. Such payments are not deductible from receipts for the purposes of arriving at profits, but must be included in profits for tax purposes. In the leading case of *Lewis* v. *I.R.C.*[24] revenue practice received its *imprimatur* in relation to such payments. The proper course is to deduct from the statutory income (including payments of the sort described) the sum of those payments, and then to distribute the balance amongst the partners in the proportions in which they share profits, crediting each of the partners with the payments which he has received. The argument was rejected that one ought to proceed by working out the respective shares of the partners by adding up each partner's share of profits, salary, interest, commission and the like, and then finding out what percentage of the total income of the partners each of those shares constitute. An example may serve to clarify the correct *modus operandi*.

EXAMPLE 6. Black and White have been in partnership for many years sharing profits and losses in the proportion 60 per cent. to 40 per cent. after charging interest on capital, Black £1,500, and White £900, and partner's annual salary, White £3,000.

Profits as adjusted for income tax purposes have been:

	£
Year ended July 5, 1975	24,000
Year ended July 5, 1976	27,000

On July 6, 1976, Grey, a senior employee, was admitted to partnership. He contributed no capital but was to be entitled to a partner's salary of £2,400 per annum and 20 per cent. of the balance of profits. Black and White's interest on capital and White's salary remained unchanged, but the profit-sharing ratios became Black 50 per cent., White 30 per cent., and Grey 20 per cent.

Notice was duly given under section 154 of the Income and Corporation Taxes Act 1970.

The assessment for 1976/77 is £24,000 based on the profits of the year ended July 5, 1975 (Grey's remuneration as an employee being allowed as a deductible expense).

The division of the assessment will be:

Period April 6, 1976 to July 5, 1976

	Total £	Black £	White £
Interest on Capital	600	375	225
Salary	750	—	750
Balance 60:40	4,650	2,790	1,860
	6,000	3,165	2,835

Period July 6, 1976 to April 5, 1977

	Total £	Black £	White £	Grey £
Interest on Capital	1,800	1,125	675	—
Salary	4,050	—	2,250	1,800
Balance 50:30:20	12,150	6,075	3,645	2,430
	18,000	7,200	6,570	4,230
Total 1976/77	24,000	10,365	9,405	4,230

Reliefs

The partners may claim reliefs (such as those relating to small incomes, wives, earned income, children, dependent relatives and insurance premiums) under sections 5 to 19 and 22 of the Income and Corporation Taxes Act 1970. The appropriate relief may be claimed against the partner's share of profits in the partnership, if not already claimed in respect of other private or personal assessments; if all the partners claim reliefs against the income from their partnership shares as opposed to their separate and individual incomes, if any, the effect is to reduce the amount of tax charged on the partnership. If, as is not unlikely, partner A is entitled to considerable reliefs under the sections referred to, whereas partner B has only modest claims thereunder, the result is a reduction of tax by the total of the reliefs of both partners. The tax attributable to each partner is then calculated and charged to his drawings account.[25]

Investment income, meaning by that term any income other than earned income, is in this country taxed more heavily than earned income. This means that income derived immediately by a partner from the trade, profession or vocation carried on by the partnership in which he personally acts is taxed less heavily than the income which a sleeping partner derives from the partnership profits. The distinction between earned income and investment income was formerly emphasised by the personal relief of " earned income relief " available to the former type of income but now abolished. Earned income relief was refused to a solicitor in *Hale* v. *Shea* [26] who had retired from a partnership, subject to the right of the continuing partner to call upon his services as a " consultant," on the ground that his post-retirement " services " could not be related to the quarter share of profits to which he became entitled, inasmuch as the latter was given in respect of the share of assets which the retiring solicitor had transferred to the continuing solicitor. Buckley J. felt unable to dissect the consideration so as to apportion a quantified part thereof to the transfer of assets and the rest to " services." If, however, the consultant's remuneration could have been based solely on his services there is no reason why earned income relief (now earned income rates of tax) should not have been available. In any event, a separate consultancy agreement is obviously desirable although not in itself conclusive.

It may be appropriate to note here that certain deductions are available to partners in respect of interest. The first relates to that given to a partner who pays interest on a loan applied (a) in purchasing a share in the partnership, or (b) in contributing money to a partnership by way of capital or premium, provided such money is used wholly and exclusively for the purposes of the partnership business, or (c) in paying off another loan where relief on the interest on the other loan could have been obtained had it not been paid off. This is only granted to partners who are active in the firm and is of course reduced *pro tanto* by any recovery of capital from the firm. The second concerns a partner who pays interest on a loan to purchase machinery or plant *used* by the partnership (note, *not owned* by the partnership).

Partnership losses

Whether as the result of imprudence or fortuitous factors (such as the materialisation of an unusually high number of bad debts), the partnership receipts may be less than the expenses incurred in earning those receipts. Such a loss is computed in like manner to the computation of profits under Cases I and II of Schedule D and is apportioned between the partners in the same way as profits are apportioned. The treatment of losses, however, discloses some significant variations from the treatment of profits.

(i) Loss is treated on an actual basis, *i.e.* as occurring in the year of assessment in which it is suffered. If the partnership accounts over an accounting period reveal a loss, it has been said that two results follow: " first, that there is no profit for the year of assessment for which that period is the basis period, and secondly, that there is a loss for the year of assessment represented by the accounting period, the loss being apportioned between different years if more than one." [27]

(ii) A partner upon whom a share of the loss falls may either (a) set it off against his general income for the same year, provided that (and subject to some special cases) it is set off primarily against income of the corresponding class (*e.g.* a sleeping partner could set it off against unearned income) [28] or (b) carry forward loss against his share of profits in subsequent years of assessment.[29] If the business is discontinued, the share of the loss cannot in general be carried forward into a new business. We have already seen that a change in the partners operates as a discontinuance unless one or more partners remain as continuing partners and all the partners elect to treat the business as continuing. For present purposes, however, the position is that, irrespective of any election to treat the business as continuing, (a) an incoming partner cannot claim any of the unabsorbed loss of an outgoing partner, and (b) a continuing partner may carry forward his share of the loss.[30]

(iii) A third possibility is that a " terminal loss " may occur,

meaning thereby a loss sustained by the firm in the 12 months prior
to its discontinuance, including a statutory discontinuance following
a change of partners (except that a continuing partner cannot claim
loss relief under this head).[31] Such a terminal loss can be carried *back*
over the three years of assessment preceding that in which the business
was discontinued.[32] It may be added here that if capital allowances
for a year of assessment exceed the assessment of profits to tax, the
balance may be carried forward.[33]

Corporate partners

The fundamental differences between partnership and companies
(considered in the Introduction to this work) are reflected in the
differing tax treatment accorded each of these *genera* and discussed
earlier in this chapter. Partnerships are, as we have seen, subject to
the régime of income tax whereas, since 1965, companies have been
subjected to the régime of corporation tax in respect of their profits,
including those arising under a partnership. A form of miscegenation
between the two jurisprudential creatures occurs in the partnership
the membership of which includes, or indeed, consists of corporate
members. The problem posed for tax law by this unholy union is
dealt with by section 155 of the Income and Corporation Taxes 1970,
which provides that a partnership including one or more companies
amongst its members shall have its trading profits and losses (including any terminal loss) treated for the purposes of corporation tax as
though the partnership were a company and without regard to any
change of members. Corporation tax is payable on the company's
share of profits or losses as though that share were derived from a
trade carried on by it alone. Individual partners are chargeable with
income tax in respect of their shares of income, except that such
income tax is charged (and the reliefs given) by reference to the
computations made for corporation tax.

Owing to the circumstance that the statutory income of the individual is normally calculated on the " preceding year basis " (see p. 197,
above), whereas corporation tax is paid on a " current year basis,"
it was, prior to the Finance Act 1968, possible that some of the profits
escaped tax completely. Those who felt that this was not only " a
consummation devoutly to be wish'd " but something to be brought
about, were deprived of their opportunity of tax avoidance by a
provision, currently section 155 (5) of the Income and Corporation
Taxes Act 1970, to the effect that the individual partners' incomes

for a year of assessment are to be deemed to be not less than the profits of the basis period reduced by the share apportioned to the company for that period.

III. CAPITAL GAINS TAX

Since its introduction in 1965, capital gains tax has been levied on chargeable gains occurring in the year of assessment by virtue of a disposal of assets. Without going into the details of the tax and its computation (on which reference should be made to the specialist works on tax law), it suffices here to state that a chargeable gain will be the difference between the cost of the asset and the consideration received on its disposal. The main attributes of the tax are that it applies (i) to wide forms of property, (ii) to persons resident or ordinarily resident in the United Kingdom, and (iii) on a disposal of an asset. As regards (i), the separate treatment of certain development gains from land (formerly treated as income and chargeable to " development gains tax ") has been superseded by a new tax— " development land tax "—which came into operation on August 1, 1976. Section 31 of the Development Land Tax Act 1976 provides that two or more persons carrying on a trade or business in partnership shall be treated as dealing individually in respect of partnership dealings and development land tax in respect of realised development value accruing to the partners on the disposal of an interest in land or for which the partners otherwise become liable shall be charged on them separately.

So far as partnerships are concerned, the tax applies to partners who are resident or ordinarily resident in the United Kingdom, unless the control and management of the partnership business is situated abroad, in which case partners resident (note, not *ordinarily* resident) in the United Kingdom are treated as being resident outside the United Kingdom. For the purposes of the tax, partnership dealings in chargeable assets are treated as dealings by the individual partners and not by the partnership firm as such, each partner being regarded (contrary to the general rule) as owning a share of the asset itself.

On the disposal of a partnership asset to an outsider, *e.g.* where the partnership assets are sold on a dissolution, each partner is treated as disposing of his share in the asset and is charged separately to the tax. How that share is to be ascertained depends upon the circumstances. If a particular method of sharing asset surpluses has been agreed or appears from the partnership accounts, that method will be used; if no particular method can be ascertained in those ways, it may be necessary to fall back on profit-sharing ratios to determine shares in asset surpluses.

The application of the tax, however, is not limited to disposals of assets to outside persons. Thus " internal " arrangements within the partnership may well have capital gains tax implications, *e.g.* the division of assets in kind among the partners, the variation or altera-tion of partnership shares, changes in the composition of the firm (as where an incoming partner is given a share in the firm without payment) and the revaluation of assets. The tax treatment of these arrangements is to be found in the Statement of Practice issued by the Revenue after discussions with interested bodies.

An important consideration in determining liability to capital gains tax is whether or not an asset has been acquired otherwise than by way of a bargain made at arm's length, *e.g.* a gift (where the disposal to the donee will be deemed to be for a consideration equal to the market value of the asset). In this respect it is relevant to note that transactions between " connected persons " are treated as transactions otherwise than by way of a bargain at arm's length. The definition of " connected persons " need not detain us here, except to note that it includes partners, unless they acquire or dispose of partnership assets " pursuant to bona fide commercial arrangements " (see the Statement of Practice referred to above).

Turning now to companies, chargeable gains made by companies are liable to corporation tax and not to capital gains tax. Corpora-tion tax therefore is charged on a company's profits which must in-clude chargeable gains. Bearing in mind that the rate of corporation tax has so far been consistently and substantially higher than the rate of capital gains tax applicable to individuals, some relief was given by section 93 (2) of the Finance Act 1972, which provides for a reduction by a certain fraction of a company's chargeable gains. For companies other than authorised unit trusts or investment trusts the fraction was fixed at 11/26ths by section 10 (1) of the Finance Act 1974 thereby producing an effective rate of corporation tax on gains of 30 per cent. by such companies.

It does not follow from the foregoing that there is little to choose between the company and the partnership so far as capital gains tax is concerned. On the contrary, the balance of advantage in this respect lies clearly with the partnership.

First, although the burden of capital gains tax would seem to fall equally on the company and the partnership, there is the further consideration that the tax may fall on the shareholder in the company when he disposes of his share. This double charge to tax—on the company and the shareholder—is absent in the case of partnerships and affords the latter a distinct advantage from this point of view.

Secondly, individuals may benefit from the so-called " half-income rule " whereby chargeable gains of £5,000 or less bear only tax on half of the amount on which they would be chargeable to income tax if charged under Case VI of Schedule D. This means that the basic-rate taxpayer pays capital gains tax at the rate of 17½ per cent. and not the full rate of 30 per cent. which will apply when his income tax rate exceeds 60 per cent. However charged, the gain is added to the other income of the individual; personal reliefs, other than life insurance relief, go to reduce the gain, a valuable concession to individuals, including partners, but not to companies.

IV. CAPITAL TRANSFER TAX

The Finance Act 1975 introduced a new tax—the capital transfer tax—on transfers of value by virtue of which a person's estate after the transfer is less than it would have been but for the disposition. Where two or more persons are liable for the same tax each of them is liable for the whole of the tax; a provision which is of interest to partnerships which make a transfer of value within the scope of the new tax. The tax encompasses gifts *inter vivos*, dispositions of property on death and settled property subject to certain exemptions (*e.g.* gifts not exceeding £2,000 in any tax year) and certain forms of excluded property (*e.g.* property situated abroad). The broad aim of the tax is to end the separate tax régimes for lifetime gifts and gifts on death and, thereby, a distinction which had provided an important device for tax avoidance *viz.* the use of lifetime transfers in preference to transfers on death. Nevertheless, despite the broad assimilation of the two types of gift for the purposes of the tax, certain differences remain, such as the higher rates of tax on death (including gifts within three years of death). The primary liability to pay the tax rests upon the donor (or trustees in the case of settled land) with a secondary liability on the donee or, in certain circumstances, later transferees of the property subject to the tax.

Partners are liable to the tax where they make a chargeable transfer within the meaning of the Act, *e.g.* on an allocation without payment of a share in the firm to an incoming partner, or on a transfer of value to a person whether partner or non-partner. An exception exists in the case of a transfer of value to the extent to which it increases the value of the estate of the transferor's spouse.

In a provision important for partnerships, it is provided that a disposition is not a transfer of value (*i.e.* is outside charge to the tax) if it is shown that it was not made in a transaction intended to confer any gratuitous benefit on any person and either (a) that it was made in a transaction at arm's length between persons not connected with each other, or (b) that it was such as might be expected to be made in a transaction at arm's length between persons not connected with each other (s. 20 (4)). The definition of " connected persons," as in the case of capital gains tax, includes partners except that transfers of partnership assets between partners (and, it is thought, an in-coming partner) are not treated as transactions between connected persons if they are pursuant to bona fide commercial arrangements. The extent to which these intra-partnership transactions will escape capital transfer tax remains to be worked out, although it is thought that a Boden-type of arrangement will escape the tax as was the case with estate duty. Under the old law, the share of a deceased partner in the partnership assets, including any goodwill, whether purchased by an incoming partner, or taken over by the surviving partners was normally available to attract estate duty under the Finance Act 1894, as amended. In *Attorney-General* v. *Boden* (1912)[34] it was held that goodwill passing to co-partners by virtue of a partner's death was exempt from estate duty on the ground that it had been purchased bona fide for full consideration in money or money's worth and that such consideration had passed to the vendor for his own use or benefit. In *Boden*, a father had entered into a partnership agreement with his two sons under which the sons were to take over the father's share of the goodwill without payment on the latter's death. The sons, for their part, agreed to devote their time to the business and not to engage in any other business without their father's consent, whilst the father, for his part, only agreed to devote such time and attention to the business as he thought fit. It was held that the sons' services ranked as full consideration for the share of goodwill passing to them. The " *Boden* Clause " proved to be a popular device to minimise estate duty and, it is thought, will be used to avoid capital transfer tax on transfers of goodwill.

Where a person, otherwise than in a transaction at arm's length between persons not connected with each other, allows another the use of money or other property without consideration or full consideration, he is treated as making a transfer of value. Because of the harsh way in which this provision would bear upon partnerships which are allowed the use of money or property (such as premises) provided by a partner, the Government agreed to defer the operation of this provision (s. 41) until April 6, 1976, and has now made special provision for the exemption of such loans by a partner to his firm (s. 115 (7), Finance Act 1976).

A transfer of value made in the carrying on of a trade, profession or vocation is an exempt transfer for the purposes of the present tax if it is allowable as a deduction in computing the profits or gains of that trade, profession or vocation for the purposes of income tax.

---

[1] See the abortive attempt by the female staff of a firm of solicitors to create a partnership of their earnings for national insurance purposes in *Rennison & Son* v. *Minister of Social Security* (1970) 10 K.I.R. 65.

[2] *Hillerns and Fowler* v. *Murray* (1932) 17 T.C. 77; *Pattullo's Trustees* v. *I.R.C.* (1955) 36 T.C. 105.

[3] *Lindsay* v. *I.R.C.* (1932) 18 T.C. 43, leaving open the position of a partnership criminal by its very nature, *e.g.* one formed for housebreaking.

[4] [1942] A.C. 402; see also Lord Devlin in *I.R.C.* v. *Four Seas Co. Ltd.* [1962] A.C. 161 at p. 168.

[5] [1966] 2 W.L.R. 183 at p. 188.

[6] [1954] 1 W.L.R. 1340.

[7] [1966] Ch. 619.

[8] *Ibid.* at p. 191.

[9] T.M.A. 1970, ss. 34, 36 and 41.

[10] I.C.T.A. 1970, ss. 108, 109. Case 1 would appear to apply to any trade wheresoever carried on, but its ambit is cut down by Case V and would not, therefore, cover a trade carried on wholly abroad. Note that in connection with a partnership firm controlled and managed abroad its trade or business is deemed to be carried on by persons resident outside the U.K. notwithstanding that some partners are resident in, and some trading operations are conducted in, the U.K.: I.C.T.A. 1970, s. 153 (1). But the profits of trading operations in this country are chargeable to U.K. taxation and may be assessed on any partner resident here: *ibid.* s. 153 (2).

[11] " But that is not quite accurate " said Lord Reid in *B.S.C. Footwear* v. *Ridgway* [1972] A.C. 544 at p. 552, referring to the example of the field manured in year one so that a harvest may be reaped therefrom in year two, a situation in which the cost of manure may properly be set against the receipts of year one.

[12] (1952) 33 T.C. 97.

[13] *Watson and Everitt* v. *Blunden* (1933) 18 T.C. 402.

[14] *Heastie* v. *Veitch* [1934] 1 K.B. 535.

[15] [1933] 2 K.B. 557, and see I.C.T.A. 1970, s. 26.

[16] [1933] 2 K.B. 557 at p. 568, pointing out that the statutory income may differ widely from the actual income enjoyed during the year of charge.

17 I.C.T.A. 1970, s. 115.
18 I.C.T.A. 1970, ss. 116, 117.
19 I.C.T.A. 1970, s. 118.
20 *Ibid.* s. 154 (2).
21 I.C.T.A. 1970, s. 154 (2), Finance Act 1971, s. 17.   :
22 I.C.T.A. 1970, s. 154 (5). The apportionment need not be based upon entitlement to profits, but may take cognisance of other factors, *e.g.* time and effort devoted to the business.
23 I.C.T.A. 1979, s. 26.
24 n. 15, *supra*. *I.R.C.* v. *McCash and Hunter* (1955) 36 T.C. 181: payment out of profits of partnership assessed on cash basis in respect of deceased's share of profits earned before his death but received later must be included in total income of partnership: *secus* an agreement on the retirement of a partner to share last year's profits in a particular manner.
25 See *Stevens* v. *Britten* [1954] 1 W.L.R. 1340, at p. 1342, *per* Evershed M.R.
26 [1965] 1 W.L.R. 290.
27 *British Tax Encyclopaedia*, pp. 1–662.
28 I.C.T.A. 1970, s. 168.
29 *Ibid.* s. 171.
30 *Ibid.* s. 171 (1), (4).
31 *Ibid.* s. 174 (10) (*a*).
32 *Ibid.* s. 174 (1).
33 *Ibid.* s. 169.
34 [1912] 1 K.B. 539.

Chapter Nine

LIMITED PARTNERSHIPS

IT was not until 1906 and after several rather inconclusive reports during the nineteenth century that the Company Law Amendment Committee recommended that the commandite system of partnership, then prevailing in France, Germany and elsewhere, might advantageously be introduced into the United Kingdom. The main characteristics of such partnerships were, according to that Committee, (a) the limited liability of certain partners for the debts and obligations of the firm, and (b) some system of registration to publicise this limited liability. It is ironical that when at long last limited partnerships were finally introduced by the Limited Partnerships Act 1907,[1] their thunder, to a large extent, was stolen by the new private company introduced by the Companies Act of the same year. The private company could be formed with as few as two members and enjoyed certain privileges with regard to publicity in addition to the advantage of separate corporate personality. If, as was claimed during the second reading of the Limited Partnerships Bill, commercial development had been held up by the lack of a legally recognised limited partnership, it is clear that businessmen since 1907 have preferred the private company to the limited partnership. In 1974, a mere 63 limited partnerships were registered in England and Wales, bringing the number of live limited partnership registrations at Companies House to 784. These numbers are dwarfed by the corresponding registrations of companies. There were 40,371 new registrations of companies in 1974, 40,254 of which were of private companies; of the 569,376 companies then on the register, 555,138 were private. No doubt the preference is largely attributable to the advantages of corporate status but it is possible that some penumbral aspects of the law pertaining to limited partnerships may have made legal advisers chary of recommending this form of organisation. Stamp duty and fees exigible from limited partnerships have constituted another deterrent to those who might otherwise have adopted this form of unincorporated status. Since the Finance Act 1973, the limited partnership has ranked as a " capital company " on which capital duty is payable *ad valorem* at the rate of £1 for every £100 on the capital contributed to the firm, whether originally or by way of increase in an existing contribution, the term " capital " meaning the actual value of assets of any kind contributed by members. This capital duty replaces the former stamp duty of 50p per £100 which was levied on the nominal value of capital furnished to the firm. The forms used and fees payable to the Registrar of Companies in connection with registration, inspection of statements, certificates of registration and extracts from registered statements are to be found in the Limited Partnerships Rules 1907, S.R. & O. 1907 No. 1020, as amended by S.I. 1972 No. 1040 and S.I. 1974 No. 560. At the present time the limited partnership lies fecund upon the Statute Book but little used. It is possible that the private company will in the future be subjected to greater legal regulation, in which event it may be that minds will turn to the possibilities of the limited partnership, as yet little explored.

Definition and constitution

According to section 4 (1) of the Limited Partnerships Act 1907, " limited partnerships may be formed in the manner and subject to the conditions by this Act provided." Because the Act constitutes an exception to the legal postulate of unlimited liability, those who wish to negative unlimited liability by invoking the Act must show that they have complied with its terms. It is interesting to note that in the United States of America the limited partnership statutes similarly received a strict construction because of their derogation from the common law principle of unlimited liability, with the result that this form of association came to be widely recognised as commercially impracticable. To alleviate the position, section 11 of the widely adopted Uniform Limited Partnership Act 1916 gives relief to a person who has contributed to the capital of a business conducted by another person or partner, erroneously believing that he has become a limited partner in a limited partnership, provided that on ascertaining the mistake he promptly renounces his interest in the profits of the business or other compensation by way of income; such a person will not be adjudged to be a general partner or subject to the obligations of a general partner. The absence of such statutory relief in this country underlines the need for meticulous compliance with the terms of the 1907 Act, although non-compliance does not render the partnership a nullity, inasmuch as it may still be held to be an ordinary partnership.

The Limited Partnership Act 1907, s. 4 (2), states that a limited partnership " must consist of one or more persons called general partners, who shall be liable for all debts and obligations of the firm, and one or more persons to be called limited partners, who shall at the time of entering into such partnership contribute thereto a sum or sums as capital or property valued at a stated amount, and who shall not be liable for the debts or obligations of the firm beyond the amount so contributed " (" firm " has the same meaning as in the Partnership Act 1890). Section 3 defines a general partner as " any partner who is not a limited partner as defined by this Act." Section 4 (4) allows that " A body corporate may be a limited partner " without, it would appear, dispensing with the requirement that such a body (chartered corporations excepted) is only authorised to engage in activities which are *intra vires*. Nor does there appear to be any impediment, other than the *vires* doctrine, to prevent a corporate body from becoming a general partner. If such a corporation were a limited company, the directors of which were the " active " partners, the practical result would be limited liability. As already mentioned, the possibilities of limited partnerships do not seem to have been fully explored, particularly with regard to taxation.

The capital contributed by the limited partner may take the form of cash or other property; in the latter event, the property must be given a fair valuation. " What the Act contemplates," said Wright J. in *Rayner and Co.* v. *Rhodes*,[2] " is that either actual money or the equivalent of money in the form of property should be transferred to the company for their use." In that case, an arbitrator's award in the sum of £780 had been given in respect of a breach of contract by a firm in which Rhodes claimed to be a limited partner. It was held that despite a deed of partnership, which expressed that he was to be a limited partner, he was subject to unlimited liability because he had not contributed capital or property but merely a running bank guarantee of £5,000 in respect of the firm's debts, terminable by three months' notice. This was merely the assumption of a future contingent liability. This requirement that capital must be contributed *in limine* puts limited partners at a disadvantage compared with private company shareholders who are not necessarily obliged to pay the full nominal value on their shares when they are issued.

The Limited Partnerships Act 1907, s. 4 (3), provides that once a limited partner has made his capital contribution he cannot " during the continuance of the partnership, either directly or indirectly, draw out or receive back any part of his contribution, and if he does so draw out or receive back any such part shall be liable for the debts and obligations of the firm up to the amount so drawn out or received back." It is worth stating that although the limited partner's capital contribution provides the measure of his liability, the contribution itself may either be credited to the limited partner contributing it or be divided between the partners, including general partners (who are not obliged by law to make a capital contribution), in a manner agreed. Thus, for example, there is nothing to prevent A, the limited partner who contributes all the capital, agreeing with B, the general partner, that each of them shall share equally in the capital, an arrangement which entitles B, with A's concurrence, to take out his share of capital. The view is expressed in Lindley [3] that any payment to a limited partner which directly or indirectly comes out of his contribution, whether in the form of interest on capital or a share of profits or other form, will constitute a receipt of the limited partner's contribution. If this is intended to mean that receipt of interest on capital or of a share of profits renders the limited partner *pro tanto* liable even where his capital contribution has not been received back, etc., it is, with respect, difficult to see how this can be so under the terms of the Act or, indeed, if limited partnerships are to have any real use. Provided the change is registered, the partners may agree to an increase in a limited partner's contribution, and it would seem that no objection could be taken to an agreement providing for an original contribution from a limited partner with a further contribution to follow, subject to the *caveat* that such an agreement is not a colourable attempt to limit liability in a way which is at variance with the reality of the limited partner's rights.

Registration

There is no requirement that the firm name of a limited partnership should give any indication of limited liability. The proposal that the name should do so was dropped from the Limited Partnerships Bill. Section 439 of the Companies Act 1948 renders use of the word " limited " as the last word in the firm name unlawful for an unincorporate body. Because of the obvious dangers in allowing partnerships to be formed with limited liability, but without publicity, the Limited Partnership Act contains provisions for the registration of such firms and for public inspection of the registers. Before considering the mandatory registration of all limited partnerships with the Registrar of Companies it should be borne in mind that such partnerships may also require to be registered under the Registration of Business Names Act 1916.

Registration is effected by sending by post, or delivering to the Registrar (who, by s. 15 as amended, is the Registrar of Companies, with offices in London, Edinburgh and Belfast) at the Register Office in that part of the United Kingdom in which the principal place of business of the limited partnership is situated or proposed to be situated, a statement signed by the partners and containing the following particulars:

(a) the firm name;

(b) the general nature of the business;

(c) the principal place of business (normally the headquarters of the firm);

(d) the full name of each of the partners;

(e) the term, if any, for which the partnership is entered into and the date of its commencement (if no term is fixed, details of the conditions of existence of the partnership are required by Form L.P. 5, appended to the Limited Partnership Rules 1907);

(f) a statement that the partnership is limited and the description of every limited partner as such; and

(g) the sum contributed by each limited partner, and whether paid in cash or how otherwise.[4]

In addition to the initial registration, certain changes occurring during the continuance of the firm require to be registered and this is done by posting or delivering within seven days to the Registrar at the appropriate office a statement by the firm specifying the nature of the change. The changes requiring to be registered are those involving:

(a) the firm name;

(b) the general nature of the business;

(c) the principal place of business;

(d) the partners or the name of any partner;

(e) the terms or character of the partnership;

(f) the sum contributed by any limited partner; and

(g) the liability of any partner by reason of his becoming a limited instead of a general partner or a general instead of a limited partner.[5]

Section 9 (2) provides that default in registering these changes renders every general partner liable to a fine not exceeding £1 for each day during which the default continues.

Section 10 of the Act requires that notice of any arrangement or transaction under which any person will cease to be a general partner in any firm and will become a limited partner therein, or under which the share of a limited partner in a firm will be assigned to any person, must be advertised forthwith in the *Gazette*, and until notice of the arrangement or transaction is so advertised shall be deemed to be of no effect for the purposes of the Act. The *London Gazette*, the *Edinburgh Gazette* and the *Belfast Gazette* are used for partnerships registered in England, Scotland and Northern Ireland, respectively.

On receiving any statement made under the Act, the Registrar is required by section 13 to file the same and to send to the firm from whom the statement was received a certificate of registration. He is also required by section 14 to keep a register and index of all registered partnerships at the appropriate register offices including all statements registered in relation to such partnerships. Section 16 (1) provides that any person may inspect the statements filed by the Registrar at the respective register offices on payment of such fees not exceeding one shilling (5p) as may be appointed by the Board of Trade; also, any person may require a certificate of registration of any limited partnership, or a copy of or extract from any registered statement to be certified by the Registrar at such fees as may be appointed by the Board of Trade but not exceeding two shillings (10p) for the certificate of registration or sixpence (2½p) for each folio of 72 words, or in Scotland for each sheet of 200 words.

The Board of Trade is empowered by section 17 to make rules concerning certain matters arising under the Act, *viz.* fees to be paid to the Registrar, duties of the Registrar, the performance by Assistant Registrars and other officers of acts required to be done by the Registrar, forms to be used and, generally, the conduct and regulation of registration and matters incidental thereto. Under the present rules, the Limited Partnerships Rules 1907, S.R. & O. 1907 No. 1020, as amended by S.I. 1972 No. 1040, fees cannot exceed £2 for an original registration and there is no charge for the registration of a change. The forms to be used are appended to the Limited Partnerships Rules by S.I. 1974 No. 560. Form L.P. 5 is used for applications for registration and for statements of particulars and amounts contributed by limited partners; Form L.P. 6 is used for changes in the particulars and increments in the amounts contributed.

Compliance with the terms of the Act is secured by criminal and civil actions. In addition to the particular sanction imposed on those who make default in notifying changes in the partnership by section 9 (2), there is the more general provision of the Perjury Act 1911, s. 5 which makes it an indictable misdemeanour (punishable with up to two years' imprisonment, or a fine, or both) for any person knowingly and wilfully to make a statement false in a material particular in any statement or notice required by the Act. The civil sanction is contained in section 5 of the Act which requires every limited partnership to be registered in accordance with the Act, default in which results in the partnership being deemed to be a general partnership and every limited partner a general partner.

As in the case of ordinary partnerships, the Companies Act 1967 has removed the upper limit on the number of partners in certain types of limited partnership. Section 121 of that Act dispenses limited partnerships of solicitors, accountants (as defined) and members of stock exchanges from the restriction on numbers, whilst the Limited Partnerships (Unrestricted Size) No. 1 Regulations 1971 (S.I. 1971 No. 782), made under section 121, free partnerships carrying on one or more of the following activities, *viz.* surveying, auctioneering, valuing, estate agency, land agency and estate managmeent, provided that in each case not less than three-quarters of the total number of members are members of one of the bodies scheduled to the Regulations and that not more than one-quarter of the total number of the partnership members are limited partners.

For partners not affected by the Companies Act 1967, the upper limits remain those fixed by section 4 (2) of the Limited Partnerships Act 1907, *viz.* 20, except for banking partnerships for which 10 is the maximum number. Whichever Act governs numbers of partners, there is no stipulated ratio between general and limited partners, although obviously there must be at least one of each.

The statutory regulation of numbers may not be the only matter which professional partners need to consider. Quite apart from statutory or professional rules concerning " non-professional " partners, there is the separate question of the legality or professional propriety of the partner with limited liability. A perusal of several professional by-laws shows that whilst some professional bodies prohibit the use of the limited liability company, others go further, like the Royal Institute of British Architects, which also prohibits " any act which will have the effect of avoiding his (*i.e. the architect's*) responsibility to his client." Since full legal accountability lies at the heart of the professional ethos, those contemplating the device of the limited partnership with professional limited partners will doubtless consult their professional organisations.

Limited partners and third persons

The law applicable to ordinary partnerships, that is to say the Partnership Act 1890 and the relevant rules of equity and common law, are applied to limited partnerships by the important section 7 of the Limited Partnerships Act 1907, subject to such modifications as are introduced by the latter Act. Thus, section 5 of the 1890 Act applies to a general partner and he has the same authority to bind the firm as a partner in an ordinary partnership. As in the case of ordinary partnerships, the general partner is subject to liability *ex contractu* (which is joint) and liability *ex delicto* (which is joint and several) whether or not he has personally performed the acts giving rise to the liability. With the limited partner the position is different.

A limited partner cannot, as such, take part in the management of the partnership business and has no power to bind the firm, although under section 6 (1) he may himself or through an agent inspect the books of the firm and examine the state and prospects of the partnership business and may advise with the partners thereon. Consonant with this lack of authority, it seems that a limited partner cannot make an admission or representation concerning the partnership affairs and in the ordinary course of its business so as to constitute evidence against the firm, nor would notice to such a partner operate as notice to the firm, as is the case, under sections 15 and 16 respectively of the 1890 Act, with partners in an ordinary partnership and general partners in a limited partnership.

Section 4 (2) of the 1907 Act enacts that the limited partner " shall not be liable for the debts and obligations of the firm beyond the amount so contributed," *i.e.* as capital. This limited liability is undoubtedly the central feature of limited partnerships, but the privilege so conferred by the Limited Partnerships Act is subjected to three important qualifications.

Section 6 (1) provides that:

(a) If a limited partner takes part in the management of the partnership's business he will be liable for all debts and obligations of the firm as though he were a general partner. As already noted, inspecting the books, examining the state and prospects of the business and advising thereon with other partners are activities in which the limited partner may engage without bringing down upon himself the Damocles sword of unlimited liability. Apart from these activities, what does the term " management " include? It is arguable that if it connotes that degree of control and direction associated with the proprietor-entrepreneur there ought to be no objection to the limited partner acting and binding the firm *qua* employee or agent.

Such an argument might be difficult to support bearing in mind that a salaried partner is nonetheless a partner, and also the further consideration that there is an incompatibility between the roles of partner and employee combined in one person,[6] in contrast to the accepted dualism in the partner who may be both agent and principal at the same time. Olympian detachment would seem to be the safest course (apart from the permitted instances of intervention). It may be noted here that the Act recognises those amphibious creatures, namely, the limited partner who becomes a general partner and, conversely, the general partner who becomes a limited partner. Section 9 (1) (*g*) provides that such legal metamorphoses must be registered and, in the case of the latter change (*i.e.* general to limited partner), section 10 provides that notice in the *Gazette* is needed in order that it may be effectual.

(b) If the partnership is not registered in accordance with the Act it will be deemed by section 5 to be a general partnership and every limited partner will be deemed to be a general partner.

(c) If, during the continuance of the partnership, a limited partner either directly or indirectly draws out or receives back any part of his contribution, he becomes liable under section 4 (3) for the debts and obligations of the firm up to the amount so drawn out or received back.

The partners " inter se "

The terms of a limited partnership are ascertained by reference to the agreement between the partners, the provisions of the Limited Partnerships Act 1907 and, by section 7 of the 1907 Act, the law concerning ordinary partnerships as contained in the Partnership Act 1890 (to the extent that these are not modified by the 1907 Act), and the relevant rules of equity and common law. Although only those incidents of the relationship peculiarly applicable to limited partnerships are discussed here, it is opportune to stress that difficult-ies will be avoided or minimised if agreement on certain matters is explicitly recorded in a partnership deed, notably on questions such as the duration of the partnership, the duration of the limited partner's membership therein, the division of partnership capital including the limited partner's share therein, the dissolution of the firm, the retirement of partners and the disposition of surplus assets on dissolution.

As already noted, the 1907 Act makes it clear that the privilege of limited liability will only be enjoyed by the limited partners during such time as they refrain from participation in the management of the business, a function which is confided to the general partners. Section 5 of the Act provides that any difference arising as to ordinary matters connected with the partnership business may be decided by a majority of the general partners, subject to any agreement, expressed or implied, between the partners. If there is no such agreement, the general partners may decide the differences in question without seeking or taking into account the views of the limited partners. If there is agreement to give the limited partners a voice in the resolution of differences arising out of ordinary matters connected with the partnership business, such partners must take great care that in exercising their right they do not cross over the threshold into " management " of a day-to-day nature if they are not to lose the prize of limited liability. The management of a business must inevitably create differences of opinion in " ordinary matters." The provision seems to be a rather clumsy attempt to permit limited partners to secure some say in the direction of the business, perhaps on the analogy of shareholders' control of companies through meetings. As is the case with ordinary partnerships, by section 24 (8) of the Partnership Act 1890, changes in the nature of the partnership business (on which s. 5 is silent) require the concurrence of all the partners, whether general or limited.

Save for the requirement that the limited partner must make a capital contribution (the same applies when a general partner becomes a limited partner), the interests of the partners in capital and in the partnership property are determined in the first place by agreement, if any, between the parties. If there is no such agreement, section 24 (1) of the Partnership Act 1890 applies and all partners are entitled to share equally in the capital and profits of the business and must contribute equally towards losses, including losses of capital. As in the case of ordinary partnership, it would appear that inequality of capital contribution would raise an implied agreement against the equal sharing of capital but would not, at the same time, preclude the application of the rule concerning the equal sharing of profits and losses, subject to the overriding consideration that the limited partner cannot be made liable as such for the debts and obligations of the firm beyond the amount which he has contributed, a consideration which, it is apprehended, also governs the making good of losses between the partners.

The presumption applicable to ordinary partnerships whereby community of profit affords a prima facie indication of community of loss does not apply to the limited partnership in which the limited partner, whilst he is entitled to an equal share of profits in the absence of agreement to the contrary, is not liable for losses, including deficiencies of capital, beyond the amount of his agreed capital contribution. For this reason, it is doubly important that the articles of partnership should set forth unequivocally the interest of the respective partners in capital, partnership property, profits and losses (including deficiencies of capital).

In contrast to section 24 (7) of the Partnership Act 1890, which forbids the introduction of a partner to an ordinary partnership without the consent of all the existing partners, section 6 (5) (b) of the Limited Partnerships Act 1907 permits a limited partner, subject to any agreement expressed or implied between the partners, to assign his share in the partnership, but only with the consent of the general partners, and upon such assignment the assignee becomes a limited partner with all the rights of the assignor. Notice of the assignment must be advertised in the *Gazette* if it is to be effective. A partner in an ordinary partnership may assign his share but, by section 31, the assignee is only entitled to receive a share of the profits; he cannot require accounts, inspect books or interfere in the management or administration of the partnership. An assignment by a limited partner without the consent of the general partners would take effect under section 31. Another contrast to ordinary partnership is provided by the introduction of fresh partners; section 6 (5) (d) provides that this does not require the consent of the existing limited partners, unless there is an agreement to that effect.

Dissolution

By virtue of section 7 of the 1907 Act (which extends to limited partnerships the application of the Partnership Act 1890 and the relevant rules of equity and law to the extent that these are not expressly modified by the 1907 Act), a limited partnership may be dissolved, whether by court intervention or otherwise, in the same way as an ordinary partnership. On the dissolution of a limited partnership, its affairs are by virtue of section 6 (3) of the Act to be wound up by the general partners unless the court otherwise orders. Before proceeding to the special rules applicable to limited partnerships, it might be mentioned that a limited partnership may cease to exist as such but remain in existence as a general partnership, as, for example, when a limited partner departs from the firm, leaving only general partners.

Death, bankruptcy and mental disorder of a limited partner

Section 6 (2) provides that the death or bankruptcy of a limited partner should not automatically dissolve a limited partnership, while that limited partner's mental disorder need not necessitate the dissolution of the partnership by the court, unless it is impossible to ascertain his share by any other means. The effect of the death or bankruptcy of a limited partner is therefore, with one difference, the converse of the rule applicable to ordinary partnerships, stated by section 33 (1) of the Partnership Act 1890. The difference is that whilst ordinary partners are at liberty to agree that the death or bankruptcy of a partner shall not work a dissolution, the rule for limited partnerships is not expressed to operate subject to any contrary agreement between the partners. Despite this omission, it seems that no objection could be taken to an agreement providing for termination of membership in the case of a limited partner who dies or is adjudicated bankrupt or even, if so desired, for termination of the partnership itself.

The mental disorder of a limited partner (but not a general partner) has an effect on limited partnerships which is different to the effect of a partner's mental disorder on an ordinary partnership. The Court of Protection may, under section 103 (1) (f) of the Mental Health Act 1959, give orders and directions for " the dissolution of a partnership of which the patient is a member." However, section 6 (2) of the Limited Partnerships Act 1907 provides that the mental disorder of a limited partner will only justify the court in dissolving the partnership if there is no other method of ascertaining or realising the share of the mentally disordered, limited partner. If the patient's share cannot be ascertained or realised without a dissolution the other partners will have to take steps, such as buying out the share in question or arranging for its purchase, if they wish to avoid such a result.

Charging order on limited partner's share

Section 6 (5) (*c*) affords yet another contrast with the Partnership Act 1890 when it states that, subject to any agreement, express or implied, between the partners, the other partners shall not be entitled to dissolve the partnership by reason of any limited partner suffering his share to be charged for his separate debts. No reference is made in the section to the position which arises when a general partner suffers his share to be charged for separate debts so that, apparently, the matter is governed by section 33 (2) of the Partnership Act 1890, *i.e.* the other partners (including, in the present context, limited partners) may join together to exercise their option to dissolve the partnership.

Notice

The Limited Partnerships Act 1907, s. 6 (5) (*e*) provides that subject to any agreement, express or implied between the partners, a limited partner is not entitled to dissolve the partnership by notice. In the absence of any such agreement, the partnership, whether formed for a fixed term, for the accomplishment of a single adventure or even for an indefinite time, will continue in existence notwithstanding any purported notice of dissolution from a limited partner. This fits in with the rule that a limited partner who draws out or receives back any part of his contribution during the continuance of the partnership remains liable up to the amount so drawn out or received back. The effect of notice of withdrawal by a limited partner (in pursuance of an agreement conferring such a right), not intended to work a dissolution of the firm, is unclear. Such a withdrawal, or retirement, whilst contractually permissible, would seem to leave the limited partner liable for capital withdrawn, unless he can obtain the consent of the general partners to the assignment of his share.

Except for section 6 (3), which provides that in the event of dissolution the affairs of a limited partnership will be wound up by the general partners unless the court otherwise orders, the 1907 Act contains no special provision for the distribution of assets on dissolution. The Bankruptcy Act of 1914 applies to limited partnerships in like manner as if they were ordinary partnerships and section 127 states that on the adjudication in bankruptcy of all general partners, the assets of the limited partnership vest in the trustee.

Certain bankruptcy provisions, however, reflect the distinction between general and limited partners which is peculiar to limited partnerships. Rule 286 of the Bankruptcy Rules 1952 provides that a receiving order made against a firm registered under the 1907 Act operates as if it were a receiving order made against each of the persons who, at the date of the order, is a general partner in the firm. Rule 290 (*a*) provides that no present or past limited partner is liable to contribute as such to the assets of the limited partnership more than the amount of any part of his contribution which he has failed to pay into, has drawn out or received back from the partnership assets since he became or whilst he remained a limited partner, but this limitation of liability to contribute to partnership assets does not apply to a present limited partner who was formerly a general partner in the firm, or to a present general partner who was formerly a limited partner. Paragraph (*b*) of Rule 290 provides that a past general partner is only liable to contribute to the assets of the partnership in relation to partnership debts and obligations incurred whilst he was a general partner. However, by Rule 290 (*a*) a general partner who has become a limited partner is liable, in addition to the liability just noted, to contribute an amount equal to the amount of any part of his contribution as limited partner which he has failed to pay into or has drawn out or received back from the assets since he became or whilst he remained a limited partner. Finally, paragraph (*c*) of Rule 290 states that contributions from past partners, general or limited, will not be required unless it appears to the court that the partnership assets are insufficient to meet partnership liabilities and the costs, charges and expenses of the administration in bankruptcy of the partnership estate.

Apart from the special rules applicable to partners who undergo the transmogrification from general to limited status, and vice versa, it will be seen that the chief consideration to be borne in mind is the limitation of the limited partner's liability for the debts and obligations of the firm to the amount of his capital contribution, a limitation which obtains not only *vis-à-vis* creditors of the firm, but *vis-à-vis* the other partners. Thus, section 44 of the Partnership Act 1890, which determines that losses, including losses and deficiencies of capital, are to be paid out of profits, capital and by the partners in their profit-sharing ratios, in that order, must be read subject to the overriding limitation on the liability of the limited partner. If there is a deficiency of assets to meet the debts and liabilities of the firm, the limited partner cannot (any more than the shareholder with fully paid-up shares) be called upon to contribute over and above his capital contribution.

As Farwell J. explained in *Re Barnard*,[7] " The result is that, so far as applicable, the method of administering an estate in bankruptcy in the case of an ordinary partnership is to be applied as far as possible in the case of a limited partnership." This means that the principle contained in section 33 (6) of the Bankruptcy Act 1914, whereby joint estate bears joint debts and separate estate bears separate debts, is applicable to limited partnerships, even where, as in the *Barnard* case itself, there is no joint estate as such. In that case, B was the sole general partner in two limited partnerships, Firm A and Firm B. Five bills of exchange had been drawn on Firm B and accepted by that firm by B as general partner. Receiving orders were made against both firms and B was adjudicated bankrupt in each case. It was held that the holders of the bills of exchange were entitled to prove in the bankruptcy of Firm A on the ground that, under the Bills of Exchange Act 1882, section 23 (2), Firm B's acceptance of the bills was in effect acceptance by B, against whom the receiving order made against Firm A operated.

Farwell J.'s exposition, although not necessary for his decision, is instructive.

" The Barnard firm [Firm A] assets must first be applied in discharging the firm's debts, *i.e.* the debts incurred by or on behalf of that firm. The surplus must be applied in repaying the limited partners their actual contributions. The balance will form part of B's separate estate, and out of that will be paid B's own private debts and any other debts incurred by him on behalf of other limited partnerships. The same thing applies *mutatis mutandis* in the case of the Scrap Metal Co. [Firm B]." [8] (*brackets supplied.*)

In this way, injustice to the limited partners is avoided in that a receiving order made against the firm, whilst it operates against the general partners, does not preclude the limited partners from proving for their capital contributions before the separate creditors (or other limited partnerships) of the general partners.

Winding up as Companies

We have seen that certain ordinary partnerships may be wound up by the Court as unregistered companies under the Companies Act

1948 (p. 127, above) as an alternative to winding up under the Partnership Act 1890. In the case of limited partnerships, the intention of the 1907 Act, as revealed in section 6 (4), was that limited partnerships should be wound up by petition under the prevailing companies' legislation, a provision which was overtaken by the Companies (Consolidation) Act 1908, which enabled such partnerships to be wound up as unregistered companies. The application of the rules applicable to companies was modified for limited partnerships by the Limited Partnership Rules 1907. An example of the old procedure is provided by *Re Hughes and Co.*[9] in which a limited partner was held to be entitled to an order winding up a limited partnership, the business of which had been conducted by the general partner in a manner which justified a winding up.

The modern position is that whilst partnerships, whether limited or not, may be wound up as unregistered companies under Part IX of the Companies Act 1948, section 398 (*d*) of that Act specifically excludes limited partnerships registered in England or Northern Ireland which, accordingly, fall to be wound up by the Court as ordinary partnerships, save for the special rules discussed above. Provided they have not less than eight members, limited partnerships registered in Scotland may be wound up as unregistered companies, subject to the Limited Partnership Rules 1907, the position with regard to those limited partnerships having less than eight members being less clear. A limited partnership of less than eight members which cannot be wound up as an unregistered company may still be wound up in an ordinary partnership action.

---

[1] The Act recognises the limited partnership but " does not create it a legal entity ": *per* Farwell J. in *Re Barnard* [1932] 1 Ch. 269 at p. 272.

[2] (1926) 24 Ll.L.R. 25 at p. 27.

[3] (13th ed.), p. 802.

[4] s. 8, and see Finance Act 1973, s. 47 (4).

[5] s. 9 (1), and see Finance Act 1973, s. 47 (4).

[6] *Ellis* v. *Joseph Ellis and Co.* [1905] 1 K.B. 324.

[7] [1932] 1 Ch. 269 at pp. 273–274.

[8] [1932] 1 Ch. 269 at p. 274.

[9] [1911] 1 Ch. 342.

CHAPTER TEN

REGISTRATION OF BUSINESS NAMES

ENGLISH law, unlike some continental systems, starts from the legal postulate that persons may engage in trade or business without need of State *imprimatur* or even State registration. One notable exception to this admirable postulate (in any event now somewhat eroded) was introduced in 1916 by the Registration of Business Names Act which had three aims. First, it was designed to protect sellers when they gave credit to a firm having a name other than the true names of the proprietors. Secondly, it was designed to enable those dealing with the firm to know the identity of the proprietors " both as to individuality and nationality," [1] the latter referring to the xenophobic and especially anti-German feeling of that time. Thirdly, it was considered useful for the State to have knowledge of the nationality of those who had traded with the enemy.

There can be little doubt that the Act fulfils a public need, but at the same time it has certain defects which were adverted to in the Report of the Company Law Committee in 1947 (Cmd. 1749). Widespread disregard of the obligation to register, whether due to ignorance of the law by small traders or to the lack of any advantage attaching to registration, has resulted in an incomplete Register. The second defect resides in the practice of the Registrar who " does not regard as undesirable . . . a business name which is identical with or too like one already on the register " (*ibid.* para. 443).

Although the Act applies mainly to partnerships, it also applies to individual traders, whether natural persons or companies. Only the provisions which apply to partnerships are now discussed. They apply equally to ordinary and limited partnerships.

Firms and persons to be registered

Section 1 of the Registration of Business Names Act 1916 stipulates that registration is necessary if a firm is carrying on business in the United Kingdom under a business name other than the true names of all the partners who are individuals and the corporate names of those partners which are corporations. " True names " include surnames alone, or surnames accompanied by Christian (fore-) names or initials. If the Christian name or initials of any partner are used, all his names or initials must appear, otherwise registration will be necessary [2]; but the use of the Christian name or initials of one partner does not oblige the other partners to do likewise.

Paragraph (c) of section 1 states that registration is also necessary where a partner in a firm having a place of business in the United Kingdom changes his name, but excepts from this requirement a woman who marries. This provision must now be read subject to section 116 (4) of the Companies Act 1947, which dispenses a firm from registration if a member thereof has changed his name before reaching the age of 18 years, or if not less than 20 years have elapsed since the change took place. In *Seymour* v. *Chernikeef*,[3] a lady carried on business in the name of " Jean Frances," which consisted of one of her Christian names and her surname, and continued the business in that name after marrying Mr. C. The court held that paragraph (c) applies only to a man who carries on business in his own name and then changes his name and the name of the business and not to a woman who changes her name on marriage. If the defendant had carried on business in her married name she would not have needed to register the change. However, she had carried on in her maiden name and had committed an offence by not registering her change of name. It would appear that the same result would ensue in the event of a woman partner changing her name on marriage, *i.e.* where the firm ABC carrying on business under that name continues after the marriage of C who has become Mrs. D.

Section 1 further provides that registration is not necessary if the business is carried on by a trustee in bankruptcy, if an " s " is added at the end of the common surname of two or more partners or if an addition to the name " merely indicates that the business is carried on in succession to a former owner of the business."

Registration by nominee, etc.

Section 2 of the Act provides for the registration of a firm which carries on business wholly or mainly as the nominee or trustee of a person, persons or corporation or which acts as a general agent for a foreign firm. Registration is not however necessary if the business is carried on by a trustee in bankruptcy or by a receiver or manager appointed by the court. Form R.B.N. 1A is used (see *infra*).

Manner and particulars of registration

Section 3 sets out the particulars which the firm must furnish in writing to the Registrar at the Register Office in that part of the

United Kingdom in which the firm's principal place of business is situated. They are as follows:

" (a) The business name [or each name, if there are more than one, s. 3 (2)];

(b) The general nature of the business;

(c) The principal place of the business;

(d) . . . the present Christian name and surname, any former Christian name or surname, nationality, . . . the usual residence and the other business occupation (if any) of each of the individuals who are partners, and the corporate name and registered or principal office of every corporation which is a partner;

. . .

(g) If the business is commenced after the passing of this Act, the date of the commencement of the business."

Form R.B.N. 1A appended to the Business Names Rules 1949 must be used (see *infra*).

Statement to be signed by persons registering: section 4

The statement setting out the above particulars must be signed either by all the partners or by only one partner. If the partner is a corporation then a director or the secretary signs. If the statement is signed by only one partner then it must be verified by a statutory declaration made by him in accordance with Form R.B.N./S.D. appended to the Business Names Rules 1949 (see *infra*). This statutory declaration is not evidence for or against other partners or alleged partners, but if the name of a partner is omitted or a name wrongfully included, the person concerned can apply under section 4 for rectification of the Register. Unless this action is taken, he may, in the first case, find himself liable for penalties under section 7, and the firm may be subject to disabilities under section 8 (see p. 233, *infra*) and in the second case he might be held liable as a partner for having knowingly allowed himself to be held out as a partner (see Partnership Act, s. 14 and comments, on that section *supra*, and s. 36).

Time for registration: section 5

The particulars specified under section 3 must be furnished to the Registrar within 14 days after the firm commences business. The same time limit applies where registration is required because of a change of name; the particulars must be furnished within 14 days of such change.

Registration of changes in firm

Section 6 states that if there is a change in any of the registered particulars then the firm must, within 14 days of the change, furnish to the Registrar a statement in writing on Form R.B.N. 3A specifying the nature and date of the change. This statement must be signed and, if necessary, verified in the manner required under section 3 for the statement on registration. On application in a particular case the Board of Trade may allow a longer period within which to furnish the particulars. The Industrial Expansion Act 1968, s. 14 states that anything required, by any enactment, to be done by the Board of Trade may be done by the " President of the Board or any person acting with his authority." This section replaced section 20 of the Registration of Business Names Act 1916 which was in the same terms but which applied only to that Act.

Section 1 of the Act deals with the case where C, a partner in a firm consisting of A, B and C, and trading under the name of " A, B and C " is replaced by D; in such a case there arises the obligation to register for the first time. But if C is replaced by D in a firm registered as " X, Y and Z " but consisting of A, B and C, then the present section requires registration of the change within the requisite period. Note that registration is needed for changes other than those appertaining to names, *e.g.* changes in the nature of the business, place of business, etc., (see s. 3, *supra*). Strictly, a change in the constitution of the firm should oblige the old firm to give notice of cessation under section 13 and the new firm to register fresh particulars, but the quasi-corporate existence of the partnership firm seems to be tacitly accepted by the notes to Form R.B.N. 3A which envisage action under section 6. The Registrar's practice is to accept a notice of change under this section unless the firm is reduced to one individual, or unless A and B have been replaced at one time by C and D. Only in the latter two cases will the Registrar insist on a notice of cessation under section 13 and the registration of new particulars, although it is always open to the firm to take this action if they prefer. In any event, a retiring partner should ensure that his name is deleted from the registered particulars, since otherwise he might find himself under a continuing liability for the firm's debts (see comments on Partnership Act 1890, s. 36, *supra*) and, possibly, to penalties under section 8, *infra*.

The wording of this section and the notes to Form R.B.N. 3A imply that the form need only be signed by the continuing members of the firm, but to avoid the position which sometimes arises where a person denies that he has ceased to be a partner, it is the practice of the Registrar to ask for the signatures of both continuing and retiring partners, unless the application is supported by a statutory declaration, or unless it is impossible to obtain the signature of a retiring partner because, for example, of death or absence abroad.

Penalty for default in registration

Section 7 stipulates that if any firm does not furnish a statement of particulars or of any change in particulars in the manner and within the time prescribed by the Act then, unless there is a reasonable excuse for not doing so, every partner shall be liable on summary conviction for a fine of up to £5 per day for every day the default continues. Thus, default in the matter of furnishing particulars (or a change in particulars) is a continuing offence by every partner. That the offence is not one of strict prohibition is shown by the availability of the defence of " reasonable excuse," a phrase which is not further elaborated, unlike the grounds for relief from civil disability under section 8, *infra*.

By virtue of section 116 (2) of the Companies Act 1947, where registration is refused under section 14 of the present Act, any person carrying on business under that name in such circumstances as to require registration under that Act shall be liable under section 7 to the same penalties as if he had without reasonable excuse made default in furnishing a statement of particulars with respect to that name.

Disability of persons in default

Complementary to the criminal sanction in section 7, section 8 imposes the civil disability of unenforceability on the defaulter and then provides for cases in which relief from such disability may be sought.

Section 8 provides that where there has been a default in providing a statement of particulars or change in particulars as required by the Act the defaulter cannot enforce any rights under or arising out of any contract made by him or on his behalf, while he was in default, in relation to the carrying on of the business. In an *obiter dictum* in *O'Connor* v. *Ralston*,[4] Darling J. thought " that the word ' default ' . . . means not furnishing any particulars at all and does not mean furnishing insufficient particulars." This opinion was rightly doubted in *Pollock on Partnership* [5] on the ground that it would allow partners to escape liability where insufficient particulars were given, *e.g.* failing to give the names of all the partners, There is no " default " until the time allowed for registration (see s. 5) has elapsed. In *Re A Debtor*, a creditor was allowed to bring a petition in bankruptcy on a bill of exchange given within 14 days of the creditor commencing business. " Here Shaffer (*i.e.* the creditor) " said Horridge J., " made the contract when he was not in default. He made it during the period allowed to him to register, and, not being then in default, he was, in my view, not prevented from enforcing the contract." [6]

A contract affected by section 8 is not void but merely unenforceable, and even then its effect is limited. In the first place, the disability imposed on the defaulter " is limited to proceedings between the parties to the contract." [7] It was pointed out that serious consequences might ensue from any other interpretation. The section was not intended to punish innocent third parties, such as the holders of negotiable instruments for value, assignees of book debts and possibly third persons holding goods purchased by the defaulter, none of whom would be disabled from asserting their rights by section 8. [8] In the second place, rights exercisable independently of contract remain unaffected. In *Daniel* v. *Rogers*,[9] it was held that Miss F, who carried on the business of dressmaking in the name of L and who had acquired ownership and possession of R's business, was entitled to resist execution on the goods put in by R inasmuch as she was asserting a right independent of contract. Serious consequences might ensue from any other interpretation. For example a foreign butcher carrying on business under an English name and not registered, might find people walking into his shop and taking meat without liability to pay for it. Scrutton L.J. was clear that possession sufficed to maintain trover and that it was unnecessary to show the manner in which possession had been obtained.

Section 8 (1) (*a*) provides that the defaulter may apply to the court (which is defined as " the ' High Court ' or a judge thereof " by s. 8 (2)) for relief against the disability imposed. The court may grant, subject to such conditions as it may impose, either general or special relief if satisfied that " the default was accidental, or due to inadvertence, or some other sufficient cause or that on other grounds it is just and equitable to grant relief." Relief may be granted on special application under Order 81, rule 1 or in an action to enforce the contract. In the latter event it is grantable after the commencement of the action and even after judgment in the action has been signed. An order for relief is retrospective in that it validates contracts according to the scope of the order and also proceedings and judgments upon such orders. The court has a wide discretion under the section. In *Weller* v. *Denton* [10] it took into account the fact that the defendant knew that the plaintiffs were proprietors of the business and also the plaintiff's ignorance of the Act. That there are limits, however, to its exercise is shown by *Watson* v. *Park Royal (Caterers) Ltd.,* [11] where, in the absence of proof of accidental or inadvertent default, the only other sufficient cause suggested appeared to be, in the words of Edmund Davies L.J., " I did not apply for relief simply because I thought that relief would be mine for the asking." " That," said the same judge, " is not the law." Relief will not be granted if any party to the contract satisfies the court that he would not have entered into the contract if the Act had been complied with.

Paragraphs (*b*) and (*c*) of section 8 (1) state that the rights of other parties in respect of the contract are not affected by the operation of paragraph (*a*) and that if any action is brought by such a party the defaulter may enforce in that action such rights as he has against that party in respect of the contract.

Penalty for false statements

Section 9 imposes penalties on those *signing* a false statement as opposed to those *in default*, who are dealt with in sections 7 and 8. It provides that if the statement of particulars, or change of particulars, is false in any material particular to the knowledge of any signatory then that signatory shall be liable on summary conviction to a term of imprisonment not exceeding three months or a fine not exceeding £20 or both.

Duty to furnish particulars to Board of Trade

Section 10 empowers the Board of Trade to require any person to furnish any information it considers necessary to determine whether the firm of which he is a partner should be registered or whether an alteration should be made in the registered particulars. If he does not furnish the requested information or if he furnishes information which is false in any material particular he will be liable on summary conviction to a term of imprisonment not exceeding three months, or a fine not exceeding £20 or both. If the Board infers from the information furnished that the firm ought to be registered or an

alteration made in the registered particulars it may require the firm
to furnish the required particulars to the Registrar within such time
as it allows. If the Board has discovered a default under the Act no
action may be taken in respect of that default until the time limit
allowed by the Board has expired.

Registrar to file statement and issue certificate of registration

Section 11 states that the Registrar must file any statement or
statutory declaration made in pursuance of the Act and that he must
issue a certificate of registration to the firm registering (using Form
R.B.N. Cert. 2, appended to the Registration of Business Names
Rules 1949). If this certificate or a copy thereof is not " exhibited in a
conspicuous position at the principal place of business of the firm "
every partner shall be liable on summary conviction to a fine not
exceeding £20.

Where a firm no longer requires to be registered by reason only of
a change in the name of a member either because such member has
since reached the age of 18 years or because 20 or more years have
elapsed since the change, the Registrar must remove the firm from
the register at its request and the firm is dispensed from the need to
exhibit the certificate of registration or a copy thereof (Companies
Act 1947, s. 116 (4) and (5)).

Index to be kept

The Registrar of each register office is required by section 12 to
keep an index of all the firms registered at that office. Section 15
stipulates that there must be register offices in London, Edinburgh
and Belfast for the registration of firms whose principal places of
business are respectively situated in England and Wales, Scotland
and Northern Ireland. Unless the Board of Trade determines otherwise the Registrar is the Registrar of Companies in each city.

Section 16 provides that any person may inspect the documents
filed by the Registrar, require a certificate of registration or a
certified copy of any registered statement on payment of the fee
prescribed by that section. The Fees (Increase) Act 1923, imposed a
search fee which is payable in addition to any inspection fees payable
under section 16.

Removal of names from the register

Section 13 deals with a cessation of business, as opposed to a
change which is dealt with in section 6. It provides that within three

months of a firm ceasing to carry on business, the partners must send or deliver to the Registrar a notice in Form R.B.N. 4 (appended to the Registration of Business Names Rules 1949) that the firm has ceased to carry on business. Failure to comply with this provision renders each partner liable on summary conviction to a fine not exceeding £20. When the Registrar receives such a notice he must remove the firm from the register.

All those who were partners at the time of cessation must sign the prescribed form. If, therefore, a partnership is dissolved, but one partner continues to carry on business in the same name, both parties should sign the notice of cessation under this section, and the partner who continues the business should re-register. If either partner refuses to sign the notice of cessation, probably the most effective course for the other to take would be to notify the Registrar so that action may be taken under subsection (3). This subsection provides that if the Registrar has reasonable cause to believe that a firm is not carrying on business he may send the firm a notice that unless he receives a reply within one month the firm will be removed from the register. Subsection (4) enables him to take this action if he does not receive an answer or if he receives an answer that the firm is not carrying on business. Where the partnership determines, owing to the death of one partner, it presumably suffices if the survivor signs the notice of cessation and it is not the practice of the Registrar to require the personal representatives of the deceased to sign also. In any case the personal representatives are not much concerned in view of the provisions of section 36 (3) of the Partnership Act, *supra*.

Section 58 (3) of the Companies Act 1947 extends section 13 of the 1916 Act to companies which are registered under the latter Act (see p. 229 above) and which ceases to carry on business, with the substitution of " directors " or " liquidators " for the word " partners."

Misleading business names

Section 14, as supplemented, gives the Registrar powers to refuse registration similar to those of the Companies' Registrar under the Companies Act 1948, s. 17. It provides that if a business name contains the word " British " or any other word " calculated to lead to the belief that the business is under British ownership or control " and the Registrar is satisfied that the nationality of those persons who wholly or mainly own or control the business is not British then he must refuse to register such name or he must remove such name from the register, whichever action is appropriate. The section gives any person aggrieved a right of appeal to the Board of Trade, but the decision of that body is final. Section 116 of the Companies Act 1947 extends this power so as to enable the Registrar to refuse to register any business name " which is in his opinion undesirable." It also provides that any person carrying on business under a name which the Registrar has refused to register is liable under section 7 of the Registration of Business Names Act 1916 as if he had, without reasonable excuse, defaulted in furnishing a statement of particulars to the Registrar. It seems unfortunate that nothing is said about the disabilities imposed by section 8, for it must now be a matter of doubt whether the firm would in such a case be subject to them.

However, it is not the practice of the Registrar to search the existing Register when particulars are lodged, so that, unlike the case of companies, identical or similar names may be registered in respect of several firms. Moreover, it will be observed that the extension contained in the 1947 Act is limited to a refusal to register, it gives no power to remove a name from the Register, which can only be done when section 14 of the 1916 Act applies, and there is no general power similar to the Companies Act 1948, s. 18 (2). Hence registration under the Act confers nothing in the nature of a monopolistic right to the name, and once a firm has registered its name, it is useless for a firm with earlier registration of a similar name to complain to the Registrar; its only remedy is in a passing-off action or one for infringement of a registered trade mark, if either is appropriate. If, however, the complaint was made before the registration was completed and the Registrar was satisfied that confusion between the two firms was likely, he would then refuse registration.

In his *Notes for Guidance*, the Registrar gives the warning contained in section 14 (2) that registration " gives no authority to use the name if its use could be prohibited for other reasons." He goes on to state that registration does not " imply that the name will necessarily prove acceptable subsequently as a company name. In particular it should be noted that registration does not give sole rights to a name nor protection against duplication." Before expenditure on stationery and the like is incurred, consultation with the Registrar is recommended. Examples of names which will not be accepted for registration are given, *viz*. names which are misleading (such as a name suggesting that a small concern is trading on a great scale), names suggesting a connection with the Crown or Royal Family, including patronage, names suggesting a connection with a government department, local authority, chartered or statutorily incorporated body or any Commonwealth or foreign government, names which include the words " Bank," " British," " Commonwealth," " Co-operative," " Corporation," " Limited," etc., (unless justified by the circumstances), names which include any surname other than the names of the proprietors of the business, and names including a registered trade mark for goods in which it is proposed to deal without production of the consent of the owners of the trade mark.

Power for Board of Trade to make rules

The Board of Trade is empowered by section 17 of the Act to make rules concerning the general conduct and regulation of registration under the Act, including matters such as fees, the forms to be used, and the duties of the Registrar under the Act. The Business Names Rules 1949, S.I. 1949, No. 2441 (as amended by S.I. 1969, No. 1330) have been made under section 17 and are mainly concerned with two matters.

First, they require notification to the firm or person concerned of a refusal by the Registrar under section 14 (1) of the Act, as amended by section 116 of the Companies Act 1947, to register a business name or to remove a business name from the register. A right of appeal from any decision of the Registrar under section 14 (1) is given by the Rules and lies to the Board of Trade, with a right to a " hearing," if the appellant so requires in his notice of appeal.

Secondly, the forms to be used are set out in full as an appendix to the Business Names Rules 1949. The forms which are relevant to partnership are:

1. **Form R.B.N. 1A.** Application for registration under section 1 (*a*) and (*c*) of the Act which, as we have seen may be necessary not only upon the initial formation of the firm but also upon a change in the composition of the firm.

2. **Form R.B.N./2/2A.** Statement of additional particulars required for a partnership having a place of business in the United Kingdom but carrying on business wholly or mainly as nominee or trustee for another person or persons (including a corporation) or acting as general agent for any foreign firm.

3. **Form R.B.N. 3A.** Statement of a change in particulars under section 6 (see above, p. 232).

4. **Form R.B.N. 4.** Notice under section 13 of the Act as amended (see p. 236, above) of cessation of business by a registered firm or individual company.

5. **Form R.B.N. 6.** Form of appeal from a decision of the Registrar under section 14 (1).

6. **Form R.B.N. 7A.** Request by a firm for amendment of particulars. This Form and Form R.B.N. 8A (request for removal from Register) have been withdrawn from use and are now replaced by Forms 3, 3A, 3B and 4. A firm need not register by reason only of a change of a partner's name if the change took place before the partner reached the age of 18 years or if not less than 20 years have elapsed since the change—section 116 (4) of the Companies Act 1947 (see also subs. (5) under which the Registrar may be required to amend the register either (a) by removing the firm name or (b) by omitting the name of the member affected).

7. **Form R.B.N./S.D.** Form of statutory declaration verifying a statement furnished under the Act. If not signed by all the partners, the statement required for registration may be signed by a partner provided the latter verifies it by statutory declaration.

8. **Form R.B.N. Cert. 2.** Certificate of registration issued by the Registrar of Business Names.

Publication of true names, etc.

Section 18 adds to the obligation to register the obligation to reveal the names of the partners where they carry on business in a name other than their own. Subsection (1) provides that all trade catalogues, trade circulars, showcards, and business letters on or in which the business name appears shall " have mentioned in legible characters . . . the present Christian names, or the initials thereof and present surnames, any former Christian names and surnames, and the nationality if not British . . . of all the partners in the firm or, in the case of a corporation being a partner, the corporate name." Subsection (2) states that if this provision is not complied with, every partner shall be liable on summary conviction for each offence to a fine not exceeding five pounds. However, proceedings may only be instituted with the consent of the Board of Trade. Of course, neither failure to register nor to disclose the name of a dormant partner will free the latter from liability for the acts of an active partner as described in Chapter 3. The position was stated in *Wintle* v. *Crowther*: " Where a partnership name is pledged, the partnership of whomsoever it may consist, and whether the partners are named or not, and whether they are known or secret partners, will be bound, unless the title of the person who seeks to change them can be impeached." [12]

For the converse case where a person is wrongfully shown as a partner, see *Tower Cabinet Co.* v. *Ingram* [13] and the comments on sections 14 and 36 of the Partnership Act 1890. Neither the present Act, nor the Limited Partnerships Act 1907, make it necessary to distinguish between general and limited partnerships in letter-headings and the like. Provided the limited partnership is registered and the limited partners do nothing to draw unlimited liability upon themselves there is nothing to be gained from making such a distinction. Nevertheless some limited partners may well feel that it is desirable to make the matter explicit *ex abundanti cautela*.

Interpretation of terms

Words and expressions used in the Act are defined by section 22.

" 22. In the construction of this Act the following words and expressions shall have the meanings in this section assigned to them, unless there be something in the subject or context repugnant to such construction:

' Firm ' shall mean an unincorporate body of two or more individuals, or one or more individuals and one or more corporations, or two or more corporations, who have entered into partnership with one another with a view to carrying on business for profit, but shall not include any unincorporated company which was in existence on the second day of November eighteen hundred and sixty-two:

' Business ' shall include profession:

' Individual ' shall mean a natural person and shall not include a corporation:

' Christian name ' shall include any forename:

' Initials ' shall include any recognised abbreviation of a Christian name:

In the case of a peer or person usually known by a British title different from his surname, the title by which he is known shall be substituted in this Act for his surname:

References in this Act to a former Christian name or surname *shall not, in the case of natural-born British subjects, include a former Christian name or surname where that name or surname has been changed or disused before the person bearing the name had attained the age of eighteen years, and* shall not, in the case of any person, include a former Christian name or surname where that name or surname has been changed or disused before the person bearing the name had attained the age of eighteen years or has been changed or disused for a period of not less than twenty years; and, in the case of a married woman, shall not include the name or surname by which she was known previous to the marriage:

References in this Act to a change of name shall not include, *in the case of natural-born British subjects, a change of name which has taken place before the person whose name has been changed has attained the age of eighteen years*; or, in the case of a peer or a person usually known by a British title different from his surname, the adoption of or succession to the title; [and an individual or firm shall not require to be registered under this Act by reason only of a change of his name, or of the name of a member of the firm, if the change has taken place before the person who has changed his name has attained the age of eighteen years or if not less than twenty years have elapsed since it took place]:

' Business name ' shall mean the name or style under which any business is carried on, whether in partnership or otherwise:

' Foreign firm ' shall mean any firm, individual, or corporation whose principal place of business is situate outside His Majesty's dominions:

' Showcards ' shall mean cards containing or exhibiting articles dealt with, or samples or representations thereof:

' Prescribed ' shall mean prescribed by rules made in pursuance of this Act."

As a result of the Companies Act 1947, ss. 116 and 123 and Sched. IX, Pt. II, the words in italics no longer apply, and those in square brackets have been inserted by implication.

Application to Scotland and Northern Ireland

Sections 23 and 24 as amended make provision for the Act to be applied to, respectively, Scotland and Northern Ireland.

1 Parl.Deb. Vol. 86, col. 1597 (1916).
2 *Brown* v. *Thomas and Burrows* (1922) 39 T.L.R. 132 (C.A.).
3 [1946] K.B. 434.
4 [1920] 3 K.B. 451 at p. 457.
5 (15th ed.), p. 205.
6 (*No. 5 of* 1919) (1919) 89 L.J.K.B. 40 at p. 42.
7 *Per* Scrutton L.J. *obiter* in *Daniel* v. *Rogers* [1918] 2 K.B. 228 at p. 234.
8 *Hawkins* v. *Duché* [1921] 3 K.B. 226 at p. 235.
9 See n. 7 *supra*.
10 [1921] 3 K.B. 103.
11 [1961] 1 W.L.R. 727.
12 (1831) C. & J. 316 at p. 318, cited with approval by Thesiger L.J. in *York-shire Banking Co.* v. *Beatson* (1880) 5 C.P.D. 109, at p. 124.
13 [1949] 2 K.B. 397.

PARTNERSHIP ACT 1890
(c. 39)

Nature of Partnership

Definition of partnership

1.—(1) Partnership is the relation which subsists between persons carrying on a business in common with a view of profit.

(2) But the relation between members of any company or association which is:

(*a*) Registered as a company under the Companies Act 1862, or any other Act of Parliament for the time being in force and relating to the registration of joint stock companies; or

(*b*) Formed or incorporated by or in pursuance of any other Act of Parliament or letters patent, or Royal Charter; or

(*c*) A company engaged in working mines within and subject to the jurisdiction of the Stannaries:

is not a partnership within the meaning of this Act.

Rules for determining existence of partnership

2. In determining whether a partnership does or does not exist, regard shall be had to the following rules:

(1) Joint tenancy, tenancy in common, joint property, common property, or part ownership does not of itself create a partnership as to anything so held or owned, whether the tenants or owners do or do not share any profits made by the use thereof.

(2) The sharing of gross returns does not of itself create a partnership, whether the persons sharing such returns have or have not a joint or common right or interest in any property from which or from the use of which the returns are derived.

(3) The receipt by a person of a share of the profits of a business is *prima facie* evidence that he is a partner in the business, but the receipt of such a share, or of a payment contingent on or varying with the profits of a business, does not of itself make him a partner in the business; and in particular—

(*a*) The receipt by a person of a debt or other liquidated amount by instalments, or otherwise out of the accruing profits of a business does not of itself make him a partner in the business or liable as such:

(b) A contract for the remuneration of a servant or agent of a person engaged in a business by a share of the profits of the business does not of itself make the servant or agent a partner in the business or liable as such:

(c) A person being the widow or child of a deceased partner, and receiving by way of annuity a portion of the profits made in the business in which the deceased person was a partner, is not by reason only of such receipt a partner in the business or liable as such:

(d) The advance of money by way of loan to a person engaged or about to engage in any business on a contract with that person that the lender shall receive a rate of interest varying with the profits, or shall receive a share of the profits arising from carrying on the business, does not of itself make the lender a partner with the person or persons carrying on the business or liable as such. Provided that the contract is in writing, and signed by or on behalf of all the parties thereto:

(e) A person receiving by way of annuity or otherwise a portion of the profits of a business in consideration of the sale by him of the goodwill of the business is not by reason only of such receipt a partner in the business or liable as such.

Postponement of rights of person lending or selling in consideration of share of profits in case of insolvency

3. In the event of any person to whom money has been advanced by way of loan upon such a contract as is mentioned in the last foregoing section, or of any buyer of a goodwill in consideration of a share of the profits of the business, being adjudged a bankrupt, entering into an arrangement to pay his creditors less than twenty shillings in the pound, or dying in insolvent circumstances, the lender of the loan shall not be entitled to recover anything in respect of his loan, and the seller of the goodwill shall not be entitled to recover anything in respect of the share of profits contracted for, until the claims of the other creditors of the borrower or buyer for valuable consideration in money or money's worth have been satisfied.

Meaning of firm

4.—(1) Persons who have entered into partnership with one another are for the purposes of this Act called collectively a firm, and the name under which their business is carried on is called the firm-name.

(2) In Scotland a firm is a legal person distinct from the partners of whom it is composed, but an individual partner may be charged on a decree or diligence directed against the firm, and on payment of the debts is entitled to relief *pro ratâ* from the firm and its other members.

Relations of Partners to persons dealing with them

Power of partner to bind the firm

5. Every partner is an agent of the firm and his other partners for the purpose of the business of the partnership; and the acts of every partner who does any act for carrying on in the usual way business of the kind carried on by the firm of which he is a member bind the firm and his partners, unless the partner so acting has in fact no authority to act for the firm in the particular matter, and the person with whom he is dealing either knows that he has no authority, or does not know or believe him to be a partner.

Partners bound by acts on behalf of firm

6. An act or instrument relating to the business of the firm and done or executed in the firm-name, or in any other manner showing an intention to bind the firm, by any person thereto authorised, whether a partner or not, is binding on the firm and all the partners.

Provided that this section shall not affect any general rule of law relating to the execution of deeds or negotiable instruments.

Partner using credit of firm for private purposes

7. Where one partner pledges the credit of the firm for a purpose apparently not connected with the firm's ordinary course of business, the firm is not bound, unless he is in fact specially authorised by the other partners; but this section does not affect any personal liability incurred by an individual partner.

Effect of notice that firm will not be bound by acts of partner

8. If it has been agreed between the partners that any restriction shall be placed on the power of any one or more of them to bind the firm, no act done in contravention of the agreement is binding on the firm with respect to persons having notice of the agreement.

Liability of partners

9. Every partner in a firm is liable jointly with the other partners, and in Scotland severally also, for all debts and obligations of the firm incurred while he is a partner; and after his death his estate is also severally liable in a due course of administration for such debts and obligations, so far as they remain unsatisfied, but subject in England or Ireland to the prior payment of his separate debts.

Liability of the firm for wrongs

10. Where, by any wrongful act or omission of any partner acting in the ordinary course of the business of the firm, or with the authority of his co-partners, loss or injury is caused to any person not being a partner in the firm, or any penalty is incurred, the firm is liable therefor to the same extent as the partner so acting or omitting to act.

Misapplication of money or property received for or in custody of the firm

11. In the following cases; namely—

(a) Where one partner acting within the scope of his apparent authority receives the money or property of a third person and misapplies it; and

(b) Where a firm in the course of its business receives money or property of a third person, and the money or property so received is misapplied by one or more of the partners while it is in the custody of the firm;

the firm is liable to make good the loss.

Liability for wrongs joint and several

12. Every partner is liable jointly with his co-partners and also severally for everything for which the firm while he is a partner therein becomes liable under either of the two last preceding sections.

Improper employment of trust-property for partnership purposes

13. If a partner, being a trustee, improperly employs trust-property in the business or on the account of the partnership, no other partner is liable for the trust-property to the persons beneficially interested therein.

Provided as follows:—

(1) This section shall not affect any liability incurred by any partner by reason of his having notice of a breach of trust; and

(2) Nothing in this section shall prevent trust money from being followed and recovered from the firm if still in its possession or under its control.

Persons liable by " holding out "

14.—(1) Every one who by words spoken or written or by conduct represents himself, or who knowingly suffers himself to be represented, as a partner in a particular firm, is liable as a partner to any one who has on the faith of any such representation given credit to the firm, whether the representation has or has not been made or communicated to the person so giving credit by or with the knowledge of the apparent partner making the representation or suffering it to be made.

(2) Provided that where after a partner's death the partnership business is continued in the old firm-name, the continued use of that name or of the deceased partner's name as part thereof shall not of itself make his executors or administrators estate or effects liable for any partnership debts contracted after his death.

Admissions and representations of partners

15. An admission or representation made by any partner concerning the partnership affairs, and in the ordinary course of its business, is evidence against the firm.

Notice to acting partner to be notice to the firm

16. Notice to any partner who habitually acts in the partnership business of any matter relating to partnership affairs operates as notice to the firm, except in the case of a fraud on the firm committed by or with the consent of that partner.

Liabilities of incoming and outgoing partners

17.—(1) A person who is admitted as a partner into an existing firm does not thereby become liable to the creditors of the firm for anything done before he became a partner.

(2) A partner who retires from a firm does not thereby cease to be liable for partnership debts or obligations incurred before his retirement.

(3) A retiring partner may be discharged from any existing liabilities, by an agreement to that effect between himself and the members of the firm as newly constituted and the creditors, and this agreement may be either express or inferred as a fact from the course of dealing between the creditors and the firm as newly constituted.

Revocation of continuing guaranty by change in firm

18. A continuing guaranty or cautionary obligation given either to a firm or to a third person in respect of the transactions of a firm is, in the absence of agreement to the contrary, revoked as to future transactions by any change in the constitution of the firm to which, or of the firm in respect of the transactions of which, the guaranty or obligation was given.

Relations of Partners to one another

Variation by consent of terms of partnership

19. The mutual rights and duties of partners, whether ascertained by agreement or defined by this Act, may be varied by the consent of all the partners, and such consent may be either express or inferred from a course of dealing.

Partnership property

20.—(1) All property and rights and interests in property originally brought into the partnership stock or acquired, whether by purchase or otherwise, on account of the firm or for the purposes and in the course of the partnership business, are called in this Act partnership property, and must be held and applied by the partners exclusively for the purposes of the partnership and in accordance with the partnership agreement.

(2) Provided that the legal estate or interest in any land, or in Scotland the title to and interest in any heritable estate, which belongs to the partnership shall devolve according to the nature and tenure thereof, and the general rules of law thereto applicable, but in trust, so far as necessary, for the persons beneficially interested in the land under this section.

(3) Where co-owners of an estate or interest in any land, or in Scotland of any heritable estate, not being itself partnership property, are partners as to profits made by the use of that land or estate, and purchase other land or estate out of the profits to be used in like manner, the land or estate so purchased belongs to them, in the absence of an agreement to the contrary, not as partners but as co-owners for the same respective estates and interests as are held by them in the land or estate first mentioned at the date of the purchase.

Property bought with partnership money

21. Unless the contrary intention appears, property bought with money belonging to the firm is deemed to have been bought on account of the firm.

Conversion into personal estate of land held as partnership property

22. Where land or any heritable interest therein has become partnership property, it shall, unless the contrary intention appears, be treated as between the partners (including the representatives of a deceased partner), and also as between the heirs of a deceased partner and his executors or administrators, as personal or moveable and not real or heritable estate.

Procedure against partnership property for a partner's separate judgment debt

23.—(1) After the commencement of this Act a writ of execution shall not issue against any partnership property except on a judgment against the firm.

(2) The High Court, or a judge thereof, or the Chancery Court of the county palatine of Lancaster, or a county court, may, on the application by summons of any judgment creditor of a partner, make an order charging that partner's interest in the partnership property and profits with payment of the amount of the judgment debt and interest thereon, and may by the same or a subsequent order appoint a receiver of that partner's share of profits (whether already declared or accruing), and of any other money which may be coming to him in respect of the partnership, and direct all accounts and inquiries, and give all other orders and directions which might have been directed or given if the charge had been made in favour of the judgment creditor by the partner, or which the circumstances of the case may require.

(3) The other partner or partners shall be at liberty at any time to redeem the interest charged, or in case of a sale being directed, to purchase the same.

(4) This section shall apply in the case of a cost-book company as if the company were a partnership within the meaning of this Act.

(5) This section shall not apply to Scotland.

Rules as to interests and duties of partners subject to special agreement

24. The interests of partners in the partnership property and their rights and duties in relation to the partnership shall be determined, subject to any agreement express or implied between the partners, by the following rules:

   (1)   All the partners are entitled to share equally in the capital and profits of the business, and must contribute equally towards the losses whether of capital or otherwise sustained by the firm.

(2) The firm must indemnify every partner in respect of payments made and personal liabilities incurred by him—

(*a*) In the ordinary and proper conduct of the business of the firm; or,

(*b*) In or about anything necessarily done for the preservation of the business or property of the firm.

(3) A partner making, for the purpose of the partnership, any actual payment or advance beyond the amount of capital which he has agreed to subscribe, is entitled to interest at the rate of five per cent. per annum from the date of the payment or advance.

(4) A partner is not entitled, before the ascertainment of profits, to interest on the capital subscribed by him.

(5) Every partner may take part in the management of the partnership business.

(6) No partner shall be entitled to remuneration for acting in the partnership business.

(7) No person may be introduced as a partner without the consent of all existing partners.

(8) Any difference arising as to ordinary matters connected with the partnership business may be decided by a majority of the partners, but no change may be made in the nature of the partnership business without the consent of all existing partners.

(9) The partnership books are to be kept at the place of business of the partnership (or the principal place, if there is more than one), and every partner may, when he thinks fit, have access to and inspect and copy any of them.

Expulsion of partner

25. No majority of the partners can expel any partner unless a power to do so has been conferred by express agreement between the partners.

Retirement from partnership at will

26.—(1) Where no fixed term has been agreed upon for the duration of the partnership, any partner may determine the partnership at any time on giving notice of his intention so to do to all the other partners.

(2) Where the partnership has originally been constituted by deed,

a notice in writing, signed by the partner giving it, shall be sufficient for this purpose.

Where partnership for term is continued over, continuance on old terms presumed

27.—(1) Where a partnership entered into for a fixed term is continued after the term has expired, and without any express new agreement, the rights and duties of the partners remain the same as they were at the expiration of the term, so far as is consistent with the incidents of a partnership at will.

(2) A continuance of the business by the partners or such of them as habitually acted therein during the term, without any settlement or liquidation of the partnership affairs, is presumed to be a continuance of the partnership.

Duty of partners to render accounts, etc.

28. Partners are bound to render true accounts and full information of all things affecting the partnership to any partner or his legal representatives.

Accountability of partners for private profits

29.—(1) Every partner must account to the firm for any benefit derived by him without the consent of the other partners from any transaction concerning the partnership, or from any use by him of the partnership property name or business connexion.

(2) This section applies also to transactions undertaken after a partnership has been dissolved by the death of a partner, and before the affairs thereof have been completely wound up, either by any surviving partner or by the representatives of the deceased partner.

Duty of partner not to compete with firm

30. If a partner, without the consent of the other partners, carries on any business of the same nature as and competing with that of the firm, he must account for and pay over to the firm all profits made by him in that business.

Rights of assignee of share in partnership

31.—(1) An assignment by any partner of his share in the partnership, either absolute, or by way of mortgage or redeemable charge, does not, as against the other partners, entitle the assignee, during the continuance of the partnership, to interfere in the management or administration of the partnership business or affairs, or to require any accounts of the partnership transactions, or to inspect the partnership books, but entitles the assignee only to receive the share of profits to which the assigning partner would otherwise be entitled, and the assignee must accept the account of profits agreed to by the partners.

(2) In case of a dissolution of the partnership, whether as respects all the partners or as respects the assigning partner, the assignee is entitled to receive the share of the partnership assets to which the assigning partner is entitled as between himself and the other partners, and, for the purpose of ascertaining that share, to an account as from the date of the dissolution.

Dissolution of Partnership, and its consequences
Dissolution by expiration or notice
32. Subject to any agreement between the partners a partnership is dissolved—

(*a*) If entered into for a fixed term, by the expiration of that term:

(*b*) If entered into for a single adventure or undertaking, by the termination of that adventure or undertaking:

(*c*) If entered into for an undefined time, by any partner giving notice to the other or others of his intention to dissolve the partnership.

In the last-mentioned case the partnership is dissolved as from the date mentioned in the notice as the date of dissolution, or, if no date is so mentioned, as from the date of the communication of the notice.

Dissolution by bankruptcy, death, or charge
33.—(1) Subject to any agreement between the partners, every partnership is dissolved as regards all the partners by the death or bankruptcy of any partner.

(2) A partnership may, at the option of the other partners, be dissolved if any partner suffers his share of the partnership property to be charged under this Act for his separate debt.

Dissolution by illegality of partnership
34. A partnership is in every case dissolved by the happening of any event which makes it unlawful for the business of the firm to be carried on or for the members of the firm to carry it on in partnership.

Dissolution by the Court

35. On application by a partner the Court may decree a dissolution of the partnership in any of the following cases:

(a) When a partner is found lunatic by inquisition, or in Scotland by cognition, or is shown to the satisfaction of the Court to be of permanently unsound mind, in either of which cases the application may be made as well on behalf of that partner by his committee or next friend or person having title to intervene as by any other partner:

(b) When a partner, other than the partner suing, becomes in any other way permanently incapable of performing his part of the partnership contract:

(c) When a partner, other than the partner suing, has been guilty of such conduct as, in the opinion of the Court, regard being had to the nature of the business, is calculated to prejudicially affect the carrying on of the business:

(d) When a partner, other than the partner suing, wilfully or persistently commits a breach of the partnership agreement, or otherwise so conducts himself in matters relating to the partnership business that it is not reasonably practicable for the other partner or partners to carry on the business in partnership with him:

(e) When the business of the partnership can only be carried on at a loss:

(f) Whenever in any case circumstances have arisen which in the opinion of the Court, render it just and equitable that the partnership be dissolved.

Rights of persons dealing with firm against apparent members of firm

36.—(1) Where a person deals with a firm after a change in its constitution he is entitled to treat all apparent members of the old firm as still being members of the firm until he has notice of the change.

(2) An advertisement in the London Gazette as to a firm whose, principal place of business is in England or Wales, in the Edinburgh Gazette as to a firm whose principal place of business is in Scotland, and in the Dublin Gazette as to a firm whose principal place of business is in Ireland, shall be notice as to persons who had not dealings with the firm before the date of the dissolution or change so advertised.

(3) The estate of a partner who dies, or who becomes bankrupt, or of a partner who, not having been known to the person dealing with the firm to be a partner, retires from the firm, is not liable for partnership debts contracted after the date of the death, bankruptcy, or retirement respectively.

Right of partners to notify dissolution

37. On the dissolution of a partnership or retirement of a partner any partner may publicly notify the same, and may require the other partner or partners to concur for that purpose in all necessary or proper acts, if any, which cannot be done without his or their concurrence.

Continuing authority of partners for purposes of winding up

38. After the dissolution of a partnership the authority of each partner to bind the firm, and the other rights and obligations of the partners, continue notwithstanding the dissolution so far as may be necessary to wind up the affairs of the partnership, and to complete transactions begun but unfinished at the time of the dissolution, but not otherwise.

Provided that the firm is in no case bound by the acts of a partner who has become bankrupt; but this proviso does not affect the liability of any person who has after the bankruptcy represented himself or knowingly suffered himself to be represented as a partner of the bankrupt.

Rights of partners as to application of partnership property

39. On the dissolution of a partnership every partner is entitled, as against the other partners in the firm, and all persons claiming through them in respect of their interests as partners, to have the property of the partnership applied in payment of the debts and liabilities of the firm, and to have the surplus assets after such payment applied in payment of what may be due to the partners respectively after deducting what may be due from them as partners to the firm; and for that purpose any partner or his representatives may on the termination of the partnership apply to the Court to wind up the business and affairs of the firm.

Apportionment of premium where partnership prematurely dissolved

40. Where one partner has paid a premium to another on entering into a partnership for a fixed term, and the partnership is dissolved before the expiration of that term otherwise than by the death of a partner, the Court may order the repayment of the premium, or of such part thereof as it thinks just, having regard to the terms of the partnership contract to the length of time during which the partnership has continued; unless:

    (*a*) the dissolution is, in the judgment of the Court, wholly or chiefly due to the misconduct of the partner who paid the premium, or

    (*b*) the partnership has been dissolved by an agreement containing no provision for a return of any part of the premium.

Rights where partnership dissolved for fraud or misrepresentation

41. Where a partnership contract is rescinded on the ground of the fraud or misrepresentation of one of the parties thereto, the party entitled to rescind is, without prejudice to any other right, entitled—

    (*a*) to a lien on, or right of retention of, the surplus of the partnership assets, after satisfying the partnership liabilities, for any sum of money paid by him for the purchase of a share in the partnership and for any capital contributed by him, and is

    (*b*) to stand in the place of the creditors of the firm for any payments made by him in respect of the partnership liabilities, and

    (*c*) to be indemnified by the person guilty of the fraud or making the representation against all the debts and liabilities of the firm.

Right of outgoing partner in certain cases to share profits made after dissolution

42.—(1) Where any member of a firm has died or otherwise ceased to be a partner, and the surviving or continuing partners carry on the business of the firm with its capital or assets without any final settlement of accounts as between the firm and the outgoing partner or his estate, then, in the absence of any agreement to the contrary, the outgoing partner or his estate is entitled at the option of himself or his representatives to such share of the profits made since the dissolution as the Court may find to be attributable to the use of his share of the partnership assets, or to interest at the rate of five per cent. per annum on the amount of his share of the partnership assets.

(2) Provided that where by the partnership contract an option is given to surviving or continuing partners to purchase the interest of a deceased or outgoing partner, and that option is duly exercised, the estate of the deceased partner, or the outgoing partner or his estate, as the case may be, is not entitled to any further or other share of profits; but if any partner assuming to act in exercise of the option does not in all material respects comply with the terms thereof, he is liable to account under the foregoing provisions of this section.

Retiring or deceased partner's share to be a debt

43. Subject to any agreement between the partners, the amount due from surviving or continuing partners to an outgoing partner or the representatives of a deceased partner in respect of the outgoing or deceased partner's share is a debt accruing at the date of the dissolution or death.

Rule for distribution of assets on final settlement of accounts

44. In settling accounts between the partners after a dissolution of partnership, the following rules shall, subject to any agreement, be observed:

(*a*)   Losses, including losses and deficiencies of capital, shall be paid first out of profits, next out of capital, and lastly, if necessary, by the partners individually in the proportion in which they were entitled to share profits:

(*b*)   The assets of the firm including the sums, if any, contributed by the partners to make up losses or deficiencies of capital, shall be applied in the following manner and order:

1. In paying the debts and liabilities of the firm to persons who are not partners therein;

2. In paying to each partner rateably what is due from the firm to him for advances as distinguished from capital;

3. In paying to each partner rateably what is due from the firm to him in respect of capital;

4. The ultimate residue, if any, shall be divided among the partners in the proportion in which the profits are divisible.

Supplemental
Definitions of " court " and " business "

45. In this Act, unless the contrary intention appears—
The expression " court " includes every court and judge having jurisdiction in the case:

The expression " business " includes every trade, occupation, or
profession.

Saving for rules of equity and common law

46. The rules of equity and of common law applicable to partnership shall continue in force except so far as they are inconsistent with
the express provisions of this Act.

Provisions as to bankruptcy in Scotland

47.—(1) In the application of this Act to Scotland the bankruptcy
of a firm or of an individual shall mean sequestration under the
Bankruptcy (Scotland) Acts, and also in the case of an individual the
issue against him of a decree of cessio bonorum.

(2) Nothing in this Act shall alter the rules of the law of Scotland
relating to the bankruptcy of a firm or of the individual partners
thereof.

Repeal

48. The Acts mentioned in the schedule to this Act are hereby
repealed to the extent mentioned in the third column of that schedule.

Commencement of Act

49. This Act shall come into operation on the first day of January
one thousand eight hundred and ninety-one.

Short title

50. This Act may be cited as the Partnership Act, 1890.

SCHEDULE

ENACTMENTS REPEALED

Section 48

Session and Chapter	Title or Short Title	Extent of Repeal
19 & 20 Vict. c. 60	The Mercantile Law Amendment (Scotland) Act, 1856	Section seven
19 & 20 Vict. c. 97	The Mercantile Law Amendment Act, 1856	Section four
28 & 29 Vict. c. 86	An Act to amend the law of partnership	The whole Act

INDEX

Jacinta

Presley Lafferty
732222 ext 610
304217 Home